Aristotelian Logic and the Arabic Language in Alfārābī

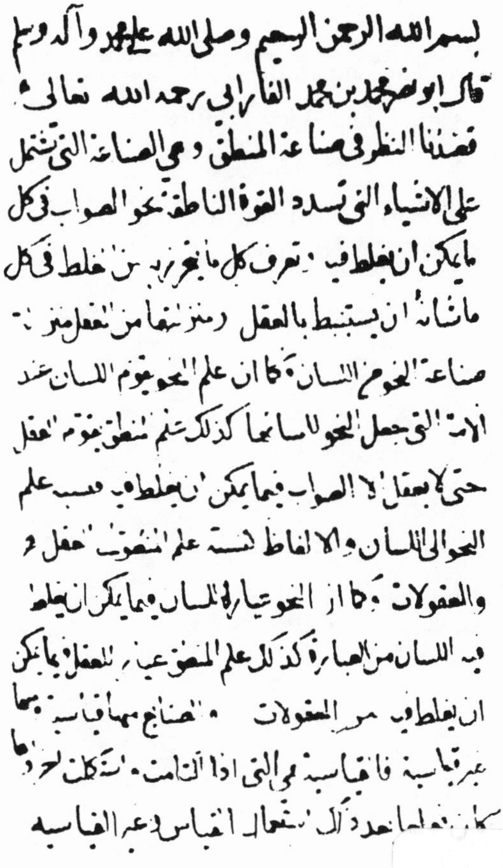
بسم الله الرحمن الرحيم وصلى الله على محمد وآله وسلم
قال ابو نصر محمد بن محمد الفارابي رحمه الله تعالى
قصدنا النظر في صناعة المنطق وهي الصناعة التي تشتمل
على الاشياء التي تسدد القوة الناطقة نحو الصواب في كل
ما يمكن ان يغلط فيه وتعرف كل ما يتحرز به من الغلط في كل
ما شأنه ان يستنبط بالعقل ومنزلتها من العقل منزلة
صناعة النحو من اللسان فكما ان علم النحو يقوم اللسان عند
الامة التي جعل النحو للسانها كذلك علم المنطق يقوم العقل
حتى لا يعقل الا الصواب فيما يمكن ان يغلط فيه ونسبة علم
النحو الى اللسان والالفاظ نسبة علم المنطق الى العقل و
المعقولات وكما ان النحو عيار اللسان فيما يمكن ان يغلط
فيه اللسان من العبارة كذلك علم المنطق عيار للعقل فيما يمكن
ان يغلط فيه من المعقولات . والصنائع منها قياسية ومنها
غير قياسية فالقياسية هي التي اذا التأمت اجزاؤها كان فعلها
بعد ذلك ان تستعمل القياس وغير القياسية

First page of the manuscript, "Risālah ṣudira bihā ʾl-kitāb" (Alfārābī's Introductory Risālah on Logic) (Bratislava 231). Reproduced from Al-manṭiq ʿind Alfārābī *(Alfārābī's Logic), part one, ed. Rafīq al-ʿAajam (Beirūt: Dār al-Mashriq, 1986), p. 15.*

SUNY Series, Toward a Comparative Philosophy of Religion
Frank E. Reynolds and David Tracy, Editors

A publication of the Harry S. Truman Research Institute
of the Hebrew University of Jerusalem

Aristotelian Logic and the Arabic Language in Alfārābī

Shukri B. Abed

State University of New York Press

Published by
State University of New York Press, Albany

Printed in the United States of America

For information, address the State University of New York Press,
State University Plaza, Albany, NY 12246

Library of Congress Cataloging-in-Publication Data

Abed, Shukri.
Aristotelian logic and the Arabic language in Alfarabi / Shukri B. Abed.
p. cm.
Includes bibliographical references.
ISBN 0-7914-0397-1. —ISBN 0-7914-0398-X (pbk.)
1. Fārābī—Language. 2. Fārābī—Contributions in logic.
3. Logic—Terminology—History. 4. Aristotle—Contributions in Logic. 5. Language and logic. I. Title.
B753.F34A62 1991
160'.92—dc20 89-77651
CIP

10 9 8 7 6 5 4 3 2 1

To my wife Joanne,
whose patience, devotion, scholarly comments and insightful suggestions have been my greatest asset in writing this book.

Contents

Preface

Many people have contributed in various ways to this book: Professors A. I. Sabra and Wolfhart Heinrichs, of Harvard University, both of whom have helped, advised and supported me throughout my work on the manuscript; Professors Joel Kraemer and Marcello Daskal, of Tel Aviv University, who read the manuscript and made invaluable suggestions; Professors Hilary Putnam and Muhsin Mahdi, of Harvard University, who inspired me; Dr. Judith Roumani, of the Truman Institute, whose professional editing of the final manuscript has been a major contribution to the quality of this work; and last but not least, my wife Joanne, who spent an enormous amount of time and energy going over the various drafts of this work. To all these people I am greatly indebted.

I would like to express my deepest appreciation to the Harry S. Truman Research Institute for the Advancement of Peace at the Hebrew University of Jerusalem for its constant support, institutionally and on the staff level, without which I would not have been able to complete this book. Special thanks are due to the Department of Publications and Information. My sincere gratitude goes too to the State University of New York Press, particularly for their meticulous and thorough copy-editing of the typescript.

For references, I have used the following conventions: "(**Alfāẓ**, 47: 5)" or "**Alfāẓ** (p. 49:12)" are both example of citations (the form depending on the context). "(**Ḥurūf**, 99, par. 65)" means page 99, paragraph 65 of **Ḥurūf** (in many cases, there is more than one paragraph on any given page of this work). My explanations within quotations are indicated thus: [. . .]. The system of transliteration is that of *IJMES*. I have adopted the spelling "Alfārābī" except when it is within a quotation from other authors and commentators; names within quotations are always spelled as they appear in the source work. When an Arabic work is quoted, the first letter only is capitalized, even if that name begins with "Al" (the definite article in Arabic), or the term *kitāb* [treatise or book], which is a part of many of the titles in Arabic.

Introduction

Medieval Islamic scholars widely referred to Aristotle as the "First Teacher," evidence of the high regard in which they held the ancient Greek philosopher. The man ranked by his contemporaries in the Arab world as second only to Aristotle was a tenth-century Muslim thinker by the name of Abū Naṣr Alfārābī.

It was Alfārābī who comprehensively collected and systematized previous translations of the "first teacher's" writings, translations that on the whole were over-literal, and therefore at times confusing.[1] According to Moritz Steinschneider, Alfārābī is said to have called his collection and commentary on Aristotle's works "The Second Teaching" [*al-taʿlīm* <*al-thānī*>], but it was the vigor, wisdom, and sensitivity Alfārābī brought to his task and the humble, scholarly life he led that earned him the respect of his peers and the reverent title of "The Second Teacher" [*al-muʿallim al-thānī*].[2]

In medieval Latin texts, Alfārābī (A.D. 870–950) is referred to as Alfarabius or Avennasar, and over a hundred works of varying length are attributed to him by Arab bibliographers. Of Turkish origin, he was most likely born in the town of Wasīj, Turkistan, in the district of the city of Fārāb. A major portion of Alfārābī's adult life was spent in Baghdād, where he was exposed to the teachings of such learned Nestorian Christian scholars as Abū Bishr Mattā Ibn Yūnis (A.D. 870–939) and Yuḥannā Ibn Ḥaylān (A.D. 860–920), from whom he studied logic, and Abū Bakr al-Sarrāj (d. A.D. 928), from whom he studied Arabic grammar. From Baghdād Alfārābī moved to Aleppo in Syria, where he spent the last eight years or so of his life, enjoying the patronage of the ruler Sayf al-Dawlah al-Ḥamadānī.[3]

Despite the fact that other Muslim philosophers — such as Avicenna (Ibn Sīnā [A.D. 980–1037]) and Averroes (Ibn Rushd [A.D. 1126–1198]) — have been more influential outside the Arab world than Alfārābī, Alfārābī's contributions were clearly recognized by the most perceptive among his contemporaries. The twelfth-century Jewish philosopher Ibn Maymūn (known in the West as Maimonides, A.D. 1135–1204) wrote to Ibn Tibon, translator of his *Guide to the Perplexed* from Arabic into Hebrew:

> You should always follow this rule: in studying logic, deal only with what was written by the wise Abū Naṣr Alfārābī, for all that

> he wrote, and particularly his work **Mabādi' al-mawjūdāt** [The principles of beings],[4] is a pure meal. . . . The books of ʿAli Ibn Sīnā [Avicenna], on the other hand, although they are very accurate, do not match the writings of the above-mentioned Alfārābī.[5]

Arab sources describe Alfārābī in similar terms. The well-known biographer Ibn al-Qifṭī (d. A.D. 1248), not given to hyperbole, describes him as the "unrivalled [*ghayr mudāfaʿ*] Philosopher of Muslims."[6] Ibn Khallīkān (A.D. 1211–82), considered by a contemporary historian "the foremost biographer Islam produced,"[7] describes Alfārābī's intellectual enterprise as follows: "No Moslem ever reached in the philosophical sciences the same rank as al-Fārābī; and it was by the study of his writings and by the imitation of his style that Ibn-Sīnā attained proficiency and rendered his own work so useful."[8]

Even Ibn Taymiyyah, the thirteenth-century theologian who launched one of the harshest attacks on Aristotelian logic, describes Alfārābī as "the greatest of the *falāsifah* [philosophers] in the exposition of logic and its branches."[9]

A growing number of current scholars of Islamic thought have also recognized Alfārābī's significance in the history of Islamic philosophy. Thus Muḥsin Mahdī, a leading scholar of Islamic studies, in describing Alfārābī's importance from the point of view of Islamic intellectual history:

> Behind this public or exoteric aspect of al-Fārābī's work stood a massive body of more properly philosophic or scientific inquiries which established his reputation as the greatest philosophic authority after Aristotle, the great interpreter of the thought of Plato and Aristotle and their commentators, and the master to whom almost all major Muslim as well as a number of Jewish and Christian philosophers turned for a fuller understanding of the controversial, troublesome, and intricate questions of philosophy. . . . He paid special attention to the study of language and its relation to logic. In his numerous commentaries on Aristotle's logical works he expounded for the first time in Arabic the entire range of the scientific and non-scientific forms of argument and established the place of logic as the indispensable prerequisite for philosophic inquiry.[10]

In order to fully appreciate the intellectual enterprise of Abū Naṣr Alfārābī, one must understand the intellectual climate of tenth-century Baghdād where he spent most of his life. This seminal logician lived in a time and place that subjected both Aristotelian logic and the Arabic language to intense and serious scholarly scrutiny. Tenth-century Baghdād witnessed vibrant developments in the study of Arabic grammar, as well as major advances in the Arabic interpretation of Aristotle's logic.

These two disciplines—grammar and logic—interacted variously and often explosively with one another. Resulting from an uneasy union between the two was Alfārābī's linguistic philosophy, or what I should like to refer to as *Arabic logic* per se.

Baghdād, political capital of the Abbasite Khalifate (A.D. 750–1258), was also the center of intellectual life during much of that period. The Baghdād of that time attracted many prominent scholars and translators, who flourished in one of the most stimulating intellectual atmospheres in mankind's history. In the words of the Arabist Joel Kraemer:

> The city of Peace was then the scene of vibrant cultural renaissance. . . . With its vast number of scholars, its bookstores, its meeting places for learned discussions, its diversified population, the sophistication of its intellectual elite, the ambition and energy of its rulers, this great urban center witnessed a splendor hardly equalled in the entire medieval world.[11]

In addition to Alfārābī, distinguished scholars such as Abū Bishr Mattā, Abū Zakaryā Yaḥyā Ibn ʿAdī (d. A.D. 974), Abū Sulaymān al-Sijistānī (d. A.D. 985), Ibn Zurʿah (d. A.D. 1008), Ibn Suwār (d. A.D. 1017), Abū ʾl-Faraj Ibn al-Ṭayyib (d. A.D. 1043), Ibn al-Khammār (born A.D. 942), and others came to Baghdād. They focused their collective attention on the study of Aristotle's corpus, translating into Arabic (mostly through Syriac mediation) those portions that had not already been translated by eighth- and ninth-century translators, and revising older versions of previous translations.[12] Aristotle's *Organon* was accorded an important position in the program of philosophic studies, and special emphasis was placed "on the importance of the scientific method as embodied in the *Posterior Analytics* (of Aristotle) and on the distinction between this method and dialectical, sophistical, rhetorical and poetical arguments."[13]

The main purpose of these translators and commentators was to expose Arab students of philosophy and logic to the teachings of Aristotle and his Greek commentators [notably Alexander of Aphrodisias (ca. A.D. 200), Porphyry (ca. A.D. 200),[14] Themistius (A.D. 317–387), John Philoponus (late fifth and early sixth century A.D.), and Simplicius (A.D. 527–565)]. By coining Arabic terminology for the Greek concepts and, in general, producing very accurate (if too literal) translations of Greek philosophical and logical works, they took an important first step in initiating interaction between (Greek) logic and (Arabic) grammar. Their efforts stirred up a considerable and not entirely positive reaction among intellectual circles (grammarians, theologians, and philosophers) in the Islamic world, in the ninth and tenth centuries in particular.

The Arab logicians [*manṭiqiyyūn*] adhered to Aristotle's teachings and presented them as the right path, indeed the only path, to true knowledge. This position is echoed in the following passage quoted from a debate concerning the relative merits of logic and grammar that took place in A.D. 932 in Baghdād between grammarians (represented by Abū Saʿīd al-Sīrāfī) and logicians (represented by the Nestorian Christian Abū Bishr Mattā, "whose recent arrival to teach at Baghdād had attracted wide attention in learned circles").[15] Mattā said: "I understand by logic an 'instrument' [*ālah*] of 'speech' [*kalām*], by which correct 'speech' is known from incorrect, and unsound 'meaning' [*maʿnā*] from sound: like a balance, for by it I know overweight from underweight and what rises from what sinks."[16]

The issue of the relationship of the Arabic language (and Islamic culture) to Greek logic arose in the early stages of the philosophical movement in the Islamic world. The first Arab philosopher, al-Kindī (d. A.D. 873), did not address this question directly. His student Aḥmad Ibn al-Ṭayyib al-Sarakhsī (d. A.D. 899), however, was reportedly the first in the Arab world to write about the difference between logic and Arabic grammar. Although his treatise on "the difference between the grammar of the Arabs and logic" is not extant, al-Sarakhsī, we are told, considered logic to be a *universal grammar* and as such superior to Arabic grammar[17] and to any other particular grammar, for that matter.

The famous Muslim physician and philosopher Abū Bakr al-Rāzī (d. A.D. 925) tells in his essay "Al-ṭibb al-rūḥānī" [The spiritual medicine] of a debate he had with someone who believed that "knowledge can be achieved only through the Arabic language and its grammar"[18] and that "everything other than that is empty [*rīḥ*]."[19] Al-Rāzī resents this attitude, which according to him prevailed among certain groups (probably a reference to the grammarians). He tells his opponent that wise men do not consider these disciplines (Arabic language and grammar) sciences at all, nor do they consider anyone who masters them a wise man. A "wise man," according to al-Rāzī, is he who masters the theory of demonstration and the rules that govern logic, mathematics, physics, and metaphysics.

This view—according to which logic is superior to language because the former is a necessary science dealing with meanings and with what is universal, whereas the latter is conventional and accidental—is a view that prevailed among Arab logicians throughout the tenth and eleventh century. In fact, according to the Arab logicians of this period, language should not even be considered an issue for logicians in their logical inquiries. Logic, they claimed, is concerned with utterances [*alfāẓ*] only accidentally and only insofar as these utterances signify the concepts [*maᶜānī*] themselves, which (in the logicians' view) are the only proper subject matter of logic. Mattā is even quoted[20] as having claimed that "there was no way to know truth from falsehood, verity from lying, good from bad, proof from sophism, doubt from certainty except through logic."[21]

It is not difficult to comprehend why the logicians' position drew a strong reaction from the circle of Arab grammarians who criticized the logicians on the grounds that the intelligible meanings they present as universal and eternal can only be achieved through mastering a specific language. Al-Sīrāfī, representing the grammarians' point of view, criticized Mattā on the grounds that there is no such thing as "language" in general, rather we speak and express meanings by using a particular language, and each language has its own tools and instruments by which one determines what is correct and what is incorrect when that language is used. "Abū Saᶜīd [al-Sīrāfī] said: You are mistaken, for correct speech is distinguished from incorrect by the familiar rules of composition and by the accepted inflection [*iᶜrāb*] when we speak in Arabic; unsound meaning is distinguished from sound by reason when we investigate meanings."[22]

Elsewhere in this debate the logicians are urged to concentrate on the knowledge of a particular language (Arabic in this case) as a necessary condition for mastering the art of logic. Knowledge of the Arabic language is required if logicians wish to convey the logical theories of the Greeks to speakers of the Arabic language, Abū Saᶜīd al-Sīrāfī concludes:

> This [Arabic] language in which you dispute or agree with us, you should instruct your friends in accordance with the way it is understood by those who speak it, and interpret the books of the Greeks according to the custom of those whose language it is. For then you will come to know that you can dispense with the meanings of the Greeks as well as you can dispense with the language of the Greeks.[23]

According to al-Sīrāfī, there is no separation between logic and language.[24] Logic for him is the logic of a particular language, and there is no such thing as universal logic. The logic that the logicians are presenting is a purely Greek logic, derived from Greek language and grammar.[25]

This debate was the grammarians' strongest reaction — at least, the strongest we know of — to the introduction of Greek logic into the Arab world and to its presentation as the only safe path to true knowledge.[26] The logicians' reported defeat[27] in this particular confrontation with the grammarians did not alter their position that logic is concerned with meaning rather than with utterances as such, while Arabic grammar [*naḥw*] is concerned exclusively with utterances.[28] It did, however, lead them to take the grammarians and their field of endeavor more seriously.

The Achilles' heel of the first generation of Arab logicians had been their profound ignorance of the discipline they so summarily dismissed. Witness the following blunt admission by Abū Bishr Mattā in the debate that took place between him and the grammarian al-Sīrāfī:

> This is grammar, and I have not studied grammar. The logician has no need of grammar, whereas the grammarian does need logic. For logic enquires into the meaning, whereas grammar enquires into the utterance. If, therefore, the logician deals with the utterance, it is accidental, and it is likewise accidental if the grammarian deals with the meaning. Now, the meaning is more exalted than the utterance, and the utterance humbler than the meaning.[29]

The next wave of logicians — including Alfārābī, Ibn ʿAdī (both disciples of Mattā), and al-Sijistānī (a disciple of Ibn ʿAdī)—was broader in its approach to the relationship between logic and language. They still believed that logic is a universal grammar and therefore more significant than any particular language which, by definition, is restricted to a particular nation. But the defeat of Abū Bishr Mattā, whose openly admitted ignorance of Arabic grammar had left him vulnerable to the Sīrāfian attacks, suggested that a serious logician might do well to master his own language as a firm basis from which to pursue his logical studies. Unlike their predecessors, then, these men realized that language and logic are closely interrelated.

Alfārābī, Ibn ʿAdī, and al-Sijistānī all engaged in serious study of Arabic grammar and were able to argue their position much more convincingly than Mattā, leader of the tenth-century Baghdād logicians, had been able to do. These logicians continued to maintain that logic is superior to grammar, with the only utterances seriously considered by the logician being those that signify universal concepts or meanings.

Ibn ʿAdī wrote an essay[30] in which he tried to prove that the subject matter and purpose of logic involve the domain of utterances that signify universal meanings and their composition.[31] The subject of grammar, on the other hand, is all the utterances, significant and nonsignificant, and the purpose of grammar is to investigate the vocalization (i.e., the writing in of the vowels) of these utterances rather than their meaning.[32]

This theme was echoed by al-Sijistānī[33] (known simply as "The Logician" [*al-manṭiqī*]), as reported by his student al-Tawḥīdī.[34] Al-Tawḥīdī also reports similar ideas held by a certain Abū Bakr al-Qawsamī, described as "highly ranked among the philosophers."[35]

Abū Naṣr Alfārābī, however, was the most thorough and systematic among the second generation of Arab logicians in presenting the relationship between Arabic grammar and Greek logic. He continued to maintain that logic is superior to language, emphasizing the theme that logicians deal with utterances only insofar as these utterances signify concepts or meanings. Thus, Alfārābī in his *Iḥṣāʾ al-ʿulūm* [Enumeration of the sciences]: "The objects with which the rules of logic are concerned are the intelligibles [*maʿqūlāt*] insofar as they are signified by the utterances [*alfāẓ*], and the utterances insofar as they signify the intelligibles."[36] Unlike the other Arab thinkers who supported this position, however, Alfārābī buttressed his belief with comprehensive philosophical analysis.

According to Alfārābī (see chapter 6 below), language acquisition is based on an epistemological process, the first step of which is man's encounter with sensible material objects. In Alfārābī's view, the first stage of comprehension begins with the individual material objects, which have certain properties such as 'this thing is a man and it is white and it is tall.' Thus we form the first intelligibles, or concepts, that we acquire directly through sense perception.

While in this early stage of perception, we develop concepts such as 'man,' 'white,' and 'tall.' Yet at this stage, each of these first intelligibles represents only a single material object, with the result that we acquire only an individual concept of 'man,' of 'white,' and of 'tall,' a preliminary distinguishing of the categories from one another.

The three Arabic terms *mushār ilayh* [an individual material object or simply a "this"], *maʿqūl* [an intelligible], and *maqūlah* [a category] are the three basic terms that represent three different levels in Alfārābī's epistemological scheme. The first of these represents the realm of sensible objects, the second that of thought, and the third the realm of language. The *maʿqūlāt* [plural of *maʿqūl*] are the mental counterparts we acquire from encounters with the external world. This is followed by the process of *naming* these mental entities, a process Alfārābī considers entirely conventional and dependent upon human consensus, whereas the former process of concept acquisition is natural, as may be seen from the following passage from one of his major logico-linguistic works, a commentary on Aristotle's *De Interpretatione:* "The relationship of thoughts within the soul to the entities outside the soul is based on nature. By contrast, the relationship of thought to speech, i.e., the relationship of being signified by speech, is based on sheer legislation" (*ʿIbārah*, 27).[37]

For Alfārābī, then, thoughts are natural and depend on things as they are, whereas language is based on human consensus. It is in this sense that Alfārābī and the other Arab logicians defended their thesis concerning the superiority of logic over language.[38] According to the Arab logicians, the realm of logic, i.e., of thought, is superior to that of language since the former is universal, natural and nonconventional.

While in Baghdād, where he spent a significant portion of his intellectual life, Alfārābī studied both disciplines, Greek logic and Arabic grammar. There is no doubt that he knew the details of the debate between Mattā and Sīrāfī and he was probably often questioned by his students about the relationship between logic and grammar, as Mahdī suggests in his introduction to **Kitāb al-ḥurūf** [Book of letters], one of Alfārābī's major logical works.[39] One should mention in this regard Alfārābī's close association with the grammarian Abū Bakr al-Sarrāj, who was taught logic and music by Alfārābī in return for teaching the latter Arabic grammar. Many of al-Sarrāj's students became famous grammarians. One was no other than Abū Saʿīd al-Sīrāfī, the same individual who represented the grammarians in the previously mentioned debate between Arab grammarians and the defenders of Greek logic. It is possible that some of the elements of Greek logic that we find in the writings of the tenth- and eleventh-century grammarians were introduced to the grammarians through this contact between Alfārābī and al-Sarrāj, as Versteegh has suggested.[40]

Alfārābī's logical writings clearly indicate that he recognized the importance of the relationship between logic and language and the importance of linguistic analysis in logical inquiries. Two of these works (**Kitāb al-alfāẓ al-mustaʿmalah fī ʾl-manṭiq** [Book of utterances employed in logic][41] and **Ḥurūf**) are devoted almost exclusively to the question of philosophical and logical terminology with a clear attempt on Alfārābī's part to reconcile Aristotle's logic to the Arabic language and vice versa.

In the opening paragraph of his **"Kitāb al-qiyās al-ṣaghīr"** [A short commentary on the prior analytics],[42] a work addressed to the Islamic community at large, Alfārābī states that his intention is not only to present Aristotle's laws of logic accurately, but also to inquire how to present these laws by means of well-known expressions in the Arabic language [*bi-alfāẓ mashhūrah ʿinda ahl al-lisān al-ʿarabī*]. Alfārābī also promises that he will provide examples that are well known to his contemporaries, in order to illustrate clearly the Aristotelian principles of logic. Aristotle, according to Alfārābī, uses expressions that were known to the speakers of his language (Greek) and examples with which his (i.e., Aristotle's) contemporaries were familiar. However, Alfārābī's argument continues, since these expressions are not the same as those used by the speakers of the Arabic language and the examples are not the same examples, it was inevitable that what Aristotle intended to show would be incomprehensible to Alfārābī's contemporaries. This led to the unfortunate result, Alfārābī says, that many of his contemporaries thought Aristotle's books of logic had no value [*lā-jadwā lahā*]; consequently they tended to dismiss them.

Alfārābī believes that the task of following [*iqtifāʾ*] Aristotle's teaching does not mean that one has to use the same examples and expressions as those used by Aristotle himself in order to explain his principles. "Rather," Alfārābī says,

> following him [Aristotle] means that we should follow his intention in this respect.[43] It is not Aristotle's intention to treat the subject matter of his books by means of those examples alone excluding all others. Rather, his intention is to make these rules known to people by means of whatever happens to be most familiar to them. Nor is it the case that following [Aristotle] should mean that one has to present [his rules] to the speakers of our language [*ahl lisāninā*] by means of Greek expressions. (Ibid., 245)

Therefore, Alfārābī's task, as he sees it, is to contribute to the efforts begun by the translators, to make the Aristotelian principles comprehensible to Arab students of logic. The issue for Alfārābī, however, was not a matter of mere translation from Greek into Arabic. The task of rendering Greek words and sentences in a literal sense into Arabic had already been carried out by the translators many decades before Alfārābī began his logical career.

Essentially Alfārābī changed the task-focus from a literal and passive translation of Greek logical works into Arabic to an active translation accompanied by actual philosophical analysis, thus embarking on a systematic treatment of logical issues in a new medium, the Arabic language. What mattered to Alfārābī, in other words, was the *meaning* [*maʿnā*] rather than the *utterance* [*lafẓ*]. Although his extant works do not indicate that he has theoretical views on translation, it is clear that Alfārābī believes in universal inter-translatability, whereas his grammarian opponents believe in some sort of linguistic relativism a la Sapir/Whorf, a dichotomy we will return to at the conclusion of this study.

Believing in universal inter-translatability, Alfārābī thus presupposes that languages are basically external expressions of one and the same thing, namely the concepts of the mind, which are enduring, universal, and common to all nations, and therefore languages can be adjusted in order to encompass ideas expressed in other languages. Thus he justifies one of the major logical tasks he sets himself, namely, giving the Arabic language a new impetus so that it can encompass the ideas of the Greeks. Similarly, he realizes that the Aristotelian corpus must be interpreted in such a way as to be rendered comprehensible and acceptable to his fellow Muslims—a second major task.

Realizing that these two tasks are interrelated, Alfārābī undertakes both simultaneously. His works describing the first of these tasks are masterpieces that have contributed significantly to the development of a major theme in tenth-century Arabic logic, namely the relationship between Arabic grammar and Aristotelian logic. By "Aristotelian logic" we mean not only the logical works of Aristotle (known as the *Organon*) but also many of the commentaries by later Greek logicians on these works, particularly Porphyry's *Isagoge*,[44] on which many of Alfārābī's analyses are modeled.

The shift from passive to active translation of Greek logical and philosophical works into Arabic, a shift to interpretation and commentary, not only enabled Alfārābī to produce a well-developed philosophical dictionary in Arabic, but assisted Arab logicians in analyzing the Arabic language from a logical point of view. The purpose of this shift is not only to extend the meanings of certain existing terms but also (and primarily) to modify or explain in a simple manner certain structural features of the language which Alfārābī considers inadequate to the new task, i.e., the introduction of Greek philosophy and logic to the Islamic world.

The present study describes Alfārābī's logico-linguistic enterprise in six chapters. The first five chapters discuss Alfārābī's use of language in analyzing logical theories—the theory of definition, theory of demonstration and the four Aristotelian causes. The last chapter shows Alfārābī's use of logical principles in analyzing the Arabic language or certain aspects thereof. With a view to solving philosophical problems the sixth chapter is the most deserving to be called "Alfārābī's linguistic philosophy" in the "ordinary language" sense.[45]

Throughout chapter 6 of this study, and to a lesser extent in chapter 5, an attempt will be made to compare Alfārābī's use and analysis of the Arabic language with the grammarians' views. I have tried to present the grammarians' views as reflected in Sībaweih's *Al-kitāb* [The book],[46] as well as those expressed by a number of Alfārābī's contemporaries with whom Alfārābī interacted in one way or another, such as: al-Zajjāj (d. 923), Ibn al-Anbārī (d. 939), al-Zajjājī (d. 951), al-Sīrāfī (d. 979), al-Rummānī (d. 994), Ibn Fāris (d. 1004), and al-Sarrāj (d. 928), Alfārābī's teacher in grammar and his student in logic and music.

Among the logicians, Alfārābī mostly drew on and referred to Aristotle's works, but on many occasions Porphyry's and others' ideas are strongly reflected or even explicitly mentioned in his writings. Although the present study is primarily a philosophical analysis rather than a survey of the history of ideas, some historical aspects are considered in order to place Alfārābī's work in the context of his predecessors and contemporaries.[47]

Notes to Introduction

1. Al-Kindī (ca. A.D. 800 – 873), generally referred to as the first Arab philosopher, made important contributions to the field of Islamic philosophy in general, but his activity in the field of logic was minimal. Cf. his concise definitions of Arabic logical and philosophical terms in "Fī ḥudūd al-ashāy᾽ warusūmihā" [On the definition and description of things] in *Rasā᾽il al-Kindī al-falsafiyyah* [Al-Kindī's philosophical essays], ed. Muḥammad ʿAbd al-Hādī Abū Rīdah (Cairo: Dār al-fikr al-ʿarabī, 1950), pp. 165 – 179.

2. Moritz Steinschneider, *Al-Fārābī, des arabischen Philosophen: Leben und Schriften mit besonderer Ruecksicht auf die Geschichte der griechischen Wissenschaft unter den Arabern* (Amsterdam: Philo Press, 1966), p. 8.

3. Richard Walzer, article on "Alfārābī" in the *Encyclopedia of Islam* (Leiden: E. J. Brill, new edition).

4. **Mabādi᾽ al-mawjūdāt** is another name for Alfārābī's **Al-siyāsah al-madaniyyah** [The political regime], ed. Fawzī Najjār (Beirūt: Al-maṭbaʿah al-kāthūlīkiyyah, 1964). This work does not deal with logical matters, however. Obviously Maimonides does not mean here that this work is the best among Alfārābī's logical works (as one is inclined to understand from his statement), but rather that it is the best among his works in general.

5. M. Bar-Yoseph, ed. *Igrot ha-rambam* [Maimonides: letters and biography], (Tel-Aviv: Mordechay Institute for Publishing Judaica, 1970), pp. 127 – 128 (in Hebrew).

6. Ibn al-Qifṭī, *Ta᾽rīkh al-ḥukamā᾽* [Biographies of the wise], ed. J. Lippert (Leipzig: Dieterich'sche Verlagsbuchhandlung, 1903), p. 277.

7. Philip K. Hitti, *History of the Arabs* (London: Macmillan & Co. Ltd., 1960), p. 687.

8. As quoted in ibid., p. 372.

9. Ibn Taymiyyah, *Al-radd ʿalā ʾl-manṭiqiyyīn* [Answer to the logicians], ed. al-Kutubi (Bombay: Qayyimah Press, 1949), p. 41.

10. Muḥsin Mahdī, "Islamic Philosophy: The Eastern and Western Schools," in *Islam: The Perenniality of Values*. Special issue of *Cultures*, vol. 4, no. 1 (1977), p. 41.

Another scholar, who lived at the beginning of this century, asserts the importance of Alfārābī by comparing him to Avicenna. T. J. De Boer, in his *History of Philosophy in Islam* (New York: Dover Publication, 1967), p. 132, says: "The notion that Ibn Sīnā pushed on beyond Fārābī and reached pure Aristotelianism, is perhaps the greatest error which has found a footing in the history of Muslim Philosophy."

Still another contemporary Islamicist and a specialist on Alfārābī maintains a similar view. In his *Al-Fārābī's Commentary and Short Treatise on Aristotle's De Interpretatione* (Oxford: Oxford University Press, 1981), F. W. Zimmermann states that in his view "there is little in the logic of Avicenna that is not foreshadowed in that of al-Fārābī" (p. lxxxiv, n. 2).

11. Joel L. Kraemer, *Philosophy in the Renaissance of Islam* (Leiden: E. J. Brill, 1986), p. ix.

12. For a brief history of the translation of Aristotle's work into Arabic, cf. F. E. Peters, *Aristotle and the Arabs* (New York: New York University Press, 1968), pp. 57–67.

13. Muḥsin Mahdī, "Language and Logic in Classical Islam," in ed. G. E. von Grunebaum, *Logic in Classical Islamic Culture* (Wiesbaden: Harrassowitz, 1970), p. 53.

14. Porphyry's *Isagoge*, tr. Edward W. Warren (Toronto: The Pontifical Institute of Medieval Studies, 1975), a propaedeutic work for the study of Aristotle's logical works, was known to every student of philosophy in the Islamic world; indeed it was considered indispensable to the study of the *Organon* and by the sixth century had become an integral part of it (cf. Peters, op cit., pp. 8–9).

15. Mahdī, "Language and Logic," p. 54.

16. Al-Tawḥīdī, *Al-imtāʿ wa-ʾl-muʾānasah* [On pleasure and conviviality], eds. A. Amīn and A. al-Zayn (Beirūt, n.d.), vol. 1, p. 109. [Henceforth: *Imtāʿ*]

17. Gerhart Endress, "The Debate Between Arabic Grammar and Greek Logic," in *Journal for the History of Arab Science*, vol. 1, no. 2 (Nov. 1977), p. 110.

18. In Abū Bakr al-Rāzī, *Rasāʾil falsafiyyah* [Philosophical essays] (Beirūt: Dār al-āfāq al-jadīdah, 1975), p. 44.

19. Ibid., p. 43.

20. *Imtāᶜ* p. 108: 10ff.

21. A very similar view is held by the eleventh-century philosopher and logician Avicenna (Ibn Sīnā). See, for example, his definition of logic in his *Al-najāt*, [Book of deliverance], ed. al-Kurdī (Cairo: 1938), p. 3: "I start with a detailed description of the art of logic because it is the instrument which prevents the mind from committing errors, both in conception [*taṣawwur*] and in judgment [*taṣdīq*]. It is the instrument that leads to true beliefs as well as to the reasons for and the right way to achieve them."

22. *Imtāᶜ*, p. 109.

23. Ibid., p. 113: 13–16.

24. Ibid., p. 115: 1–2.

25. Ibid., p. 111: 11: "You are not, therefore, asking us [to study] the science of logic, but rather to study the Greek language."

Al-Sīrāfī's position on this issue represents what some contemporary philosophers of language call a "naturalistic" (rather than a "constructionistic") point of view and can be summed up in the words of F. Sommers as follows: "The naturalist believes with Aristotle and Leibniz that logical syntax is implicit in the grammar of natural language and that the structure attributed by grammarians to sentences of natural language is in close correspondence to their logical form." Fred Sommers, *The Logic of Natural Language* (Oxford: Clarendon Press, 1982), p. 2. Modern parallels to these medieval debates will be dealt with further in the conclusion to this study.

26. An equally strong reaction to the logicians' position came later from the theologians, who did not, however, object in a systematic and meaningful way until the thirteenth century, when Ibn Taymiyyah wrote his *Al-radd ᶜalā ʾl-manṭiqiyyīn*.

27. At least, this is the picture painted in al-Tawḥīdī's description of this debate. At various junctures, in response to particularly incisive points made by the grammarian Abu Saᶜid al-Sīrāfī, the logician Mattā "was bewildered" (*Imtāᶜ*, p. 114: 5) or "was troubled and hung his head and was choked by his saliva" (ibid., p. 119: 2), unable to produce counterarguments.

28. Utterances not in the sense of speech-acts but rather of composite utterances, i.e., utterances in the context of sentences.

29. *Imtāᶜ*, p. 114: 6–9. This position was also defended by Avicenna. Cf. Ibn Sīnā, *Al-shifāʾ, al-manṭiq, 3: al-ᶜibārah* [De interpretatione: book of healing, part 3], ed. M. al-Khodeirī (Cairo: Dār al-Kātib al-ᶜarabī, 1970), p. 5.

Elsewhere Avicenna says that logicians need natural languages only in order to be able to address logical issues and to communicate with others about these issues. Logic, according to him, does not deal with utterances per se because these are only a tool and can theoretically be replaced by some other device [*ḥīlah*] through which one can express logical relations without the mediation of a natural language. (Ibn Sīnā, *Al-shifāʾ, al-manṭiq, 1: al-madkhal* [Isagoge: book of healing, part 1], eds. G. Anawātī, M. al-Khodeirī and F. al-Ahwānī (Cairo: Al-maṭbaʿah al-amiriyyah, 1952), p. 22.

30. Yaḥyā Ibn ʿAdī, "On the Difference Between Philosophical Logic and Arabic Grammar," ed. Gerhart Endress in *Journal for the History of Arab Science,* vol. 2 (1978), pp. 38–50.

31. Ibid., p. 49. By "universal meanings" [*al-alfāẓ al-dāllah ʿalā ʾl-umūr al-kulliyyah*], Ibn ʿAdī means the five predicables (or universal predicates): genus, species, differentia, property, and universal accidents (ibid., p. 47: 2–3). For the meaning of each of these five terms and its place in logical inquiries see chapter 1 of this study.

32. Ibid., p. 50.

33. For the position of Sijistānī on this issue consult J. Kraemer, op. cit., p. 142.

34. Al-Tawḥīdī, *Al-muqābasāt* [Adaptations], ed. M. T. Husein (Baghdād: 1970), pp. 121–125.

35. Ibid., pp. 91–92.

36. Alfārābī, **Iḥṣāʾ al-ʿulūm**, ed. ʿUthmān Amīn (Cairo: 1968), third edition, p. 74. [Henceforth: **Iḥṣāʾ**]

37. Alfārābī, **Sharḥ Alfārābī li-kitāb Arisṭūtālīs fī ʾl-ʿibārah**, [Alfārābī's commentary on Aristotle's De interpretatione], eds. W. Kutsch and S. Marrow (Beirūt: Al-maṭbaʿah al-kathūlīkiyyah, 1960). [Henceforth: **ʿIbārah**] See also **Alfārābī's Kitāb al-siyāsah al-madaniyyah**, p. 70: 6–7.

38. See Abū Bishr Mattā's position on the issue of universality of thought: "But people are equal in matters conceived by mind: cannot you see that four plus four equals eight with all nations, and similarly for things like this?" (*Imtāʿ*, p. 111: 2). Alfārābī for his part expresses this very same idea in the following manner:

> That is to say, the thoughts all men understand when expressed in their different languages *are the same for* them. The sense-object which those thoughts are thoughts of are *also* common *to all*. For whatever individual thing an Indian may have a sensation of—if the same thing is observed by an Arab, he will have the same perception of it as the Indian. (**ʿIbārah**, as translated by Zimmermann, *Al-Fārābī's Commentary,* pp. 12–13, emphasis his.)

39. Alfārābī, **Kitāb al-ḥurūf**, ed. Muḥsin Mahdī (Beirūt: Dār al-mashriq, 1970), p. 48. [Henceforth: **Ḥurūf**] Given its content—which is largely devoted to the grammatical particles, their meaning and use in philosophy, logic and

other disciplines—this title might more appropriately be translated as "Book of Particles." The word *ḥurūf* (plural of *ḥarf*) has both meanings, "particles" and "letters."

40. C. H. M. Versteegh, *Greek Elements in Arabic Linguistic Thinking* (Leiden: E. J. Brill, 1977), p. 140: "On the whole, we believe that Fārābī was Zağğāğī's primary source for the logical definitions, probably through Ibn as-Sarrāj, his pupil and Zağğāğī's teacher."

41. Alfārābī, **Kitāb al-alfāẓ al-mustaʿmalah fī ʾl-manṭiq**, ed. Muḥsin Mahdī (Beirūt: 1968). [Henceforth: **Alfāẓ**]

42. Alfārābī, "**Kitāb al-qiyās al-ṣaghīr**," ed. Mubahat Turker, in: *Ankara Üniversitesi: Dil ve Tarih-Cografya Fakultesi Dergisi*, 16 (1958): 244 – 86. [Henceforth: **Qiyās ṣaghīr**]

43. I.e., in giving certain examples and using certain terms and expressions.

44. Op. cit.

45. John R. Searle, *Speech Act: An Essay in the Philosophy of Language* (England: Cambridge University Press, 1969), p. 4. The relevance of Searle's concept of "ordinary language" to Alfārābī's linguistic views will be explained further in the conclusion of this study.

46. ʿAmr Ibn ʿUthmān Sībaweih, *Al-kitāb*, 5 vols., ed. ʿA. S. M. Hārūn (Cairo: Dār al-qalam, al-hayʾah al-miṣriyyah al-ʿāmmah li-l-kitāb, 1966–1977).

47. For a historical perspective on Alfārābī's logical views, cf. F. W. Zimmermann, *Al-Fārābī's Commentary and Short Treatise on Aristotle's De Interpretatione.*

1

Particulars and Universals: An Introduction to Alfārābī's Logical Lexicon

One of the major requirements for an understanding of Alfārābī's logical writings, or rather for an understanding of Arabic logic in general, is familiarity with the terminology used in Arabic logical texts. The major portion of the logical terminology was introduced by the translators of Aristotle's *Organon* into Arabic. The literal nature of these translations, however, makes it very difficult even for the specialized reader to comprehend the technical meaning of these terms or the logical theories with which they are associated.

Alfārābī's primary aim in a number of his logical works is to break this vicious circle by attending to the principle that in order to understand the philosophical and logical meaning of terms, one must explore their use in logical contexts. Meaning and use of terms in logical contexts is thus a major theme in Alfārābī's writings, particularly in **Alfāẓ** and **Ḥurūf.** Indeed, the former can be described as Alfārābī's metalogical work par excellence.

Alfārābī flatly declares in **Alfāẓ** (p. 43: 10–11) that he is concerned with references [*dalālāt*] and meanings [*maʿānī*] of terms only from a logical point of view. This is perhaps an example of what Abū Saʿīd al-Sīrāfī referred to in his already-outlined debate with Abū Bishr Mattā as the logicians' penchant for "building a language within a language."[1] In fact, however, this and other such statements by Alfārābī indicate not an intention to invent a new Arabic language completely divorced from the old but simply to develop a specialized "logical lexicon" of the meaning of Arabic words as used in logic. His logical lexicon is not a disregard of the everyday meanings of Arabic words, but an *extension* of their meanings for use in the field of logic, just as each art and science has its own terminology.

Alfārābī's logical lexicon is not a lexicon in the traditional sense of a dictionary based on the individual treatment of terms. Rather it is composed in such a manner that the logical meaning of each term emerges from its use in a logical system or context. This systematic treatment of Arabic terms used in logic—a methodology that might be termed "logical meaning in use"—is far more comprehensive and illuminating than the conventional lexical definition of such terms would have been and will be the primary focus of this and subsequent chapters.

In a sense, the first five chapters of the current study represent a summary of Alfārābī's logical lexicon. Chapter 1 deals with most of the basic logical terms and concepts used in Arabic, illustrating Alfārābī's approach to the analysis and systematization of these terms, and therefore is an appropriate introduction to "Alfārābī's Logical Lexicon."

Chapter 1 will be divided into 5 sections. Section 1 will involve a discussion of the terms *particular* and *universal*, what they signify, and the relationships (linguistic, ontological, and epistemological) between them in Alfārābī's writings. This discussion of particulars and universals is an important basis for future discussion of the logical theories of definition and predication, the former to be dealt with primarily in chapter 2 and the latter, throughout the present study.

Special attention is paid in section 1 of this chapter to the Aristotelian concept of "primary substances" (individual material things or "particulars") and how the various "predicates" (or "attributes") relate to them. The treatment of the primary substances and their relationships to the universals occupies a significant portion of both Aristotle's and Alfārābī's writings. In this chapter, I focus principally on Alfārābī's views, with occasional references to Aristotle. (For a more detailed discussion of the Aristotelian view see appendix I.)

In sections 2 through 5 of this chapter, the five singular universals (or "predicables") are introduced (with "genus" and "species" discussed together because of strong interrelationships between them). Discussion of two additional (compound) predicables — "definition" [*ḥadd*] and "description" [*rasm*]—is reserved for chapter 2.

In merging the Porphyrian list of five predicables (genus, species,[2] essential difference, property, and accident) with the Aristotelian (genus, essential difference, property, accident, and definition), Alfārābī paves the way for other Arab logicians to join him in accepting as standard a system of six predicables.[3] No Arab logician denies that Porphyry's "species" [*nawʿ*] is a predicable, along with "genus" [*jins*], "difference" [*faṣl*], "property" [*khāṣṣah*], and "accident" [*ʿaraḍ*], just as they interpreted Porphyry to mean. Yet neither Alfārābī nor the other Arab logicians is willing to relinquish "definition" [*ḥadd*] — Aristotle's candidate for the fifth predicable. Following Alfārābī's lead, all the Arab logicians try to marry the two approaches, thus practically adopting a system of *six* universals [*kulliyyāt*, pl. of *kullī*] or "general terms" [*maᶜānī ᶜāmmah*], as they are also called.

Porphyry's influence will also be apparent in Alfārābī's analysis of the relationships between the universals, which follows lines similar to those employed by Porphyry in his *Isagoge*. Alfārābī's analysis in this area (a la Porphyry) is based on what is today referred to as "class relations" between predicables.

Particulars and Universals in Alfārābī's Writings

In two of Alfārābī's logical works ("**Kitāb īsāghūjī ay al-madkhal**" 119;[4] **Alfāẓ**, 58–59), a "universal" [*kullī*][5] is defined as such that two or more things resemble it (lit., become similar through or by means of it [*yatashabbah bih*]).[6] In other words, it is a thing that can be predicated [*yuḥmal*] of more than one "subject" [*mawḍūᶜ*]. A "particular" (or "individual") [*shakhṣ*] is a thing that cannot be predicated of more than one thing (**Madkhal**, 119).

In **Alfāẓ** Alfārābī explains this last point in the following manner: certain notions [*maᶜānī mafhūmah*], such as the names of individual people or things (e.g., 'Zayd,' 'ᶜAmr,' 'this horse,' 'this wall'), cannot be predicated of anything at all,[7] while other individual things, such as 'this white spot' [*hādhā ʾl-bayāḍ*] or 'that coming man' [*dhālik al-muqbil*], can only be predicated of one thing [*tuḥmal ᶜalā shayʾⁱⁿ-mā waḥdah lā ghayr*]. (**Alfāẓ**, 59).[8] Thus, according to Alfārābī, *particular things* may be categorized according to whether 1) they are predicated of one thing only or 2) they are not predicated of anything at all. This distinction is of great philosophical import, as we shall see in Alfārābī's commentary on Aristotle's *Categories*.

Near the beginning of this commentary (known as "**Kitāb qāṭāghūriyās ay al-maqūlāt**" ["Al-Fārābī's paraphrase of *The Categories* of Aristotle"]),[9] Alfārābī presents this very same distinction in more abstract form:

> Individuals [*ashkāṣ*, pl. of *shakhṣ*] are of two kinds. One kind belongs to a subject [*lah mawḍūᶜ*][10] and defines [*yuᶜarrif*] what is outside the essence[11] of that subject, but does not define the essence of any subject whatsoever. These are the individual accidents [*shakhṣ al-ᶜaraḍ*].[12] The other kind [belongs to no subject and] defines neither the essence nor anything outside it whatsoever. These are the individual substances [*shakhṣ al-jawhar*]. (**Maqūlāt**, 169)

In order to reach a more complete understanding of this significant classification, one should view it in the context of the broader fourfold classification of 'what there is,'[13] which Alfārābī (following the second chapter of Aristotle's *Categories*) offers in this work (**Maqūlāt**, 169). Following is a brief summary of the Aristotelian classification, Alfārābī's view of which will be described in greater depth below.

1. things that are 'said of' but are not 'in';
2. things that are 'said of' and 'in';
3. things that are 'in' but not 'said of'; and
4. things that are neither 'in' nor 'said of.'

Alfārābī's classification, like that of Aristotle, relies on two expressions — 'said of a subject' [*al-maqūl ʿalā mawḍūʿ*] and 'said in a subject' [*al-maqūl fī mawḍūʿ*] — the definition of which Alfārābī attributes to Aristotle: "Aristotle refers to the universal predicate [*al-maḥmūl al-kullī*] that defines the essence of the subject as 'what is said of its subject,' and to that which defines an aspect of the subject that is external to its essence as 'what is said to be in a subject' "[14] (**Maqūlāt**, 169).

On the basis of the above-mentioned notions 'said of' and 'said in,' Alfārābī describes the fourfold Aristotelian classification of things (**Maqūlāt**, 169):[15]

(1) Things that are said of a subject but are never in a subject.[16] These are the "universal substances" [*kullī ʾl-jawhar*],[17] or as Alfārābī refers to them elsewhere in **Maqūlāt**, "secondary substances" [*jawāhir thawānī*] (**Maqūlāt**, 170).[18]

(2) Things that are both said of a subject and in a subject. These are the "universal accidents" [*kullī ʾl-ʿaraḍ*] (**Maqūlāt**, 169).[19] As far as Alfārābī is concerned, the universal accidents play no role whatsoever in defining the essences of substances [*mā hiyyāt al-jawāhir*]. If anything, he says, it is due to the latter that the former are comprehended and conceptualized [*an taṣīr maʿqūlah*] (**Maqūlāt**, 171). In fact, all predicates [*maḥmūlāt*] of the primary substance, other than the universal substance, have no independent existence, since they "need the [primary] substance in order to exist."

(3) Things that are in a subject but never said of a subject. These are the "individual accidents" [*shakhṣ al-ʿaraḍ*] (**Maqūlāt**, 169).[20] Alfārābī supplements this statement in **Ḥurūf** (p. 103: 4–5, par. 70) by adding that these things are never called substances, neither relatively nor absolutely [*lā bi-ʾl-iḍāfah wa-lā bi-ʾl-iṭlāq*].

(4) Things that are neither in a subject nor said of a subject. These are the "individual substances" [*shakhṣ al-jawhar*] (**Maqūlāt**, 169)[21] or as Alfārābī also calls them—following the Arabic translator of Aristotle's *Categories*—the "primary substances" [*jawāhir uwal*].[22]

Thus, for both Aristotle and Alfārābī, categories 1 and 2 (universal substances and universal accidents) encompass "universals," whereas categories 3 and 4 (individual accidents and individual substances) encompass "individuals" (introduced at the beginning of this section as 1) predicated of one thing only or 2) not predicated of anything at all).

Substances (whether individual or universal) are, therefore, never in a subject, whereas nonsubstances (accidents) are always in a subject, i.e., in a primary substance. Thus the notion 'in a subject' helps to distinguish things that have no independent existence from things that exist in their own right. This is, in other words, the distinction between substances and the attributes they possess.

Yet substances themselves are of two kinds, individuals and universals. Attributes, too, are either individuals or universals. Thus the notion 'said of a subject' is used in reference to the relationship between universals and individuals.

In one passage of his **Madkhal** (p. 119), Alfārābī describes one aspect of the universal/individual interactions on the *linguistic* level. By "interactions" I mean the five different possible groupings of these terms in a sentence, possibilities which Alfārābī presents as follows:

1. *The subject and the predicate of a proposition* [qaḍiyyah] *are both universals,*[23] such as in the proposition, 'man is an animal.' This is the kind of proposition used in science [*ʿulūm*], in dialectics [*jadal*], in sophistical arts [*ṣināʿah sūfisṭāʾiyyah*], and in many other arts.
2. *The subject and the predicate are both individuals,* for example, 'Zayd is this standing person.' This type of proposition, however, is seldom used in any discipline.
3. *The subject is an individual and the predicate is a universal,* such as in the statement, 'Zayd is a man.' This type of proposition is much used in rhetoric, in poetry, and in the practical arts.
4. *The subject is a universal and the predicate is an individual.* In this case there are two possibilities considered by Alfārābī.
   a) *The predicate of the proposition is a single individual,* such as in the statement, 'Man is Zayd.' This type of proposition is used in analogy [*tamthīl*].

b) *The predicate of the proposition is composed of several individuals,* such as in the statement, 'Man is Zayd and ʿAmr and Khālid.' This type of proposition is used in induction [*istiqrāʾ*].

Alfārābī in this passage[24] is considering neither the quality (affirmative or negative) nor the quantity ('some,' 'every,' 'all') of these propositions. He is offering a classification of indefinite propositions. His aim is not to come up with logical conclusions. Rather, he is seeking here methodological results, such as a classification of the sciences and the methods used in these sciences.

Although the passage is brief and lacks the necessary details from which to draw any far-reaching conclusions about Alfārābī's attitude toward classification of the sciences and their methodologies, there are still certain important observations to be made. Firstly, there is no precedent in Aristotle for this classification.

Secondly, the passage is evidence that for Alfārābī a proposition must have at least one term that stands for a universal in order to be of any significance for this methodological classification. When he considers the proposition whose subject and predicate are both individuals (or stand for individuals), he says that it is seldom used, implying that it has no application in any branch of science. This is the second category in the above classification (which I will call Type II, to indicate that this is a sentence in which both the subject and the predicate are Individuals).

Thirdly, note that the two major branches of knowledge (in the Aristotelian system)—i.e., theoretical and practical philosophy—are categorized by Alfārābī according to the type of propositions used in them:

(1) If the subject and predicate are both universals (the first category, which I will call Type UU), then we are in the domain of natural science, dialectics, sophistical arts, or other arts (Alfārābī does not specify), in short, the domain of Aristotle's "theoretical philosophy."

(2) However, if only the predicate is a universal (the third category above, Type IU), then we are in the domain of poetry, rhetoric, or the practical arts [*ṣanāʾiʿ ʿamaliyyah*], i.e., Aristotle's "practical philosophy."

The fourth category of Alfārābī's classification (Type UI) refers to propositions used in methods of research or proof: analogy and induction.[25]

As far as I know, this approach to classification is unique in the history of logic.[26]

We will proceed now to an examination of the individual/universal relationship from another point of view, important for our discussion of the *theory of definition* (in chapter 2). The position of "primary substances" and "secondary substances" in Alfārābī's system and their relationships to one another leads us to explore *ontological* and *epistemological* aspects of Alfārābī's **Maqūlāt.**

Alfārābī defends the primacy of the individual substances over all else, including the universals which are said of them. The former need no subject for their being; they are self-sufficient from an ontological point of view for they are 'neither in a subject nor [said] of a subject'[27] (**Maqūlāt**, 170). Alfārābī clearly emphasizes that this primacy is from the ontological point of view, or what he calls "by nature."[28] In the short paragraph in which he analyzes this topic, Alfārābī mentions the word *wujūd* [existence] and its derivatives several times. He explicitly states that primary substances "are more entitled to be substances since they are ontologically prior to their universals"[28] (**Maqūlāt**, 170, par. 4). This explains, Alfārābī argues, why the individual substances are called "primary substances" (ibid.).

In the case of secondary substances, it is clear that for Alfārābī ontological priority is the only sense in which primary substances have primacy: "universals come into existence due to their individuals, and the individuals are intellectually apprehended through their universals" (**Maqūlāt**, 171).

Although he mentions universals without any qualification, it is evident that Alfārābī in this passage is not talking about all kinds of universals. According to him, there is only one category of universals that fits this description: the secondary substances, i.e., the universal substances. Only these predicates [*maḥmūlāt*] can define or make the essence of their subjects known and thus he calls them "their universals" [*kulliyyātuhā*], with "their" referring to the individual things (**Maqūlāt**, 170).[30]

The nonsubstantial universals, on the other hand, need [*muftaqirah* or *taḥtāj*][31] the individual things in two respects: 1) they cannot exist without the primary substances and 2) they cannot be grasped (or perceived) without them (**Maqūlāt**, 171). In this case, therefore, there are two kinds of primacy of primary substances over nonsubstantial universals: ontological and epistemological.

We have seen above that according to Alfārābī no other thing would exist if the primary substances did not exist. And by "no other thing" I mean everything other than the individual objects, not even the secondary substances. This I have described as an ontological priority of the primary substances over everything else. In other words, for Alfārābī everything is dependent upon the existence of primary substances. None of the things that one can imagine may exist without the existence of the primary substances (i.e., the individual objects); the existence of everything else depends on the existence of the primary substances, and hence they have the strongest claim to independent reality, which makes them "prime applicants for the title 'substance,' " to use the words of a modern commentator on Aristotle.[32] In other words, we cannot think of any qualities without thinking of a subject to which they are attached, whereas the existence of the primary substance does not depend on any specific quality for its existence.

However, a legitimate question can be raised against Alfārābī in this regard:[33] how can we think or present or imagine any individual without certain qualities? I can think of a specific table not being red, but I cannot think of it without having *any* color. It is true that the same table will continue to exist without a specific quality in any possible (imaginable) world where it has an existence, but again, it must be red or black or some other color; it must be round or square or some other shape. It cannot be without any qualities; it is not independent of them, it cannot exist without them.

If so, then how can we determine what is prior to what: the so-called primary substance or its qualities? Moreover, one can challenge the very conception of being a "substance" without certain qualities. But first let us try to resolve the former problem: the problem of priority.

Given the above argument, it is clear that when we talk about ontological priority of the primary substance over its attributes, we cannot mean temporal priority since it can be seriously doubted whether the primary substance would be able to exist before that which characterizes it. The idea behind this priority is perhaps what might be called "durability."[34] When Aristotle or Alfārābī speak of "knowing the essence" of a thing (i.e., defining a thing), they assume the existence of a thing that undergoes various changes while it is one and the same thing (the principle of identity). Aristotle, for instance, calls this the most distinctive characteristic of substance:

> It seems most distinctive of [primary] substance that what is numerically one and the same is able to receive contraries. In no other case could one bring forward anything, numerically one, which is able to receive contraries. A [primary] substance, however, numerically one and the same, is able to receive contraries. For ex-

ample, an individual man—one and the same—becomes pale at one time and dark at another, and hot and cold, and bad and good. Nothing like this is to be seen in any other case.[35]

It is reasonable to assume that Aristotle does not mean to say that the individual men existed before colors did. It is true that the specific 'white' that characterizes a specific individual man would not have existed without the existence of that man. But from this to conclude that individual men exist before the qualities (e.g., colors) that characterize them is not accurate, since 'whiteness' will continue to exist even if this specific 'man' disappears.

Aristotle (and Alfārābī with him) seems to be assuming that permanent or stable structures of entities do exist and that not everything is in a state of constant flux (a la Heraclitus). A table or an individual man will continue to exist regardless of external changes they may undergo. The specific quality (or qualities) is not essential for the existence of the individual table qua table. Perhaps it is essential for a table's existence as that table with that certain quality, but not for a table as such. A certain color of this table persists only by virtue of the existence of the table and due to the fact that it is predicated of it.[36] Colors and other qualities change while the table is the same table that I bought from a certain place at a certain time.

In that sense, individual things are more permanent than their specific qualities; they are more durable than their specific colors and other "external" (or accidental) qualities they may have. Priority, therefore, is the ability to endure while undergoing "external" changes. This is what Alfārābī means when he says in **Ḥurūf** (p. 97, par. 61): "Whatever is an accident of a thing subsists in that thing the least [*ʿalā ʾl-aqall*]. Whatever is essential and not accidental, however, is either permanent or present in most cases [*akthar al-awqāt*]."

But then we must face the second and more serious question: What is that thing which endures while undergoing changes? What is 'the table?' or more generally, what are the primary substances? If they are not a bundle of qualities, what are they and how can they be defined?[37]

Clearly one of the central questions in philosophy is, What is the "nature" or "essence" of things? In order to determine a thing's essence, we must "define" it. And "definition," according to the Aristotelians (including Alfārābī), involves identifying the thing by means of "universals." According to the Aristotelians, the most precise knowledge of a thing is attained through identification of its "genus" and its "specific difference." The formula combining these two universals is known as "essential definition" [*ḥadd*]. Lower degrees of knowledge of a thing (such as "description") may be obtained by means of the universals "property" and "universal accident." Thus, before proceeding to our discussion of "essence," a topic that will preoccupy us in chapters 2 through 5 (beginning with "definition" and "description" in chapter 2), we must first examine the *building blocks* of "essence," i.e., the "universals."

Having introduced the meaning of *kullī* [a universal] as that which is predicated of more than one thing, Alfārābī analyzes and examines this notion more closely in the third paragraph of his **Madkhal.** He does so by analyzing the linguistic terms that signify it in a categorical judgment.

According to him, "universals" (or "general terms" [*maᶜānī ᶜāmmah*]) are of two kinds: 1) those signified by singular expressions [*alfāẓ mufradah*] and 2) those signified by composite expressions and whose composition is restrictive and conditional [*tarkīb taqyīd wa-ishtirāṭ*] rather than declarative [*tarkīb ikhbārī*], such as when we say 'the white man' and 'the rational animal' (as opposed to 'the man is white' and 'the animal is rational'). In the latter example, 'animal' is restricted by 'rational,' and similarly 'man' is restricted by 'white' (**Madkhal**, 119).

Alfārābī also claims that "it is evident that composite general terms can be divided [*tanqasim*] into the singular [general terms]." Therefore, there is no need to talk about the former since we can understand them through analyzing the latter. The remainder of this chapter will be devoted to a discussion of category 1 above (the singular universals, including "genus," "species," "essential difference," "property," and "accident"). Discussion of category 2 above (the compound universals, including "definition" and "description") will be reserved for chapter 2.

Alfārābī's next step after differentiating between the two types of universals (singular and compound) is to concentrate on analyzing the general terms that "many of the ancients had considered to be five in number"[38] (**Madkhal**, 119). He then presents these general terms in the following order:[39] *jins* [genus], *nawᶜ* [species], *faṣl* [difference], *khāṣṣah* [property], and *ᶜaraḍ* [accident]. Each of these general terms (or predicables, as they are often called),[40] the relationships between them, and the relationship of each of them to the individual things are thoroughly discussed by Alfārābī in his various logical writings. His analysis of these topics will be the subject matter of the remainder of this chapter. The first of these terms to be discussed are "genus" and "species."

"Genus" and "Species" in Alfārābī

"Genus" and "species" are defined by Alfārābī as the two universals one employs in answering the question What is this individual?: "In general, 'genus' is the more general of two universals that may be employed in reply to the question: 'what is this individual?' and 'species' is the more specific of the two" (**Madkhal**, 120). A more complete explanation of these general terms appears in another work:

> If several universals signified by singular expressions participate in the predication [*al-ḥaml*] of [certain] individuals, and if each of these universals is appropriate in answering the question 'what are they (i.e., these individuals)?' then, the most specific of these universals is called "species" and the rest, which are more general, are called "genera." An example of this: [since] 'Zayd,' "ᶜAmr' and 'Khālid' have 'man,' 'animal,' 'nourished' and 'body' as their common predicates, and [since] each of the latter is signified by a singular expression, and [since] each is employed in answering the question 'what is each of these individuals?'—which is to say, when it is asked: 'what is Zayd?' and 'what is "ᶜAmr?'—and the most specific of these universals is 'man' whereas the rest are more general, then 'man' is called "the species" of those individuals and the rest—which is to say, 'animal,' 'nourished,' and 'body'—are called "genera." (**Alfāẓ**, 66)

The expressions "more general" and "more specific" are often used by Alfārābī when he discusses problems related to universals. These expressions have a logical meaning he discusses in **Alfāẓ**. The following general discussion of the terms *general* and *specific* will distract us momentarily from our discussion of *genus* and *species* in Alfārābī, yet the two sets of terms are clearly related, and an understanding of the terms *general* and *specific* is obviously vital for an understanding of the terms *genus* and *species*, to which we will return shortly.

The expressions "more general" and "more specific" usually surface when Alfārābī compares the different universals with one another. In **Alfāẓ** (p. 60 ff.), for example, this issue is raised when Alfārābī enumerates the different possible relationships between any two given universals. Any two universals, he says, stand in one of the following relationships to one another:

1. *Two predicates (universals) are both predicated of the very same individuals but whereas the scope*[41] *of one of them is confined [yaqtaṣir]*

only to those individuals under consideration, the scope of the other universal (which Alfārābī calls "the other partner" or [*mushārikah*]) *extends beyond these individuals,* i.e., it is predicated of more individuals. His examples in this case (as indeed in most of his logical writings) are taken from the biological world: 'animal' and 'man.' Both, he says, are predicated of individual human beings, but while the latter is predicated *only* of these individuals, the former is *also* predicated of individual 'horses' and 'donkeys' and indeed of all other animals. Thus 'animal' exceeds [*yafḍul*] 'man' in predication.[42]

2. *Two universals have certain elements in common as their subject of predication but each of them is also predicated of other individuals not within the scope of the other universal.* An example of this was mistakenly given by Alfārābī to illustrate Case 1 above (see preceding footnote), namely 'white' and 'man.' These predicates overlap but they do not coincide.
3. *Two universals are predicated of the very same individuals and only of those.* This relationship exists, for example, between the universals 'man' and 'capable of laughter' [*ḍaḥḥāk*] (**Alfāẓ**, 61), or between 'animal' and 'sensitive.' For 'man' is predicated of everything whereof 'laughter' is predicated and vice versa. And similarly where the pair 'animal' and 'sensitive' is concerned. Universals in this category are called "equal in predication" [*mutasāwiyah fī ʾl-ḥaml*] or [*mutasāwiqah fī ʾl-ḥaml*] (**Alfāẓ**, 61).
4. *Two universals have no common elements within the scope of their predication.* An example of this is the two universals 'man' and 'horse.' These two universals cannot be predicated of the same individual. Nor "can they be predicated of each other" (**Alfāẓ**, 62).

This last passage in Alfārābī, which mentions universals being (or not being) predicated of one another, is a new phase in Alfārābī's analysis and an important step from a logical point of view.

In the previous discussion, we presented Alfārābī's perception of the possible relationships between universals. These relationships, however, were explored indirectly by examining their relationships to a certain number of individuals of which they are or are not predicated. Now with the introduction of the notion that "one universal can or cannot be predicated of another" we arrive at a new situation, in which the previous intuitive concepts will be refined and systematized. Alfārābī is thereby moving from an intuitive explanation of the logical relationships between universals to a more profound and sophisticated discussion.

One universal, Alfārābī explains (**Alfāẓ**, 62, par. 16), is predicated of another either without qualification [*ḥaml muṭlaq*] or in a qualified way [*ḥaml ghayr muṭlaq*]. A predication without qualification is defined by him as a statement such that "if the expression 'all'[43] is attached to the subject [of the proposition] the judgment will be true [*ṣadaqa ʾl-ḥaml*], such as when we say, 'all men are animals' " (**Alfāẓ**, 62).

A qualified predication, on the other hand, is that which becomes false [*kadhaba ʾl-ḥaml*] when the expression 'all' is attached to its subject, such as when we say 'all animals are human beings.' But if one attaches the expression 'some' [*mā*] to this subject, Alfārābī explains, the judgment[44] may be true, since it is true to say 'some animals are human beings.'

This distinction between qualified and nonqualified judgments is parallel to the classification of general judgments into particular (both affirmative and negative) and universal judgments (both affirmative and negative). The distinction is important in explaining the relationships between the different universals in a more systematic and less intuitive way. Thus we find that Alfārābī's next step is the formulation of the following rule:

> If universals are predicated of the very same individuals and one of them is more general than the other,[45] then it follows[46] that that which is more general is predicated without qualification of that which is more specific, whereas the latter is predicated of the former in a qualified way. (**Alfāẓ**, 62)

Now in light of this new definition one can revise the four possible ways of joining universals into judgments, as indeed Alfārābī does (**Alfāẓ**, 63). But before examining this and before examining what I will call the "generalization" of the above definition, I would like to introduce the relatively modern logical notions of "extension of a term" and "class relations."

In my view, Alfārābī was thinking along these lines when he presented his views on the relationships between universals (or general terms). The extension of the general term *animal*, for example, is the class of all objects that can be truly called "animals." The extension of this term is broader than that of the general term *man*, which is subordinated to the former in that sense; in other words, the term *animal* is applicable to every object of which 'man' is truly said, but it is also applicable to other objects (horses, etc.). The class of objects, one can say, to which the term *animal* is applicable *contains* the class of objects to which the term *man* is applicable, and the latter is *contained* in the former. There are, however, further general terms subordinated to the general term *animal*, such as *horse, donkey,* indeed general terms that refer to or stand for any species of animal.

Using this terminology we can sum up Alfārābī's view on the relationships between general terms, which he describes in terms of qualified and nonqualified predication, in a simpler and perhaps more accurate way. For convenience, the term *class* will be used for the phrase "the class of all objects to which the general term is applicable." Thus the "class of animal" will mean "the class of all objects to which the general term *animal* is applicable." A "member" of that class will mean "one of those objects to which the term is applicable." Now we can formulate Alfārābī's views in the following manner:

> If the objects of a certain Class 'A' are themselves classes (i.e., subclasses of Class 'A'), then the following holds: The Class 'A' is predicated of each of these classes in an unqualified way, whereas each of them is predicated of the Class 'A' in a qualified way. Using symbols:
>
> If 'Z' is a subclass of 'W' then
> $$(x)\,[\,x \in Z \rightarrow x \in W\,].$$
> But $\sim (x)\,[\,x \in W \rightarrow x \in Z\,]$ or its equivalent form
> $$(\exists y)\,[y \in W \cdot y \notin Z\,].$$

This kind of relationship exists between a "species" and each of the "genera" predicated of the same individuals. But it also exists, according to Alfārābī's scheme (and here we move to the generalization step), between the various "genera" that are ranked under each other: "In general everything that can be a subject to a more general thing that is predicated of it in reply to the question, 'what is that thing?'[47] is said to be ranked under that thing" (**Alfāẓ**, 67, par. 22).

The "genera" predicated of a "species" are ranked, according to Alfārābī, in the following manner: one of these "genera" is the most specific and it is called the "proximate genus" [*al-jins al-qarīb*]. No other "genus" predicated of this given "species" can be more specific than this "genus." On the other hand, we have the "genus" that is the most general, "the supreme genus" [*al-jins al-ʿālī* or *al-jins al-baʿīd*]. And between these two extremes we have those genera "that are more general than the proximate genus but more specific than the supreme genus" (**Alfāẓ**, 67, par. 22); these are called the "intermediate genera" [*mutawassiṭāt*].

Alfārābī explicitly mentions that this category of "intermediate genera" always has more than one "genus."[48] Although Alfārābī gives the impression that his scheme is confined to the biological sensible world, it is clear that he means it to be a general and valid description of every given situation. One starts with certain individuals (and according to Alfārābī one always starts with familiar sensible individuals, abstracting universals from them)[49] and one can always construct this kind of scheme, even when talking about abstract entities such as numbers.

As to the question of whether or not there is one or more "supreme genera" and one or more "proximate species," Alfārābī seems noncommittal with reference to "supreme genera." He can only "assume" that there is more than one: "As for the 'supreme genus,' it is not clear yet whether it is one or more than one, and if it is more than one, it is not clear yet how many there are. Let us assume [*nunzil*] that it is more than one" (**Alfāẓ**, 68–69). With reference to "proximate genus," on the other hand, Alfārābī arrives at a definite answer: namely, there is more than one. The external world provides us with things "that are different in kind" (**Alfāẓ**, 70). Thus, from observation we *know* there is more than one "proximate genus."

The above description of "genus" and "species" in Alfārābī is important for an understanding of his theory of definition, a topic central to chapter 2. The second component of the formal Aristotelian "definition" is yet another universal, the "essential difference," to be treated in the following section. The reader will note Alfārābī's frequent use of "question particles" (e.g., *mā* [what?], *kayfa* [how?]) in his analysis of "essential difference." In fact, these question particles represent an integral component of Alfārābī's *theory of definition* and will be discussed more systematically in chapters 2 through 5.

Essential Difference [*Faṣl Dhātī*]

In **Madkhal** (pp. 121–122), Alfārābī explains that if the subject of inquiry (whether a species or an individual) is introduced as an answer to the 'what?' [*mā*] question by some remote genus that does not clearly introduce and define it, then one must proceed to ask further questions until the subject of inquiry becomes distinguished from other entities that are also the subject of predication of the same universals.

According to Alfārābī, one reaches this stage only when the *faṣl dhātī* or *al-faṣl* [essential difference][50] of the subject under consideration is provided. *Al-faṣl,* Alfārābī says, distinguishes the subject of inquiry from its partners in an essential way [*fī jawharih*]. However, it is the combination of *al-faṣl* and *al-jins al-qarīb* [the proximate genus] of the species or individual under consideration that provides the appropriate answer to the question, What is it? For example, when one asks, "What is a palm tree?" the answer "It is a tree" is not an adequate answer to this question (since there are many other things of which the term *tree* is also predicated, or in other words, the genus *tree* applies to other things than the specific tree being considered). We must therefore ask, Alfārābī's argument continues, "What kind of tree is it?" If the answer to this question is, "It is a tree that bears dates," then the "essential difference," and consequently the *definition* of the subject of inquiry, is provided.

In **Alfāẓ** (pp. 71–72), Alfārābī defines *al-faṣl al-dhātī* in the following manner (which I will paraphrase rather than translate):

> *Al-faṣl al-dhātī* is a universal such that it participates with other universals that are predicated in the answer to the question What is it? (i.e., species and genus) in being predicated of certain entities and such that it fulfills the following two conditions:
>
> (1) It is appropriately employed in answering the 'how?' [*kayfa*] question when this question is asked in relation to the essence of the universal with which it participates in the predication under consideration.
>
> (2) It is predicated without qualification [*ḥaml muṭlaq*] of those universals with which it participates in this predication.

Thus, Alfārābī says, if a species is predicated of certain entities and universal 'A' that fulfills the above two conditions participates with this species in predication of these entities,[51] then 'A' is an essential difference [*faṣl dhātī*] of this species. Similarly, if a universal 'B' fulfilling conditions 1 and 2 above joins a genus in being predicated of entities (a species, in this case), then the universal 'B' is an "essential difference" of this genus.

This description is valid in the case of all the intermediate genera and also in the case of the supreme genus, Alfārābī concludes (**Alfāẓ**, 72). *Al-faṣl al-dhātī* of 'X' constitutes the second part of the definition of 'X,' the first part being its proximate genus (**Madkhal**, 122, par. 9),[52] and as such it is called *faṣl dhātī muqawwim* [essential constitutive difference] (**Alfāẓ**, 73, and **Madkhal**, 122).[53] However, the same *faṣl dhātī*, while it constitutes and specifies the essence of 'X,' also acts as a dividing factor for the genus of 'X' and as such is called *faṣl dhātī qāsim*, i.e., it is an essential difference (for 'X') and at the same time divides the genus of that 'X.' In his **Madkhal** (p. 122) Alfārābī explains this phenomenon:

> The genus is followed by [*yurdaf*] its various differences in one of the two following manners:
>
> 1) It is restricted by contrary [*mutaḍāddah*] and in general by opposite [*mutaqābilah*] differences, to which the disjunction particle [*ḥarf al-infiṣāl*] is added, such as when we say, "the garment is [made] either of wool or of linen or of cotton"; and "the body is either nourished or it is not." This is the division of a genus by differences.
> 2) The genus can be followed [directly] by each of the differences without opposition and without the disjunction particle, such as when we say, "a garment of wool and a garment of linen and a garment of cotton," or "nourished body" and "non-nourished body." The latter kind of composition [*irdāf;* lit., follow-up] is the one by which one answers the 'which?' [*ayy*] question, and this is how the definition of the species under that genus came about.

Thus, Alfārābī explains (**Madkhal**, 123, par. 10), dividing a given genus by pointing out its various differences is itself the act of defining the various species under that genus, or as he puts it:

> The division of a genus by means of the differences leads to [*tantahī ilā*] the species ranked under it [i.e., under that genus], because if you remove the disjunction particle [from the statement of division] you will get the definition of the [various] species [under that genus].

We have seen that according to Alfārābī each genus has several species ranked under it, and each of these is predicated in a qualified way of that genus (which is another way of stating what, in *class calculus terminology,* is called "inclusion" of the species in its genus). Now, according to Alfārābī, this relationship exists between the essential difference of a species and the genus of that species, namely that the essential difference of a species 'Y' is predicated of the genus of 'Y' in a qualified way (and the genus of 'Y' is predicated of the essential difference of 'Y' in an unqualified way, i.e., it includes it).[54] Now, Alfārābī mentions two other principles he has already discussed (**Alfāẓ**, 73):

> 1) Whatever can be appropriately applied in answering the question *kayfa* [how?] can also be appropriately applied in answering the question 'what sort of thing is it?' (the *ayy* question).

2) The essential difference is predicated (of its species or of its genus) in answering the *kayfa* question.

From these two principles Alfārābī implies that the specific differences of a species or of a genus can be appropriately applied in answering the question, What sort of thing is that species or that genus? In other words, each essential difference can be taken to distinguish between that of which it is specific and other things that share the same genus.

This is the reason, it is pointed out, that the "difference" is described as "that which is predicated of a universal in answer to the question *ayy*[u] *shay*ʾ[in] *huwa?*" and that it is the thing "by which one can distinguish things that are under the same genus," or that it is the thing "through which things that are not different in genus differ" (**Alfāẓ**, 74).

However, one must observe, Alfārābī says, that the essential difference distinguishes a thing from other things through their essence rather than through their external states [*fī dhātih lā fī aḥwālih*]. Hence the definition of *faṣl dhātī* as that which is predicated of a universal in answer to the *ayy* question should, in Alfārābī's opinion, be amended to read as follows: "an essential difference is the universal that is predicated of another universal in answering the question *'ayya*[u] *shay*ʾ[in] *huwa fī dhātihi?'* [as opposed to *fī aḥwālihi*]" (**Alfāẓ**, 74).

Finally, there are two more points discussed by Alfārābī in relation to the universal under consideration. The first of these is the extension of the *faṣl dhātī* in relation to the (relative) species it modifies. From what we have explained so far, it is clear that according to Alfārābī, the "unqualified predication" is transitive. By this I mean the following: if 'X' is a genus of 'Y' (i.e., 'X' is predicated without qualification of 'Y') and 'Y' is a genus of 'Z,' then 'X' is a genus of 'Z' and hence is predicated of it without qualification.

Alfārābī now also tries (**Alfāẓ**, 73, par. 29) to apply this to the essential difference saying, "Similarly, when two genera are ranked one under the other, then the essential difference of the higher genus is predicated of the lower genus in an unqualified way."

This conclusion can be easily understood if we remember that, by definition, an essential difference of a genus 'A' is a universal the extension of which must be at least as broad as that of 'A' itself. This is in effect what Alfārābī says in his **Alfāẓ**: "There are certain 'specific differences' that have the same extension [*musāwī fī ʾl-ḥaml*] as that of the universal they constitute, and there are some whose extension is broader [*aʿamm*, lit. "more general"] than that of the universal they constitute" (**Alfāẓ**, 74).

Unfortunately, Alfārābī provides no example to support this striking conclusion. In it he declares that a species (i.e., a relative species) is not necessarily convertible with its specific (i.e., essential) difference, since the latter can be broader, i.e., can appropriately be applied in answering the *ayy* question (as a follow-up for the *mā* question and after the genus has been provided) not just for its genus but also for other things as well. But does this not contradict the very meaning of being a "specific difference" of a species, or is not the essential difference of a certain 'X' supposed to differentiate 'X' from the rest of the things?

Had Alfārābī answered these questions, he would have said that the answer is a qualified "yes." For we must remember that for him the phrase "the rest of the things" means "the rest of the things that participate with 'X' in the same genus." The essential difference does not apply to (i.e., cannot be properly predicated of) other species that are partners in the same immediate genus (i.e., the genus being divided by these specific differences), but it can be properly employed in predicating things that are different in genus.

Alfārābī would, I believe, have given the following illustration: We can think of 'rational' as the "essential difference" separating 'man' from the rest of the things for which the predicate 'animal' is the common genus. 'Rational' will not be properly predicated of any other species (i.e., the subclass) of the genus 'animal.' Yet the predicate 'rational' can be properly predicated of other things that are not participants in the genus 'animal.' For example, 'rational' can be properly employed in predicating the species 'angel' or 'God.'[55] These two species are separated from the former not by a "specific difference," but rather by a genus, since they are incorporeal, whereas 'man' is under the genus 'corporeal.' In this case, the predicate 'rational' is of broader extension than that of which it is an essential difference (i.e., the species 'man'). This is probably the kind of example Alfārābī had in mind when he concluded that "Therefore, the essential difference that is broader [than its species or genus] is predicated not only of things that are numerically different, but also of things that are different in species" (**Alfāẓ**, 75).

We must remember, however, that the term *species* [*nawʿ*] is used here (and in many other passages in Alfārābī's writings) not simply as the "proximate species" [*al-nawʿ al-qarīb*] but rather as the "relative species"; namely, one of the intermediate genera that are considered by Alfārābī as a species in relationship to what is ranked above it, and a genus in relationship to what is ranked below it.

The second point I would like to discuss is Alfārābī's division of *faṣl dhātī* into two kinds (**Alfāẓ**, 73, par. 28):

1) *essential differences that cannot be properly predicated of each other in any way* [*fuṣūl mutaqābilah* or "opposite differences"], and
2) *essential differences that can be predicated of each other* (whether in a qualified or non-qualified way). Alfārābī calls this latter type of essential difference *fuṣūl ghayr mutaqābilah* [differences that are not opposite], but he provides no examples. However, it is reasonable to assume he is talking about two differences of two genera, provided these are predicated of one another. An example of this would be 'capable of moving itself' and 'capable of barking.'

Two "opposite differences," on the other hand, must be partners of the same genus. Opposite differences can be indicated either by two different symbols that have nothing to do with one another (such as 'rational' and 'capable of barking') or one can be indicated by a certain name whereas its opposite is indicated by that very name combined with the negation particle ('rational' and 'not rational'). Following, then, is a summary of the major characteristics of *faṣl dhātī* as outlined by Alfārābī:

1. *Faṣl dhātī is the second element in the formula that expresses the essence of a thing,* the first element being the proximate genus of that thing.
2. *The* ayy *question is presented as an inquiry about the difference of a thing* and that can happen only after the genus of that thing has been provided (in answer to the *mā* question).
3. *The* faṣl dhātī *modifies or constitutes [*yuqawwim*] the essence of the genus (or species) of which it is a* faṣl dhātī, i.e., it shows its essential difference from the rest of the things that participate in the same genus.
4. *Each* faṣl dhātī *divides the genus ranked immediately above the genus (or species) it modifies.* For example, 'rational' divides the genus 'animal' into 'rational animals' and 'non-rational animals' (and this class of 'non-rational animals' is divided by the different essential attributes of each of the species that participates in the genus 'animal,' i.e., that are subclasses of the class 'animal').
5. Al-faṣl al-dhātī *(or* al-faṣl al-muqawwim, *as Alfārābī sometimes calls it) is convertible with the species (or the relative species, to be*

more exact) that it modifies. (Sometimes, however, it can modify something else and can therefore be a larger class than the relative species it modifies, but this "something else" cannot be a partner in the same immediate genus with the given relative species, otherwise the concept of essential difference becomes meaningless.)

6. *The supreme genus is not constituted by any of the differences; it is only divided by those differences that constitute the relative species (or the genus) ranked immediately under it.* Similarly, the proximate species is not divided; it is only constituted or produced by means of its specific difference. As for the relative genera (i.e., the relative species), each of them is produced (or constituted) by a certain difference and is divided by certain other differences, thus constituting the subclasses, i.e., the species, of each relative genus. (**Madkhal**, 123, par. 10)

Property [*Al-Khāṣṣah*]

Having clarified the nature of the universal with the six features outlined above, Alfārābī next introduces another universal that, although it plays a significant role in definition, is *not* a part of the essential definition. With the introduction of the universal (or predicate) referred to in Arabic as *al-khāṣṣah* [property] we move away from the concept of "essence" and consequently from the definition that indicates the essence of a thing, i.e., from the phrase that states the proximate genus and the essential difference of the defined object. The predicate called *al-khāṣṣah* (and, as we shall see in the following section, also the concept of *al-ʿaraḍ* [accident] plays a role in identifying a thing by means of its attributes that are not essential, i.e., attributes that are neither the genus nor the specific difference.

In **Alfāẓ** (p. 75, par. 30)[56] Alfārābī defines *al-khāṣṣah* in the following manner (presented below as a paraphrase of the original):

A universal 'K' is called *al-khāṣṣah* if:

1) it is copredicated of certain entities with universals that are employed in answer to the question 'what is it?', i.e., with a species or a genus of the subject of predication. (I will refer to a genus or species that plays such a role as 'G');
2) 'K' is appropriately employed in answering the question, 'how are the external states of 'G'?' [*kayfa hiya fī aḥwālihā*];
3) the extension of 'K' equals that of 'G' [*musāwiyah li-l-awwal fī ʾl-ḥaml*]; and

4) 'K' is signified by a singular expression that represents a singular concept.

If 'K' fulfills all these conditions, then it is called a property of 'G.'

Conditions 2 and 3 above clearly indicate the difference between the concept of "essential difference" and that of "property." The latter describes the external states of 'G,' whereas the former is part of the phrase that describes the essence of 'G.' Moreover, from condition 3 one can see that a property 'K' of 'G' is predicated of the same entities of which 'G' is predicated and only of them, i.e., 'K' and 'G' are convertible or have the same extension. We have seen, however, that according to Alfārābī this is not always the case with a "specific difference" in relationship to the universal it modifies. Condition 4 above aims at distinguishing the concept *khāṣṣah* from certain "composite expressions" we call "definitions."

An example of the newly introduced concept is 'the capacity to laugh' in relationship to the species 'man' (**Alfāẓ**, 75–76). The following is true of this predicate:

1. 'Capacity to laugh' participates with 'man' in being predicated of individual human beings (see below in this section for the meaning of the phrase "participating in predication").
2. 'Capacity to laugh' can be properly employed in answering the question 'how are the states of the species 'man'?' (i.e., it provides a certain external description of every member of the species 'man'), since every man is capable of laughing ("not because he is always laughing but because it is natural for him to laugh," as Porphyry puts it in his *Isagoge* [p. 48] when he discusses this predicate).
3. 'Capacity to laugh' is an attribute that is predicated of those individuals of which the species 'man' is predicated and only of them. Every human being is capable of laughing and everything that is capable of laughing is a human being.
4. 'Capacity to laugh' is a singular expression (not singular in a grammatical sense, but rather in the sense that it signifies a singular universal).

Hence, the predicate 'capable of laughing' is a *khāṣṣah* of the species 'man' since it fulfills the four conditions of a property. Condition 3 above indicates that if 'K' is a property of 'G,' then every 'K' is 'G' and every 'G' is 'K.' In other words, if an individual 'x' is 'K' then 'x' is 'G,' and if 'x' is 'G' then 'x' is 'K.' In Alfārābī's terminology this amounts to saying that a thing and its property are "equal in predication," or that they are predicated of each other without qualification (**Alfāẓ**, 76). This means that if 'K' is a property of 'G,' then 'K' and 'G' can be used interchangeably as predicates: if 'x' is 'K,' then 'x' is also a 'G' and vice versa, or, to again use Porphyry's language, "For if there is a horse, there is the capacity to neigh, and if there is the capacity to neigh, there is a horse."[57] Two predicates that are equal in predication (like 'K' and 'G' above) are called "convertible" [*munʿakisah fī ʾl-ḥaml*] (**Alfāẓ**, 76; **Madkhal**, 125).

Now, the kind of property described above is called "property in the strict sense" [*khāṣṣah bi-ʾl-taḥqīq*] as opposed to the type that is "not in the strict sense" [*khāṣṣah lā bi-ʾl-taḥqīq*] (**Alfāẓ**, 76). The latter differs from the former in terms of condition 3 above.

Let us take an example given by Alfārābī to illustrate this difference. The predicate 'being an engineer' (or 'being a physician') is true only of human beings; 'being an engineer' implies 'being a man,' but not vice versa. For it is not the case that every man is an engineer. This amounts to saying that 'being an engineer' is a proper subclass of the class 'man,' or as Alfārābī puts it, "Whatever is predicated of a species (or genus) in a qualified way, and is not predicated of any other species at all, is called the property of that species. . . . And it is evident that the species is predicated without qualification of this kind of property" (**Alfāẓ**, 76).[58]

Incidentally, the expression "participating in predication" [*mushārakah fī ʾl-ḥaml*] used by Alfārābī in defining the predicate "property" requires some elaboration since it is not a self-evident expression, as was the case when it was used in relation to the term *essential difference*. In the latter case there is an actual participation in predication; when we formulate the definition 'man is a rational animal,' the essential difference 'rational' actually participates with the genus 'animal' in the predication of (the species) 'man.' However, the concept under consideration acquires a different meaning when it is applied to the predicate 'property' in relation to its species or genus. The statement, 'Zayd is a man capable of laughing,' for example, does not say more than the statement 'Zayd is a man.' For the predicate 'man' implies 'capable of laughing' (and vice versa, as we have seen). The statement 'man is capable of laughing' is an *analytic statement* because the concept 'man' includes the concept 'capacity to laugh' and the negation of 'man is capable of laughing' will result in a clear contradiction.

Thus, when we say 'x is a man,' it is implied that 'x is capable of laughing' and therefore there is no need to repeat it, whereas when you say 'Y is an animal,' it is not implied that 'Y is a rational animal.' 'Animal' can be 'rational' and can be 'nonrational,' and therefore the explicit combination of 'rational' and 'animal' is required if we want to define 'man'; thus we have an *actual* participation in predication between an essential difference and the universal it modifies.

"Property," however, does not participate actually or explicitly in predication with the universal it modifies since in this case an actual participating would result in a redundancy. The participation Alfārābī speaks of in this case is, I believe, an implicit participation or a potential one, in the sense outlined above.

The discussion concerning the predicate called "property" paves the way for future discussion concerning the nature of nonessential predicates (of which property is only one type) and their role in the broader sense of the *theory of definition*. We must therefore examine the fifth and last type of predicate, referred to in Arabic as *al-ᶜaraḍ* [accident]. This discussion will shed further light on the previously discussed concepts of "property" and "definition."

Accident [Al-ᶜAraḍ]

If a universal 'A' is co-predicated with a species or a genus 'G' and

1. 'A' is broader (lit., *aᶜamm* [more general] than 'G'
2. 'A' is properly used in answering the question, 'what sort of things are the nonessential properties of 'G'?', then 'A' is an accident of 'G,' Alfārābī concludes in his **Alfāẓ** (p. 76, par. 31).

This definition does not apply to the individual accidents and explicitly refers to a universal accident, thus excluding an important category of accidents. A similar problem occurs in Alfārābī's **"Risālah ṣudira bihā 'l-kitāb"** ["Alfārābī's Introductory Risalah on Logic"][59] (p. 229), where he defines 'accident' as "the thing through which two or more things become similar in a non-essential way." Here again he is talking about universal accidents only, thus ignoring the individual accidents [*shakhṣ al-ᶜaraḍ*] he discusses in **Maqūlāt** (p. 169), presented in section 1 of this chapter. There are, however, some adjustments made by Alfārābī in **Madkhal** (p. 125), where he discusses "accident" in general: "The accident is the singular universal which exists in a genus or species, being either more general or more specific than them without making known in any of them its essence [*dhātih*] or substance [*jawharih*], for example, white and black, standing and sitting, moving and at rest, hot and cold."

Let us examine Alfārābī's various explanations for and illustrations of these definitions, in order to see what he really understands by the concept "accident." We have already seen (in section 1 of this chapter) that on the basis of the notion 'said of' and 'being in,' Alfārābī in his **Maqūlāt** (p. 169) divides the accidents into two types:

(1) Things that are 'said of' a subject (i.e., predicated of that subject) and are 'in' a subject (i.e., are part of its attributes). These are the *universal accidents*.
(2) Things that are 'in' a subject but never 'said of' a subject. These are the *individual accidents*.

This is a twofold classification into universal accidents (such as 'black' as predicated of 'pitch' and also of 'man'), and individual accidents (such as 'sitting down' and 'greyness of the eyes'). It is obvious, however, that the statement 'all pitch is black' is true, whereas the statement 'all men are black' is false. 'Black' is a general term that is predicated of one universal ('pitch') without qualification and of another universal ('man') in a qualified way (since only the particular statement 'some men are black' is true). The universal 'black' always exists wherever 'pitch' exists, and thus it is an *"inseparable accident"* [*ʿaraḍ ghayr mufāriq*] (**Alfāẓ**, 76).[60] It is also called a "permanent inseparable accident" [*ʿaraḍ dāʾim ghayr mufāriq*, *ʿaraḍ ghayr mufāriq*, and *ʿaraḍ lāzim*]. These are all terms used by Alfārābī to denote those universals that are truly predicated of the entire species to which they apply all the time. (The same terms are also applied to another type of accident, as will be discussed below.)

This group is contrasted by Alfārābī (**Alfāẓ**, 76; **Madkhal** 125) with another type of accident he calls "separable accident" [*ʿaraḍ mufāriq*]. When this type of accident is applicable to a certain species, then it is true only of certain members of that species, in other words, of a subclass of the species,[61] such as when one applies the predicate 'black' to the species 'man.' From observation we know that only 'some men are black,' thus 'black' is predicated of 'man' in a qualified way.

For this reason, the same predicate ('black,' for example) can be a separable accident for some species and an inseparable accident for another species. When the latter is the case, it means that the attribute applies to every member of that species at all times. When the former is the case, however, then the attribute is a permanent predication, but applies only to a subclass of the species.

In **Madkhal** (p. 125) Alfārābī notes that the accidents discussed above (such as 'black' and 'white') can apply to more than one species.

This is a significant point, since it may explain what Alfārābī means in using the term *broader* for the **Alfāẓ**-version of his definition of "accident." Use of the expression "broader" would seem to connote that the term *accident* applies to more than just the species under consideration, yet it need not mean that it applies to all members of that species (like 'black' when applied to the species 'man').

In addition, Alfārābī's use of the word *broader* in this particular definition of "accident" may also explain the last two lines of page 60 in **Alfāẓ**, where Alfārābī rather inexplicably states that the two universals 'white' and 'man' are copredicated of some individuals, but that 'white' is "broader" in scope (i.e., predicated of more individuals than is 'man'). On the surface, there seems to be no philosophical basis for this statement, since just as 'white' is predicated of individuals that are not 'men,' so 'man' may be predicated of individuals that are not 'white.' However, 'man,' being itself a species, can only be predicated of individuals within the species 'man,' whereas 'white' (as an accident) can be predicated of many different species, though not necessarily of all members of any of these species.

And finally, Alfārābī's use of "broader" in defining "accident" acquires yet further significance in that it explains the difference between "property" and "accident," as we shall see below.

The terms *separable* and *inseparable* accident are also applied by Alfārābī to describe individual accidents (**Alfāẓ**, 77):

(1) *inseparable* accidents in relationship to a certain individual [*al-ʿaraḍ al-lāzim li-shakhṣ^{in}-mā*] such as 'snub-nosed,' which is a permanent quality of certain individuals. I will refer to this kind as "personal inseparable accident."
(2) *separable* accidents in relationship to certain individuals [*al-mufāriq li-shakhṣ^{in}-mā*], such as 'sitting up.' To this type I will refer as "personal separable accident."

The "personal separable accidents" of an individual change constantly and, due to this change, the individual constantly differs in its external properties (**Alfāẓ**, 77). Nevertheless, Alfārābī maintains that one can use either of these types of personal accident to distinguish between individuals; each of them will be instrumental in informing about the differences that exist between two individuals. This is the reason, he continues, they are called "differences," though not in the *strict sense* [*lā ʿalā ʾl-taḥqīq*], but rather by virtue of similarity [*ʿan ṭarīq al-tashbīh*] to the specific differences. In **Madkhal** (p. 125) Alfārābī refers to these as "qualified improper differences" [*fuṣūl lā ʿalā ʾl-iṭlāq*] and also as "accidental differences" [*fuṣūl ʿaraḍiyyah*].

Yet it is one thing to draw the distinction by means of the "personal inseparable" and quite another to draw it by means of the "personal separable," as Alfārābī states in his **Alfāẓ** (p. 77). When the former is used, one realizes one is using a more permanent thing and thus the sign used to distinguish between things is more adequate [*akmal*[u] *tamyīz*[an]] (**Madkhal**, 126, and **Alfāẓ**, 77). According to Alfārābī, it is for this reason that Porphyry refers to them as "proper differences" [*fuṣūl khāṣṣah*].[62] When the "personal separable accident" is used to distinguish between things, then the differences are called "common differences" [*fuṣūl ʿāmmah*], since the signs used are not permanent; they are common and change constantly and, therefore, are of a lower type and less specific than the "inseparable personal accidents."

In **Madkhal** (p. 125) Alfārābī says that accidents can be used to distinguish not only between individual things (as the above presentation based on **Alfāẓ** suggests), but also between different genera and different species. That is the reason, he says, they are not proper differences [*fuṣūl lā ʿalā ʾl-iṭlāq*], rather they are "accidental differences" [*fuṣūl ʿaradiyyah*]. According to him, they are so called because they are used in distinguishing one species from another not in an essential way, but by means of their external properties.

Alfārābī also compares the "accidental difference" with the universal "property." They both, he says (**Madkhal**, 125), distinguish between things in a nonessential way; the latter, however, separates the entire species from other things at all times, whereas the former distinguishes the species not from everything else, but rather from certain things and only sometimes. This is the reason the accidental difference is called a "relative property" [*khāṣṣah bi-ʾl-iḍāfah*]; for to set a thing apart from other things by referring to its accidents is always in relationship to other things and at a certain time.

This may be true for separable accidents, but this does not answer the question regarding the difference between "inseparable accident" and "property." Alfārābī's answer to this question appears in **Alfāẓ** (p. 77): "Our saying that it [the accident] is more general [*aʿamm*] distinguishes it from the property of the species." 'Black,' Alfārābī would argue, exists in every piece of pitch, but it does not exist only there.

This statement is no different in principle from Porphyry's answer to this very question (*Isagoge*, 62): "Thus, the property is predicated equally and convertibly with what it belongs to, but the inseparable accident is not convertible."

This concludes our discussion of the five singular universals in Alfārābī's system: "genus" [*jins*], "species" [*nawʿ*], "essential difference" [*faṣl dhātī*], "property" [*khāṣṣah*] and "accident" [*ʿaraḍ*]. These are the basic building blocks of Alfārābī's logical system. In chapter 2, we move to a higher level in our discussion of universals, an investigation of the various combinations of these five singular universals as employed to explore the central questions of Aristotelian philosophy, perhaps the most important being "What is [the essence of] a thing?"

According to the Aristotelians, the combination of the "genus" and the "essential difference" of a thing, for example, represents the most precise way to identify a thing. It is the formula for the "definition" of a thing that results in the highest degree of knowledge of a thing. Various combinations of the other three universals lead to lower degrees of knowledge of things (such as "description"). Let us turn, therefore, to the topics *ḥadd* [definition] and *rasm* [description], the two compound universals in Alfārābī's system.

Notes to Chapter 1

1. Al-Tawḥīdī, *Imtāʿ*, p. 122: 15.

2. Alfārābī does not seem to share the concern of some modern commentators who describe Porphyry's introduction of the "species" as a fifth predicable as a "philosophical mistake." See particularly Sir David Ross, *Aristotle* (London: Methuen, 1949), p. 57; E. A. Moody, *The Logic of William of Ockham* (New York: Russell and Russell, 1935, repr. 1965), p. 67.

3. Cf. the article on "Porphyry" in *The Encyclopedia of Philosophy* (ed. Paul Edwards [New York: Macmillan Co. Inc. & The Free Press, 1972], vol. 6, p. 412) which briefly discusses the controversy over whether or not Porphyry did indeed replace "definition" with "species" as a fifth predicable. Significant in this context is that the Arab logicians *understood him to have done so*.

4. Alfārābī, "**Kitāb īsāghūjī ay al-madkhal**" ["Al-Fārābī's Eisagoge"], ed. & tr. D. M. Dunlop, in *The Islamic Quarterly,* vol. 3 (1956 – 57): 117 – 38. [Henceforth: **Madkhal**]

5. "Universals" are also referred to by Alfārābī in **Alfāẓ** as "general terms" [*maʿānī ʿāmmah* and *maʿānī ʿāmmiyyah*].

6. Compare this to Aristotle's definition of universals in *De Interpretatione*, chapter 7, 17a38. In all my references to this work of Aristotle, I will be using the following edition: Aristotle, *Categories and De Interpretatione*, tr. (and commentary) J. L. Ackrill (Oxford: Oxford University Press, 1963).

7. The example 'that coming man is Zayd,' which appears in this passage of **Alfāẓ**, contradicts Alfārābī's own explanation, according to which individual things that correspond to proper names are not predicated of anything at all. In a statement of this sort, the relations expressed by 'is' [*huwa*] is a rela-

tion of *identity* rather than of predication per se. By identity I mean here two names (or two sounds) that refer to the same object.

For the distinction between 'is' as a sign of predication and 'is' as a sign of identity see, for example, Bertrand Russell, *Our Knowledge of the External World* (London: George Allen and Unwin, 1972), p. 48, (n. 1); also, Russell Dancy, "On Some of Aristotle's First Thoughts About Substances," *Philosophical Review* (1975): 340.

8. Cf. Aristotle's *Categories* ($1^a20 - 1^b10$), especially the last part of that passage.

9. Alfārābī, "**Kitāb qāṭāghūriyās ay al-maqūlāt**," ed. & tr. D. M. Dunlop, in *The Islamic Quarterly,* 4(1957–8): 168–97; 5(1959): 21–54. [Henceforth: **Maqūlāt**]

10. See below the expression 'in a subject.'

11. Let us ignore for a while the questions What is the essence of a thing? and What is the meaning of 'to define?' These are major questions that will be dealt with in the first four chapters of this study.

12. *Shakhṣ al-ʿaraḍ* and *shakhṣ al-jawhar* in this passage both have the singular form, but are clearly intended as plural.

13. The Arabic expression is *fa-takūn al-ashyāʾ*. It appears in the edition as *fa-yakūn al-ashyāʾ*, which I believe is a minor typographical mistake. The Arabic translation of the Greek original of Aristotle's *Categories* uses the expression *mawjudāt* [existing things or beings] [*Manṭiq Arisṭū*, 3 vols. ed. Badawi (Cairo: Maṭbaʿat dār al-kutub al-miṣriyyah, 1948 – 52; reprint: Beirūt: Dār al-qalam, 1980) vol. 1: 34].

14. A reference to Aristotle's *Categories* (1^a20 ff.). The Arabic equivalent of this last phrase is difficult to explain. It reads, *al-maqūl fī mawḍūʿ* and could be translated as 'said about a subject.' However, this raises certain philosophical difficulties if we take into consideration (and we should) the Aristotelian text on which this passage is ostensibly a commentary. In the Aristotelian text it is clear (at least in this specific case) that by introducing the notion 'in a thing,' Aristotle does not mean to talk about linguistic expressions but rather about things: "For example, the knowledge of grammar is in a subject, the soul, . . . and the individual white is in a subject, the body (for all color is in the body)" (*Categories,* chapter 2, 1^a25).

For a more complete explanation of this problem see A. J. Ackrill's commentary on the Aristotelian text (p. 75 ff.) and also William and Martha Kneale, *The Development of Logic* (Oxford: Oxford University Press, 1962; reprint ed., Clarendon Press, 1978), p. 27.

Fortunately this troublesome expression occurs only once in Alfārābī's work and one can assume either that he was careless in stating this point or that it is a textual mistake due to a careless (or perhaps an over-ambitious) scribe who wanted the sentence to resemble the one that preceded it. In any case, this phrase should be understood as 'said to be in a subject,' as if the Arabic form were, *al-maqūl annahu fī mawḍūʿ*.

15. Note that in the rest of his description of this classification, Alfārābī does not use the term *said of* or *said to be in*. He simply says 'on a subject' [*ʿalā mawḍūʿ*] and 'in a subject' [*fī mawḍūʿ*]. But there is no reason to conclude that the elimination of the term *al-maqūl* [said of, predicated of] is philosophically significant.

16. Cf. Aristotle, *Categories*, chapter 2 ($1^{a}20$).

17. The Arabic expression has the singular form.

18. These are Aristotelian terms that appear in chapter 5 of his *Categories*. The Arabic translation of this Aristotelian text (attributed to Isḥāq b. Ḥunain) uses the terms *jawāhir thawānī*, as opposed to *jawāhir uwal*, i.e., the primary substance (Badawi, ed., *Manṭiq Arisṭū*, vol. 1: 36). Alfārābī, in **Ḥurūf** (p. 102, par. 68), explains that "Aristotle refers to the individual material objects [*al-mushār ilayh*] as 'primary substance' [*al-jawhar al-awwal*] and to the universals predicated of it [*kulliyyātih*] as 'secondary substances' [*al-jawāhir al-thawānī*], since the former is the thing that has an external existence outside the soul and the latter is conceived in the soul after the former [has been established in the soul]."

19. The Arabic has the singular form. Cf. Aristotle, *Categories*, $1^{b}3$–4.

20. Cf. Aristotle, *Categories*, $1^{a}27$–28.

21. Cf. Aristotle, *Categories*, $1^{b}5$–6.

22. Cf. Aristotle, *Categories*, $1^{a}27$–28.

23. By saying that a "subject is a universal" and so forth, Alfārābī means that the subject of the sentence is a term that refers to or signifies a universal. In general, Alfārābī seems to take no pains to be consistent in making the distinction between the linguistic expressions and the concepts, which are in turn mental pictures of the external world. In English, this distinction is maintained by use of the term *universal* for the concept versus *general term* for the linguistic expression of that concept. Alfārābī, however, uses the two Arabic equivalents *kullī* and *maʿānī kulliyyah* absolutely interchangeably.

24. This fivefold (counting 4a and 4b) classification of propositions should not be confused with the well-known fourfold classification of propositions as made by Aristotle in his *De Interpretatione* and summarized in the doctrine called the "square of opposition." For further details on this doctrine, see Kneale and Kneale, op. cit., pp. 54 ff.

25. Further details about "induction" and "analogy" in Alfārābī are given in three of his published works: 1) **Alfāẓ** (p. 93), 2) **Qiyās ṣaghīr** (p. 264

ff., induction only) and 3) **Kitāb fī ʾl-manṭiq: al-khiṭābah** [Book of Rhetorics], ed. M. S. Sālim (Cairo: Al-hayʾah al-miṣriyyah al-ʿammah li-l-kitāb, 1976), pp. 27, 59, 61, 62 (analogy only).

26. For further details about Alfārābī's classification of the sciences see his celebrated work **Iḥṣāʾ**. See also the thorough analysis of this work by M. Mahdī, "Science, Philosophy and Religion in Alfārābī's Enumeration of the Sciences," in J. E. Murdoch and E. D. Sylla, eds., *The Cultural Context of Medieval Learning*, Boston Studies in the Philosophy of Science, vol. 26 (Holland: D. Reidel, 1975); for comparison see Aristotle's *Topics* 105^b15 ff., trans. E. S. Forster, *Aristotle's Posterior Analytics, Topica* (London: The Leob Classical Library, 1960), p. 175; and consult Kneale & Kneale, op. cit., p. 139.

27. Cf. Aristotle's *Categories*, chapter 5.

28. The priority of a thing "by nature" (which is the closest thing to what is called "ontological priority") is one of five types of priorities [*taqaddum*] Alfārābī postulates in "**Fuṣūl tashtamil ʿalā jamīʿ mā yuḍṭarr ilā maʿrifatih man arād al-shurūʿ fī ṣināʿat al-manṭiq**" ["Paragraphs containing the prerequisites for the study of logic"], ed. & tr. D. M. Dunlop, "Al-Fārābī's Introductory Sections on Logic" in *Islamic Quarterly* 2 (1955), p. 268. [Henceforth: **Fuṣūl**]

> Something is said to be prior to something else in five different ways: in time [*bi-ʾl-zamān*], by nature [*bi-ʾl-ṭabʿ*], in rank [*bi-ʾl-martabah*], by virtue of honor and perfection [*bi-ʾl-faḍl wa-ʾl-sharaf wa-ʾl-kamāl*] or by virtue of the fact that it is a cause for that thing's existence [*annahu sabab wujūd al-shayʾ*].

29. The Arabic text includes the phrase *akmal*[u] *wujud*[an], which literally means "more perfect from an existential point of view," but I have translated it as "ontologically prior" because the former (i.e., the literal) translation does not, I think, adequately convey Alfārābī's idea.

30. Furthermore, in **Ḥurūf** (p. 101, par. 67) Alfārābī calls both primary and secondary substances "absolute substance" [*jawhar ʿalā ʾl-iṭlāq*].

31. Alfārābī uses both terms in this passage.

32. Dancy, op. cit.

33. A question raised by many scholars of Aristotle. See, for example, G. E. M. Anscombe and P. T. Geach, *Three Philosophers: Aristotle, Aquinas, Frege* (Ithaca, NY: Cornell University Press, 1961), p. 10.

34. This idea is owed to Edwin Hartman, *Substance, Body, and Soul* (Princeton: Princeton University Press, 1977), 14–15.

35. Aristotle, *The Categories*, 4^a10–21.

36. Hartman, pp. 14–15.

37. Aristotle's analysis of this point is significant and has far-reaching consequences for Alfārābī's thought, as well as for that of other Arab philosophers. Before proceeding, the reader may wish to consult the concise summary of Aristotle's analysis found in appendix I, in order to understand the background for Alfārābī's analysis.

38. Reference to Porphyry's *Isagoge,* which is devoted to the discussion of these five predicables. (Aristotle also talks about five general terms and defines them in the *Topics,* but his list differs from that of Porphyry in one significant item, namely, "definition," which Porphyry ostensibly replaces with "species.")

39. An order slightly different from that presented in the opening sentence of Porphyry's *Isagoge.* The order there puts "difference" in second position and "species" in third.

40. See for example, Kneale and Kneale, op. cit., p. 33; and especially Ernest Moody, op. cit., passim.

41. The term *scope* (or rather, an Arabic equivalent of this term) is not used by Alfārābī, but it seems useful in conveying Alfārābī's ideas.

42. Unfortunately, Alfārābī's second illustration is not appropriate to this category. He compares 'white' [*al-abyaḍ*] with 'man' and concludes that the scope of 'white' is definitely broader than that of 'man,' i.e., that it is predicated of more things. Alfārābī fails to consider, however, that 'man' is also predicated of certain individuals (black men) of which 'white' is not predicated. Actually, this example better suits his second category.

43. Or its logical equivalents, such as 'every,' 'each.' The Arabic term is *kull.*

44. 'Judgment' is usually translated *ḥukm* or *qaḍiyyah,* but in this passage the term *ḥaml* is used. Literally, *ḥaml* means "predication," but it can also be understood as "judgment." This usage, as I see it, emerges from a similar expression in the Arabic translation of Aristotle's *Topics* (IV, 122^{a}14,16) where the phrase *ḥaml*^{an} *ṣawāb*^{an} [true predication] is mentioned twice. But since whenever you have a "judgment" [*qaḍiyyah*] you have a predication [*ḥaml*] (but not vice versa), then it can be understood when Alfārābī uses *ḥaml* in the sense of *qaḍiyyah,* although he himself does not say this.

45. There is a great deal of repetition in this passage, which I doubt adds to the meaning of the sentence. The relevant portion of the sentence reads: ". . . and if one of them is more general and the other is more specific and that which is more general is more general than the more specific . . ."

46. The expression "then it follows" translates the Arabic: *abadan fa-inna,* which literally means: "then it is always the case that," which I take to be equivalent of the expression often used in logical relations: "it follows that."

47. In Arabic: *yuḥmal ʿalayh min ṭarīq mā huwa.* This expression occurs frequently in Aristotle's *Topics* (example: chapter 1, 102a31; chapter 4, 120b21; chapter 4, 122a4–5; chapter 4, 127b26 ff.) and the above-mentioned Arabic version is used by the translator of the *Topics.* The English phrase, "in reply to the question, What is that thing?" is only one way of rendering it in English. The Loeb translation of the *Topics,* for example, uses the phrase "predicated in the category of essence."

48. In fact, if we take Alfārābī literally in his description of this scheme, we can show that he is led to an awkward position, since he says clearly that "each time you point to a more general thing [than one of the intermediates], you will find a more general thing, and each time you point to a more specific one, you will find one that is more specific" (**Alfāẓ**, 67, par. 21). If one follows this line of reasoning, then one has an infinite series of intermediates. However, given the type of examples Alfārābī presents in his logical writings as illustrations for his explanation (all taken from the biological world), one can conclude that it is most likely he was thinking in terms of three or four intermediates, depending on the case.

49. See Alfārābī's theory concerning the apprehension of first principles, presented in his **Kitāb al-mūsīqā ʾl-kabīr** [The comprehensive book of music], ed. Ghaṭṭās Khashabah (Cairo: Dār al-kātib al-ʿarabī, 1967), pp. 83–105 (particularly, pp. 92–105).

50. Cf. Aristotle's *Topics,* (144a20 ff.).

51. In this case these entities must be individual things if the species under consideration is the proximate species, referred to by Alfārābī as *al-nawʿ* or *al-nawʿ al-qarīb.*

52. See also Porphyry's *Isagoge,* p. 43: "Thus from essential differences (i.e., specific differences) 1) the divisions of genera into species arise and 2) definitions are expressed, since they are composed of a genus and such difference." See also p. 45, where Porphyry expresses the same idea.

53. The origin of this expression, as well as that of *faṣl dhātī qāsim,* to be discussed below, seems to be the Arabic translation of Porphyry's *Isagoge,* see Badawi, ed. *Manṭiq Arisṭū,* vol. 3, p. 1078. Incidentally, Alfārābī uses *faṣl muqawwim* and *faṣl dhātī* interchangeably (see, for example, **Alfāẓ**, 74).

54. Cf. Aristotle's *Topics* (128a19–30).

55. Cf. Porphyry's *Isagoge,* 45 (see note 29 in that text).

56. See also Alfārābī's **Madkhal**, 125, Section 114. Cf. Aristotle's *Topics,* Book I, Chapter V, but especially with *Topics,* Book V.

57. Porphyry's *Isagoge,* 48, an example also given by Alfārābī in his **Madkhal**, 125. See also Aristotle's *Topics,* 102a20.

58. This is only one of the three kinds of property in the nonstrict sense mentioned by Porphyry in his *Isagoge* (p. 48). The following is a full quotation of the three kinds mentioned by Porphyry:

> Our predecessors distinguish three meanings of property: 1) what occurs in one species only, although not in every member of the species, as healing and measuring occur in man; 2) what occurs in the entire species and not in it only, as being two-footed occurs in man; 3) what occurs in the entire species, in it only, and at some time, as becoming grey in old age occurs in every man.

59. Alfārābī, "**Risālah ṣudira bihā 'l-kitāb**" ["Al-Fārābī's Introductory Risālah on Logic"], ed. & tr. Ḍ. M. Dunlop, *The Islamic Quarterly,* vol. 3 (1956–57): 224-35. [Henceforth: **Risālah**]

60. A. C. Lloyd claims that Porphyry's *Isagoge* did introduce inseparable accidents, which are an uneasy intermediate between essential attributes and pure or separable accidents. See the *Encyclopedia of Philosophy,* s.v. "Porphyry," by A. C. Lloyd.

61. I prefer the term *subclass* since we are really referring to the universal/universal relationship: the one being an accident, the other being a species or genus.

62. A reference to Porphyry's *Isagoge,* 42.

2

Definition and Description in Alfārābī's System

One important aspect of the relationships between the five singular universals is the theory of *"essential definition."* The Arabic term that describes this logical theory is *ḥadd* which, like the Greek *oδos,* means "limit" or "border." Alfārābī shows how we define things by first indicating the general area to which they belong (the "genus"), then by "limiting" them, indicating the particular or the specific class to which they belong ("essential difference," also called "specific difference"). The "essential difference" can be seen as the boundary that separates neighboring objects from one another (**Alfāẓ**, 78), or as a subclass of a larger class (the genus) that contains all the objects that happen to possess a certain property no other objects possess.

An "essential definition" [*ḥadd*] is perceived by Alfārābī as merely a composite of two singular universals: "genus" and "essential difference." Similarly, "description" [*rasm*][1] is viewed as various combinations of two or more singular universals. For this reason, we will refer to "definition" and "description" as *"compound universals,"* as they are composed of more than one singular universal.

Our discussion of Alfārābī's analysis of "essential definitions" and "descriptions" will cover two major aspects. First, we will examine from a *structural* or *formal* point of view what kind of statement a definitory clause is. Second, with respect to *content*, we will examine the subject matter of which definitions and descriptions are composed. But first, let us begin with a general discussion of phrases and sentences.

General Types of Phrases and Sentences in Alfārābī

In chapter 5 of **Fuṣūl** (p. 273 ff.) Alfārābī distinguishes between two types of "compound expressions" [*alfāẓ murakkabah*]:

1. *Compounds in which each part signifies a part of the meaning [maʿnā], with the whole signifying the whole of that meaning.* Examples: 'he who chooses wisdom,' 'Zayd's friend,' 'white man.'

2. *Compounds in which the parts do not signify parts of the meaning, which is rather signified by the totality of the compound.* Example: *ʿabd shams* (lit., "slave of the sun," although the term may also be used as a proper name, usually of a tribe). This compound expression signifies an individual, but neither of the parts of which it is composed corresponds to or signifies parts of this individual. In other words, there is no correspondence between the parts of this kind of expression and the parts of the object it signifies. "Thus," Alfārābī concludes, "whenever part of a compound expression does not signify part of the whole signified by the whole compound, the expression is like a simple expression [*yajrī majrā ʾl-alfāẓ al-mufradah*]."

In "**Kitāb bārī armīniyās ay al-ʿibārah**" ["Short treatise on Aristotle's De Interpretatione"][2] (pp. 44–45), Alfārābī gives the following example in order to illustrate the two kinds of compound expressions:

> Suppose a man whose name is ʿAbd al-Malik [lit., "slave of the king"] becomes a king's servant. The name ʿAbd al-Malik applies to him in two ways: as a proper name [*laqab*] and as an attribute [*ṣifah*]. Being an attribute, each part of it signifies a part of the referent;[3] but being a proper name, parts of it do not signify parts of the referent by itself [*bi-dhātih*], but rather by accident [*bi-ʾl-ʿaraḍ*]. ʿAbd al-Malik, then, is a phrase [*qawl*] insofar as it is an attribute. But insofar as it is a proper name it is a phrase by accident, since it just so happens it has become a phrase as well.

In light of this example, Alfārābī's opening statement in the above-quoted section may be easily understood: "A phrase [*qawl*] is a compound expression that signifies a whole referent (i.e., meaning), while part of it signifies, by itself [*bi-dhātih*] and not by accident [*bi-ʾl-ʿaraḍ*], part of the referent."

Thus, Alfārābī divides the class of all "compound expressions" [*alfāẓ murakkabah*] into "phrases" and "simple compound expressions." The latter are compound expressions *only grammatically* and must otherwise be viewed as simple expressions, since they refer to, at most, one object. Some compound expressions refer to no (externally existing) object at all, such as the term *ʿanz-ayyil* [*goat-stag*][4] or a grammatical particle such as *ʿinda-mā* [lit., *when it is the case that*]. The Arabic particle *ʿinda-mā* is a combination of two words—*ʿinda* [when] and *mā* [what]—although it refers to no subject at all when considered outside a propositional context.

The English term *phrase* is used here (following Zimmermann) as a translation of the Arabic *qawl*, employed by Alfārābī in a variety of contexts with a variety of meanings: "phrase," "statement," "proposition," "definition," etc. This parallels Aristotle's use of the term *logos*, which has been translated into English in various ways, depending on Aristotle's usage of the term in a given passage.[5] The Arab translators of Aristotle, on the other hand, chose an alternative solution to the problem of the term *logos* by selecting one term *qawl* to represent *logos* in all its many meanings. It is these translations that are most probably the source of Alfārābī's usage of the term *qawl*.

In fact, Alfārābī himself explains in **Ḥurūf** (pp. 63–64, par. 6) that *qawl* in its most general usage can refer to any expression, whether that expression signifies [the external existence of] some thing or not [*dāll aw ghayr dāll*]. But more specifically, he continues, it may have any of the following meanings: "a predicate of some thing" [*maḥmūl ʿalā shayʾ*^{in}*-mā*], "an intelligible" (since *qawl* can signify a concept[6] that exists in the soul), "a definiendum" [*maḥdūd*] ("since definition is a type of phrase [*qawl*^{un}*-ma*]), and a description [*marsūm*][7] ("since a description is also a type of phrase").

The class of all phrases is itself divided by Alfārābī into two subclasses. "Phrases are either complete [*tāmm*] or incomplete [*ghayr tāmm*]," he declares in **Bārī armīniyās**, (p. 45). For convenience, *tāmm* (or "complete phrase") will subsequently be referred to as "sentence" and the term *phrase* will be applied to incomplete phrases only.

In the same passage, Alfārābī maintains that sentences [*qawl tāmm* or simply *qawl*, as he sometimes refers to them] (cf. **ʿIbārah** 16^{a}2 and 17^{a}2) are of several different types:

> Complete phrases [i.e., sentences] are, according to many of the ancients,[8] five in number: declarative [*jāzim*], imperative[9] [*amr*], entreaty [*taḍarruʿ*], request [*ṭilbah*], and vocative [*nidā'*].[10] Declarative sentences [*qawl jāzim*] are those that are either true or false[11] and composed of a subject and a predicate. The remaining four types are neither true nor false, except by accident.

In **Fuṣūl** (p. 273) Alfārābī contends that a declarative sentence is a compound so composed as to convey a message [*tarkībuh tarkīb ikhbār*]. In this passage he also mentions the various terms used interchangeably by Arab logicians for this kind of compound; *qawl jāzim*, *qaḍiyyah* [roughly, a proposition], and *ḥukm* [lit., a judgment]. There are three additional synonyms for these terms: 1) the term *ḥaml* [predication], which Alfārābī uses to mean "statement" or "judgment" (cf. chapter 1,

n. 44); 2) *taṣdīq*, often discussed by Arab philosophers in association with the term *taṣawwur* [perception, conceptualizing];[12] and 3) *khabar.*[13] Each of these Arabic terms will be rendered into English as "declarative statement" or simply "declarative."

Alfārābī further concentrates on the distinction between the two types of compound expression he considers of special significance from a logical point of view: "There are two primary kinds of compounds, one composed in order to convey a message [*tarkībuh tarkīb ikhbār*], the other to express a stipulation [*ishtirāṭ*], qualification [*istithnā*ʾ] or delimitation [*taqyīd*]"[14] (**Fuṣūl**, 273).

By using the term *primary* [*al-uwal*] in the above quotation, Alfārābī wishes to show the importance he attaches to this classification, with which he draws his limits for the domain of logic. This classification of compounds excludes not only singular compounds (i.e., compounds that are not phrases and that are to be treated as single expressions), but it also excludes a major category of sentences, namely the entire set of nondeclarative sentences (imperatives, entreaties, requests, and vocatives).

By making this distinction, Alfārābī aims at isolating those phrases he considers to be of primary importance for logicians: declarative sentences and definitory clauses. Unlike other phrases, these phrases represent central issues for logicians, Alfārābī says. He even interprets Aristotle (*De Interpretatione*, $17^{a}2$) in this way:

> But we need not elaborate further on this for it is not our concern to establish the number [of kinds][15] of sentences. All we need to establish is that, apart from statements, there are sentences shaped like commands and prohibitions [*al-amr wa-*ʾ*l-nahī*], and phrases shaped like definitions and descriptions, namely those composed in a delimitative and stipulatory way. These three are the primary kinds of sentences [*aqāwīl*]. This is why he [Aristotle] said: "Not every sentence is declarative."

And in his commentary on $17^{a}5$–7 of Aristotle's *De Interpretatione*, Alfārābī adds:

> By *other sentences* Aristotle means imperatives, requests (entreaties), and vocatives[16] (if to be considered as sentences), but not definitions. For he is here only thinking of complete phrases. But a definition is not a complete phrase. . . . [17] *Since they are* appropriately *considered in the context of speeches and poetry:* This proves that Aristotle does not here treat definitions and descriptions as sen-

tences. For it is by complete phrases excluding statements, that speeches and poetry are distinguished.[18] The study of definitions, however, is appropriate to the subjects of demonstration [*Posterior Analytics*] and disputation [*Topics*] rather than speeches [*Rhetoric*] and poetry [*Poetics*].

Later on in the above-quoted passage, Alfārābī refers to Aristotle's statement in 17ª7 of *De Interpretatione* that "the present investigation deals with declarative sentences." By this Aristotle, in Alfārābī's view, means this book (i.e., *De Interpretatione*) and the *Prior Analytics [Anālūtīqī ʾl-ūlā]*. Thus, according to Alfārābī, the two kinds of compounds that are the basis for a logician's activity are declarative sentences ('Zayd is a man,' 'man is an animal') and compounds that express stipulation, qualification, or delimitation. For the purposes of this chapter, however, I will confine my discussion to compounds of the latter type.

The three terms (*ishtirāṭ, istithnāʾ*, and *taqyīd*) are used interchangeably by Alfārābī in **Fuṣūl** (273); they are clearly not used to indicate different kinds of phrases within this category. All are used in the sense of "qualification" (the meaning of which will be explained later in this chapter).[19]

The conjunction *wa* used here is often employed in Arabic to indicate a disjunction (such as "or") rather than a conjunction (such as "and"), and this passage of **Fuṣūl** is a typical example of this usage of the *wa* particle. When Alfārābī provides examples to illustrate his meaning of these terms he says, "examples of compounds of the *ishtirāṭ* type are . . . " (ibid.). In the **Bārī armīniyās** (p. 57) he uses a derivative of *taqyīd* in order to indicate the same type of compound expression, while in his major treatise **ʿIbārah** (p. 52) he uses *taqyīd* and *ishtirāṭ* synonymously. Again in **Madkhal** (p. 122) Alfārābī uses derivatives of *taqyīd* to indicate delimitation.[20]

In any event, delimitative phrases are illustrated by Alfārābī as follows: 'Zayd the secretary,' 'white man,' and 'Zayd's friend' (**Fuṣūl**, 273); 'even number,' 'rational animal,' and 'straight line' (**Bārī armīniyās**, 57); and also 'white scribe' and 'the building doctor' (ibid., 58).

Since the language is Arabic, the second term in all of these examples is added to the first, in order to qualify or delimit it. This qualification renders an indefinite term as an indefinite phrase by attaching a certain attribute to that term, thus restricting its extension (i.e., the number of individuals to which it applies as a predicate). For example, *man* is a general and unqualified term, the extension of which is the entire set of human beings, that is to say, it is properly predicated of each member of this class. By joining an attribute such as 'white' to this term, a new situation emerges whereby the extension of the phrase no longer applies to the same class to which the term *man* standing alone applies. Rather, it applies as a predicate to a subclass of the class of 'all men,' namely to the class of 'white men.' Alfārābī's analysis suggests that this is true of any combination of terms that results in a phrase.

Yet, Alfārābī makes an important distinction between two types of phrases (**Bārī armīniyās**, 57):

> There are two kinds of notions [*maᶜānī*] delimited by one another. One type is that in which they [i.e., the two parts of the delimitation] apply to one another in an essential way, in that it is in the nature [*tibāᶜ*] of one or both of them to be delimited by the other,[21] as in 'even number,' 'rational animal,' 'straight line.' For, 'even' applies to 'number' qua number, and similarly, 'rational' to 'animal' and 'straight' to 'line.' The other type is that in which the parts apply to each other accidentally as in 'white scribe' and 'building doctor.' For it is not qua scribe that whiteness applies to the scribe or qua doctor that being a builder applies to the doctor, but by coincidence [*bal ittafaqᵃ lahᵘ dhālikᵃ ittifāqᵃⁿ*].[22] However, these delimitative phrases [*muqayyadāt*][23] whose parts apply to each other essentially are more appropriate to be [considered] as delimitative phrases, while those that apply to one another accidentally are inferior to the former [as delimitative phrases].

This distinction between essential and accidental delimitative phrases parallels the well-known philosophical distinction between *essential* and *accidental predication*, and hence between *essential definition* and other types of definition, as we shall see later in this chapter.

Figure 1.1 is a diagram of Alfārābī's major ideas concerning the compound expressions described thus far. (See Figure 1.1)

The Place of Definition and Description in This Scheme: The Structural Point of View

According to Alfārābī, there are two kinds of definitory clauses: those that represent a "definition" [*ḥadd*] and those that represent a "description" [*rasm*] of a thing. Both *ḥadd* and *rasm* are delimitative phrases, the main function of which is to clarify notions by explaining the terms that represent them. In Alfārābī's own words (**Fuṣūl**, 274):

> A definition [*ḥadd*] is a delimitative phrase [*qawl tarkībuh tarkīb taqyīd*] that illustrates [*yashraḥ*] the notion [*maᶜnā*] signified by a

Figure 1.1

Alfārābī's Ideas Concerning Compound Expressions

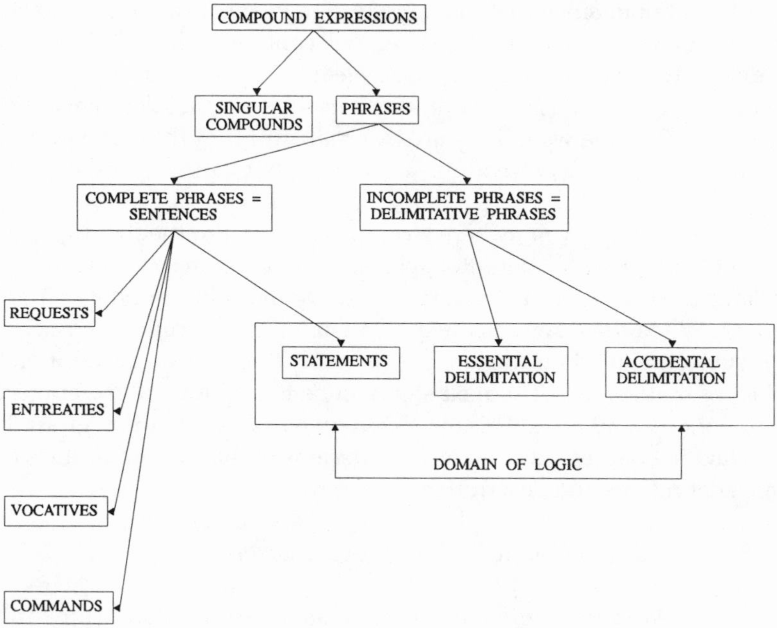

certain noun [*bi-ism*^{in}*-mā*] by means of the things that constitute that notion. And a "description" [*rasm*] is a delimitative phrase that illustrates the notion signified by a certain noun by means of things that do not constitute that notion, rather [it illustrates it] by means of its states [*aḥwālih*] or by means of the things that are constituted by that notion [*aw bi-ʾl-ashyāʾ allatī qiwāmuhā bi-dhālika ʾl-maʿnā*].

The example Alfārābī provides to illustrate his definition of these terms (*ḥadd* and *rasm*) is the following:

'Wall'[24] is a noun that signifies a notion that can be illustrated in two [different] phrases [*bi-qawlayn*]; one that it is an upright body, made of stone, brick or clay in order to carry a roof, and the other, a body to which doors are attached and in which pegs are inserted, etc.

The first case, Alfārābī explains, is an explanation of the noun *wall* in terms of things without which the wall will have no existence at all [*lā yakūn li-l-ḥā'iṭ wujūd*]. Clay and stone (or whatever the wall is made of) are a necessary condition for the wall to become a wall (but not a sufficient condition, since there is the question of the form of the subject under consideration). 'Wall,' however, will continue to be a wall, even if no doors are attached to it and nobody leans against it. These latter attributes are not *essential* for a wall, and thus their absence does not affect the existence of the wall. They are external attributes that can indicate and describe what is already in existence, but cannot provide that existence.

Alfārābī has given us here a complete answer to the first (formal) stage of our inquiry: a "definitory clause"[25] is a deliminative phrase that explains the essence or the external states of the subject under consideration. When the former is the case, then it is a "definition" [*ḥadd*] of that subject, and when the latter is the case, then it is a "description" [*rasm*] of that subject. The next step will be to inquire into the subject matter of *ḥadd* and *rasm*. This investigation will be based upon groundwork laid in chapter 1 during our discussions of the five predicables of which definitions and descriptions are composed.

Subject Matter of Definitory Clauses [*Ḥadd*]

Since Aristotle, there has reigned a standard rule concerning the nature of definition: "A definition is a phrase indicating the essence of something" (*Topics*, 101^{b}37). The "something" referred to in this statement is the subject of the definition, i.e., the "definiendum"; the defining phrase is traditionally referred to as the "definiens."

In order to analyze this Aristotelian rule, we must mention two further Aristotelian principles, which until recently had also been accepted by logicians and philosophers without challenge. I am referring to Aristotle's principles: 1) that "everything has one single essence" (*Topics*, 141^{a}35)[26] and 2) that "the framer of a good definition must define by means of genus and differentia [essential difference]" (*Topics*, 141^{b}26–7).

This last principle has come to be known as *definitio per genus et differentiam*. It is the most significant statement in Aristotle's, as well as his commentators', discussions of definition and is known as the "essential definition," since, according to Aristotle, it is said to make the *essence* of a thing known. Combination of the first and third principles (as outlined above) yields the conclusion that, according to Aristotle, the essence of a subject is expressed by means of the combination of its genus and its differentiae (or essential difference). In appendix I, I present some of the philosophical analysis that led Aristotle to these principles. Yet what is important for our study is not Aristotle as such, but rather how Alfārābī understands and interprets him.

Alfārābī, like all medieval Arab philosophers, accepts these principles and incorporates them into his system. This is the source, for example, of his statement: ''A definition is a compound universal [*kullī murakkab*] composed of a genus [*jins*] and a differentia [*faṣl*]'' (**Madkhal**, 126). This is in complete accordance with the third Aristotelian principle above.

Alfārābī's analysis of the essential definition is thorough and appears in many forms in his various writings, the most conclusive of the analyses appearing in **Alfāẓ**. In this work (pp. 77–78, par. 32) he describes essential definition as follows (paraphrase):

> *If* a universal signified by a compound expression 'D' joins a species ('S') in being predicated of individuals ('x,' 'y,' 'z,' . . .) and possesses the following characteristics:
>
> 1) 'D' is appropriately applied in answering the questions: 'what is 'S'?' and 'what is 'x' or 'y' or 'z,' etc.?';
> 2) One part of 'D' signifies the genus of 'S' and the other part signifies its differentia;
> 3) 'D' has the same extension as 'S' [*musāwī li-l-nawʿ fī ʾl-ḥaml*] or in short, 'D' and 'S' are convertible; *then* this universal is the definition of the species 'S' [*ḥadd dhālik al-nawʿ*].[27]

Of primary interest in this formal definition of ''essential definition'' is the fact that Alfārābī admits to his system a sixth category of universal (i.e., a sixth predicate); namely, universals represented by compound expressions and possessing the above-mentioned properties. The other five predicates previously introduced to his system are those discussed in Porphyry's *Isagoge* and dealt with in chapter 1 (*jins* [genus], *nawʿ* [species], *faṣl dhātī* [essential difference], *khāṣṣah* [property], and *ʿaraḍ* [accident]).

The introduction of this sixth predicate into Alfārābī's system is of philosophical import, since it represents his desire to harmonize Aristotle's conception of predicates with that of Porphyry (or rather, Porphyry as understood by Alfārābī and his contemporaries). Unfortunately, this effort is in essence an attempt to harmonize two incompatible attitudes, incompatible particularly in their treatment of the universal ''species'' (see below).

On the basis of the above-paraphrased formal definition of "essential definition" and the examples provided by Alfārābī to illustrate it,[28] we can picture that Alfārābī is thinking of the following scheme:

> Certain individuals 'x,' 'y,' 'z,' etc., are the subject of predication for the species 'S' to which they belong. This means that each of the following declarative sentences is true: 'x is S,' 'y is S,' 'z is S,' etc. Then we have a universal signified by a compound expression 'D' composed of certain terms (let us say, 'G' and 'F,' where 'G' signifies the genus and 'F' signifies the differentia of 'S'). Now by saying that 'D' and 'S' are convertible, Alfārābī also means that each of the following is true: 'x is D,' 'y is D,' 'z is D,' etc. (and vice versa, of course, namely that 'S' is properly predicated of whatever 'D' is properly predicated of).
>
> If all these conditions are fulfilled, then 'D' is the definition of 'S.'

Now in **Madkhal** (p. 126)[29] Alfārābī explains that the component 'F' of 'D' can itself be an expression composed of several differentiae of 'S.' He illustrates this by means of the following example: 'an animal is a nourished, sensitive body.' 'Nourished' and 'sensitive' are considered by Alfārābī to be differentiae of the definiendum 'animal.' He explains, however: "You ought to know that the constituent differentia [*al-faṣl al-muqawwim*] of that species[30] is the last one [of the definitory phrase]; the preceding differentiae joined to the genus comprise a definition of the genus of that species whose definition[31] was taken in place of its name."

One of the examples Alfārābī gives in this passage of **Madkhal** is the following: in defining 'man' you can say it is 'a body that is nourished, sensitive and rational.' 'Nourished body' is a genus of both animal and plant; it need not have a name in every given language, and indeed it has no name in the Arabic language. The combination 'sensitive nourished body' is another genus ranked under the genus represented by 'nourished body.' This new genus does have a name in Arabic, namely, *ḥayawān* [animal], and so forth.

In the language of symbols this process is expressed as follows:

> Suppose we have a genus 'G' and several attributes 'a_1,' 'a_2,' 'a_3,' etc. (with their nature to be discussed below), are joined to 'G' in delimitative phrases in the following manner: '$Ga_1a_2a_3$. . . . '
>
> The combination 'Ga_1' (i.e., 'nourished body' in the above example) results in a genus that may or may not have a name in a given language. Let us call it 'G_1.' Thus the original formula be-

comes '$G_1a_2a_3$,. . . .' Now the combination 'G_1a_2' yields another genus, which again may or may not have a name in a given language. Let us call it 'G_2.' Hence, the new formula will be 'G_2a_3,. . . .' (In the above example, 'G_2' stands for 'animal.') The combination 'G_2a_3' results in another genus, which we will call 'G_3,. . . .' ('G_3' represents 'man' in the above example.)

Later on in **Alfāẓ** (p. 89; see also **Madkhal**, 124) Alfārābī explains that the opposite process may also occur, especially for the purpose of illustration in teaching or for methodological reasons. In such cases, the teacher might want to replace a single expression with a compound one, if the latter is more comprehensible from the learner's point of view. In this process, which Alfārābī calls the "substitution [*ibdāl*] of the more known," a name of something can be replaced by its definition or by the definition of the parts of its definition.

Alfārābī refers to the substitution of a single expression (a name) by a compound expression (such as its *ḥadd* or *rasm*) as "the analysis of the name into its expository statement" [*qawl shāriḥ*].

In modern terminology the above process of substitution (in either direction) is called "indiscernibility of identicals." W. V. Quine summarizes the process as follows: "Given a true statement of identity,[32] one of its two terms may be substituted for the other in any true statement and the result will be true."[33]

It is reasonable to assume that this is what Alfārābī has in mind when he speaks of *ibdāl* [substitution]. In the example above (once again taken from the sensible biological world, a fact of no little philosophical significance, as we shall see) the attributes chosen are 'nourished,' 'sensitive,' and 'rational.' They are all considered by Alfārābī as differentiae, the specific role of which is to divide the genus 'body' into 'nourished body' (i.e., animals and plants) and 'nonnourished body' (i.e., all that is not animals and plants).

Let us call each of these parts a "class." Each of these classes is itself a genus that is a proper subclass of the class 'body.' The differentia 'nourished' differentiates by necessity [*bi-iḍṭirār*] (**Madkhal**, 126) things that possess this attribute from those that do not.

Each of the above classes can be divided still further. Let us take, for example, the class 'nourished body.' This class (or genus) contains all plants and all animals. There is, however, an essential difference between these two groups, Alfārābī argues. The predicate 'sensitive' applies necessarily to animals but not to plants. We may, therefore, divide this class into those things that are sensitive and those that are not. Thus 'sensitive' is a necessary dividing element in relation to the class 'nourished body,' and as such it is called a "dividing difference" [*faṣl qāsim*] or an "essential dividing differentia" [*faṣl dhātī muqassim*] in relation to the genus it divides (**Alfāẓ**, 73).

By the same token, this division (as well as the first division of the *class* 'body') has resulted in two new genera, one of which has as its essential characteristic the attribute 'sensitive,' which separates it from other things that are also 'nourished bodies.' As such, 'sensitive' is an essential differentia [*faṣl dhātī*] or a constitutive essential differentia [*faṣl dhātī muqawwim*] (ibid.) in relation to the class (or genus) it separates from other things. This process may be continued until we reach the final class, which has no subclasses that can be essentially differentiated from each other.

We have seen in chapter 1 that, according to Alfārābī, each of the entities generated in this way is called a "genus" in relation to its subclasses (also generated in this way), but it is called a "species" in relation to the class of which it is a proper subclass. Each of these classes (with the exception of the supreme genus and the infima species) is an intermediate class that can be termed a genus or a species, depending on the context.

This process of dividing by means of joining to each genus one of its dividing differentia "leads [*tantahī*] necessarily to the definitions of species and to the species themselves," Alfārābī concludes. However, "that which is employed in the sciences and is useful in obtaining definitions of species is the division of the genus by differentiae" (**Madkhal**, 126).

Alfārābī notes that there are two additional ways of dividing genera: 1) by employing the attributes called "properties" or 2) by employing accidental attributes. The first of these methods can indeed, he comments, lead *necessarily* to the various species of each genus but it *does not* provide their essential definitions (ibid.).

As for division by means of accidental attributes, Alfārābī is convinced that the results of such a division cannot be useful in science, since it does not lead (at least, not by necessity) to the desired [*al-maṭlūb*] species, such as when we divide the genus 'animal' by applying the accidental attribute 'white' to distinguish between 'white animals' and 'animals that are not white.' Such a division, he argues, does not lead by necessity to the desired conclusions, which are useful in the sciences (ibid.). By using terms like "useful" or "required species in the sciences," Alfārābī seems to agree with Aristotle, who says that "knowledge is of the universal and proceeds by necessary propositions" (*Posterior Analytics*, 88^{b}30).

This relates to another passage of Alfārābī's discussed earlier (**Madkhal**, 119). In this passage Alfārābī presents a fivefold classification of propositions, one of which has the form "UU," namely, both the subject and the predicate of the proposition are universals. In his commentary on this type of proposition, Alfārābī says this is the type used in science, dialectics, sophistical arts, and in many other arts (which he leaves unspecified).[34]

From a scientific point of view, therefore, the ultimate goal of the process described above is to reach necessary declarative sentences (i.e., those that cannot be otherwise),[35] the subjects of which are universals. These universals are the species—"not only the infima species but also the intermediate species," as Alfārābī concludes his formal definition of "essential definition" in **Alfāẓ** (p. 78).

If the ultimate goal of the definer is to answer the question 'what is the species?' and if knowledge proceeds through universals (and not through individuals),[36] why then does Alfārābī state that the compound expression 'D' must answer the question 'what are the individuals 'x,' 'y,' 'z,' . . . ?' (i.e., the individuals of which the species 'S' is composed).

If 'D' is an answer to the question 'what is Zayd?', then 'Zayd' as an individual is definable, i.e., he has an essence of his own as an individual. But this is incompatible with Alfārābī's own conception (not to mention Aristotle's) of "definition," namely, that it reveals the essence of a thing, and the essence of a thing lies in its kind or species. In fact, the term *ḥadd* itself is applicable, in Alfārābī's own system, to the species and not to the individuals belonging to that species. (For example, in the **Alfāẓ** version, Alfārābī explicitly states that the formula described above is called the "definition" of that species.)

I think Alfārābī does not really mean to state the above as a necessary condition (for 'D' to be a *ḥadd* for 'S'). Rather he is inserting a statement implied by the above definition without intending to have it as a requirement. Most probably, Alfārābī is thinking of the following Aristotelian argument when he adds this redundant requirement:

> Whenever one thing is predicated of another as of a subject, all things said of what is predicated will be said of the subject also. For example, 'man' is predicated of the individual man, and 'animal' of man, so 'animal' will be predicated of the individual man also. For the individual man is both a man and an animal.[37]

This is a position Alfārābī himself is explicit about in an earlier stage of **Alfāẓ** (p. 66), which can be described in modern terminology as the "transitivity" of the 'said of' relation.[38] This problem will arise in another form when we discuss the concept of "predication" in Alfārābī's writings later in the present study.

The fact that the concept of definition is not used by Alfārābī for individuals is explicit in his **Ḥurūf** (p. 106: par. 21–22), where he says, "Whenever we say the essence of 'Zayd,' we are really seeking his essence, which is more general than what Zayd, as an individual, stands for and which is his true essence [*māhiyyatuh fī ʾl-ḥaqīqah*]." In other words, individuals have no essence; only the species to which they belong have it. The theme that species and not individuals are the subject of scientific inquiry is repeated in **Ḥurūf** (p. 178, par. 177).

It is important to quote this passage in order to eliminate the disturbing impression that Alfārābī himself has helped create by applying the 'what is it?' question to individuals rather than to their species, implying that for him individuals have essences of their own and as such can be the subject of scientific inquiry. In that passage of **Ḥurūf**, Alfārābī explains that the predicates that make known the essences of the absolute substances (i.e., the primary substances, or simply, the individual material objects) are also called "absolute substance" [*al-jawhar ʿalā ʾl-iṭlāq*],[39] "but it is the latter that are the subject of scientific inquiry and not the former" (ibid., 178: par. 9–10).

Alfārābī concludes (**Alfāẓ**, 78: par. 22–23) that the Arabic term *ḥadd* [essential definition] as used in logic reflects its common meaning of "limit" or "border." An essential definition [*ḥadd*] makes known the essence of a thing [*yuʿarrif dhāt al-shayʾ wa-jawharah*] and at the same time answers the question 'what sort of a thing is it?' [*ayy* question], i.e., it makes known the things in which it is separated from other things.[40] Hence, the name *ḥadd*, "for it resembles the limits of country estates [*ḍiyāʿ*] and real estate [*ʿaqār*] since the limit of a house pertains to that house only and by it, it is distinguished from other houses and by it, it is isolated from other things."

Alfārābī's concept of definition, therefore, is presented as related to the intuitive notion of putting the limits between two things (houses, etc.). This explanation has its roots in the Platonic concept of "division," a concept Alfārābī addresses in **Alfāẓ** and in **Burhān**, to be discussed in chapter 4.

There is one more notion related to Alfārābi's concept of definition, one I believe introduced by Alfārābī himself. I am referring to the term *ḥadd nāqiṣ* [incomplete definition]. This term is contrasted by Alfārābī with the concept of *ḥadd* discussed above, to which he sometimes refers as *ḥadd kāmil* [complete definition] (**Alfāẓ**, 78).

Alfārābī's definition of "incomplete definition" is identical to his definition of *ḥadd* except in one requirement, namely that 'D' and 'S' are *not* equal in predication (i.e., not convertible); rather 'D' "is more general than the species with which it participates in predication [i.e., 'S' in our notation],'' to use Alfārābī's own words. An example of this, he says, is 'pedestrian animal,' which is an incomplete definition of 'man' (**Alfāẓ**, 78).

The incomplete definition of certain species, Alfārābī explains, is a complete definition of some genus higher than that species (ibid.). The phrase 'pedestrian animal,' though it does not define 'man,' is a definition of a certain[41] intermediate genus that is a genus (predicated essentially) of the species ('man,' in this case) of which that phrase is an incomplete definition.

Subject Matter of Descriptive Clauses [*Rasm*]

In a very similar fashion to that employed in discussing the concept of *ḥadd,* Alfārābī analyzes the closely related concept of description or [*rasm*] in Arabic (**Alfāẓ**, 79). This will again be paraphrased, rather than literally translated as follows:

> If a universal signified by a compound expression 'R' joins a species or a genus 'S' (in being predicated of individuals 'x,' 'y,' 'z,' . . .)[42] and has the following characteristics:
>
> 1. 'R' is not an appropriate answer to the question 'what is it?' in relation to the species or genus 'S' (and also in relation to the individuals belonging to them).[43]
> 2. The components of 'R' signify one of the following:
>   a) accidents[44] of 'S';
>   b) one part of 'R' signifies the genus of 'S'[45] and other parts signify accidents of 'S';
>   c) one part signifies the genus of 'S' and other parts signify properties [*khawāṣṣ*] of 'S';
> 3. 'R' and 'S' are convertible.
>
> If these conditions are fulfilled, then 'R' is called the description of 'S.'[46]

Alfārābī gives the following phrase as an example of the above: ''mobile, capable of knowledge,'' which has the following characteristics, he says:

1. it is co-predicated with 'man' of individuals 'Zayd,' ''ʿAmr,' etc.;
2. it is convertible with 'man';

3. it signifies (some of) the accidents of 'man' (requirement 2a above);

and (Alfārābī would have agreed to add):

4. it does not answer the question 'what is man?', i.e., it does not reveal the essence of 'man.'

Other examples given by Alfārābī as descriptions of 'man' are the following:

1. 'animal capable of laughter' (the components of 'R' in this case being a genus and a property of 'man,' requirement 2c above);
2. 'animal capable of knowledge' ('R' in this case composed of a genus and an accident of 'man,' requirement 2b above);
3. 'mobile, capable of laughter.'

This last example is of special significance since it adds a further possibility not mentioned in the above-stated definition of *rasm*. This combination is composed of an accident and a property, without the genus of 'man.' We can therefore amend the above definition of description so that requirement 2 will have a fourth possibility added to it:

2d. parts of 'R' signify accidents of 'S' and other parts signify properties of 'S.'

There is yet another problem in the above definition of *rasm*. In order to explain this problem let us analyze the first example Alfārābī provides in order to illustrate his definition of *rasm*. The phrase 'mobile, capable of knowledge' is, in Alfārābī's view, an example of a descriptive phrase that describes 'man.' It is composed, he claims, of (two) accidents of 'man.'

Now, it is true that the component 'mobile' of this phrase is an accident (an inseparable accident to be more precise), but how about 'capable of knowledge'?[47] Suppose that it, too, is an accident. Then it must be either a separable accident or an inseparable one. If the former is the case then (by Alfārābī's own standards, **Alfāẓ**, 76–77) it should modify only a subclass of the species and as such it cannot be a part of the description for the whole species 'man.'

At best, therefore, 'capable of knowledge' is an inseparable accident of 'man.' But as such it applies to more individuals than those included in the species 'man,' i.e., it is "more general" [*aʿamm*]. (This is exactly what was indicated earlier [chapter 1, section 5] as the difference between a "property" and an "inseparable accident": the former is more general than the species it modifies, while the latter is convertible with that species [**Alfāẓ**, 77].) If this is the case, then, when the predicate under consideration is mentioned, the species 'man' cannot be assumed to be its subject, since it is broader in scope than the latter. This means it is predicated of more objects than those included in 'man' as a class.

The trouble is that in the phrase under consideration, i.e., 'mobile, capable of knowledge,' the first component is assumed by Alfārābī to also be an inseparable accident of 'man,' and as such is *not* convertible with 'man,' and what was said of 'capable of knowledge' applies here, too.

If both attributes are broader in scope than 'man,' how could their combination result in a compound expression that is convertible with 'man?' Obviously, the answer is that this is impossible. At least one of the components must be convertible with the species under consideration.

The primary intention in the above analysis is not to show that 'capable of knowledge' is a property. Rather it is aimed at challenging the rule expressed in 2a) above. I believe that Alfārābī erred in assuming that a combination of two or more accidents can be a description of a species or genus. An accident (whether separable or inseparable) is never convertible with the species it modifies, and this is the key issue.

It is appropriate, therefore, to further amend the above formula of description introduced by Alfārābī to the following:

> 'R' is a description of 'S' if conditions 1, 3, and one of the following (2b, 2c or 2d) are satisfied.

In **Risālah** (p. 229) Alfārābī indeed admits that the "combination of accidental predicates alone has no single name," implying that it is neither a definition nor a description. Furthermore, this troublesome element of the **Alfāẓ** version is not repeated in any of Alfārābī's other writings, which all the more leads me to believe that Alfārābī could not have meant that a combination of accidental predicates alone can be a "description" in the strict sense outlined above.

Rasm is an important concept in Alfārābī's system, since it introduces a wide range of possible combinations of predicates, thus paving the way for discussion of another important logical topic: "nonessential predication." Consequently, *rasm* relates to a number of significant philosophical issues, as we shall see. This concept is also considered by Alfārābī, among other things, as a supplement to the notion of *ḥadd*.

On this latter question Alfārābī says that *rusūm* (pl. of *rasm*) reach where *ḥudūd* (pl. of *ḥadd*) cannot reach (**Alfāẓ**, 79). Since definitions are composed of genera and of essential differentiae only, it follows that if something has no genus, then it will not have a definition either, Alfārābī explains. Similarly, if something has no essential differentia.

Now, the argument continues:

> Since the supreme genera have no genera above them, it follows that they have no definitions. However, in the case of things that lack genera or essential differentiae [but not both][48] it is not impossible [*lam yamtaniʿ*] for them to have accidents, and consequently it is not impossible for them to have *descriptions*. (emphasis mine)
>
> It is not impossible, therefore, for the supreme genera to have a description; similarly, for the intermediate [genera].

Alfārābī's use of the plural of *khāṣṣah* [property] as a possible candidate for part of the compound 'R' raises the question as to whether anything has more than one property or has at most one property.

On several occasions, Alfārābī indicates his answer to be that every species has more than one property, even if we assume the question is about properties in the strict sense, namely about properties that are convertible with the species or genus they modify.[49] This is the kind of property Alfārābī refers to as *al-khāṣṣah bi-ʾl-taḥqīq* (the species 'man,' for example, has several properties in this sense: 'capable of laughing,' 'capable of learning,' 'capable of trade,' etc. [**Risālah**, 229]).

The nonstrict type of properties are those that are not convertible with the universal they modify, such as 'being an engineer' or 'being a physician' in relation to 'man' (**Alfāẓ**, 76).

This leads to the obvious, but important, conclusion that "each species can have several descriptions, but not several definitions. Rather each species has a single definition" (**Risālah**, 230).

The importance of this issue is that it leads to more fundamental questions, such as Why does a description not reveal the essence of the species or genus it describes, whereas a definition does?

Based on the above conclusion quoted from **Risālah**, Alfārābī can argue, for example, that since there is only one essence of any given thing, there should be a unique expression or formula that expresses that essence.

But then, one may ask, how can that formula be reached? And given that we can reach several expressions describing the subject under consideration, how do we decide which is the one that expresses the essence of that subject? Is there an objective criterion for deciding what the essence is (and consequently the formula that expresses it) or is Ibn Taymiyyah right in his charge?

> Each person can invent an essence in his soul different from that invented by other people. And if a certain person claims that the essence [of man] is 'rational animal' another person can say "it is rather the animal who is capable of laughter." (*Kitāb al-radd*, 67)

Besides, what guarantees that formulae of this sort are not equivalent?

Yet, even if Alfārābī succeeds in resolving these (related) problems, there will be further questions concerning the *scope* or the *extension* of the concept of *ḥadd* as presented thus far.

By this I mean to ask whether definitions *per genus et differentiam* may be applied to all that there is? We may ask in this regard whether a natural phenomenon such as an eclipse of the moon (where the concepts of genus, differentia, and property themselves are not clear) may be defined or described by means of the methods we have investigated up to this point.

And if no definition *per genus et differentiam* can be assigned to certain things, an obvious question arises: Does an essence of any thing exist where a definition *per genus et differentiam* cannot be formulated?

The answers to these and other related questions are inherent, as we shall see, in Alfārābī's conception of "essence" [*māhiyyah*], which stands in exactly the same need of clarification as does the notion of "definition" (*ḥadd*) itself. In Alfārābī's system these two notions, it seems, are "the two sides of a single dubious coin"[50] and it is the task of the following chapters to further elucidate their nature.

Notes to Chapter 2

1. *Rasm* [description] is virtually accepted by Alfārābī as a *seventh predicate*, on similar grounds as those on the basis of which he accepts *ḥadd* [definition] as a *sixth* predicate, namely that it is a composite of two or more singular universals (predicates).

2. Alfārābī, "**Kitāb bārī armīniyās ay al-ʿibārah**," ed. M. Kuyel [Turker] in *Arastirma*, 4 (1966), pp. 1–85. [Henceforth: **Bārī armīniyās**] This work is translated by F. Zimmermann, op. cit.

3. Translating *maʿnā,* which I usually render as "meaning." Zimmermann defends the use of "referent" (rather than "meaning" or "notion") when "it is specifically used to denote things 'outside the mind' " (Zimmermann, op. cit., p. 11, n. 2).

4. Cf. *Aristotle's Posterior Analytics,* 92b7. See also **ʿIbārah** (p. 27): "Some single expressions signify images in the soul that are not founded on anything existing outside, like *ʿanz-ayyil* [goat-stag] and *ʿanqāʾ mughrib* [sphinx]."

5. For instance, in the *Posterior Analytics* 93b29, J. Barnes translates *logos* as "an account," whereas Sir David Ross translates it in the same passage as "a statement." In *Topics* I 102a1 *logos* is rendered by Forster in the Loeb translation as "phrase," whereas the same translator renders it as "meaning" in *Topics* II 112a32–34 and as "definition" in *Topics* III 119a29–30. See also Ackrill's commentary on the term *logos* in Aristotle's *Categories and De Interpretatione,* p. 124.

6. Translating *qawl.*

7. Literally *marsūm* means the "object of description"; similarly with *maḥdūd* (which literally means the "object of definition" or the "definiendum"). I do not think this is what Alfārābī has in mind, however, especially in light of his explanation that *ḥadd* [definition] as well as *rasm* [description], rather than *maḥdūd* and *marsūm,* are kinds of statements.

8. Zimmermann (op. cit., p. 43, n. 4) explains that this fivefold classification of sentences is reported, by Ammonius among others, to be the standard peripatetic classification: *amr, ṭalab, taḍarruʿ, nidāʾ,* and *qawl jāzim.*

9. The Arabic word *amr* has the meaning of "imperative" when used as a grammatical term.

10. This list also appears in **ʿIbārah** 17a2–3. In **Ḥurūf** (p. 162, par. 159), however, Alfārābī adds to the above four nondeclarative sentences the following: permission [*idhn*], prevention [*manʿ*], urging [*ḥathth*], discouraging [*kaff*], and prohibition [*nahī*].

Incidentally, Alfārābī mentions in this passage of **Ḥurūf** an important distinction between declarative and nondeclarative sentences. By expressing any of the latter type, he says, one always seeks an action. Elsewhere in **Ḥurūf** (p. 163, par. 161), he explains that the answer to a vocative sentence, for example, is either coming [*iqbāl*] or refraining [*iʿrāḍ*] from coming, the answer for entreaties and requests is either granting [*badhl*] or refusing [*manʿ*], etc. In declarative statements, on the other hand, the purpose is to communicate knowledge [*ʿilm*].

11. Alfārābī states in this regard that some people (probably a reference to Aristotle's *Categories* 2a7 and *De Interpretatione* 17a24) hold that this feature of statements is their *definition,* while others describe it as a *property* of statements.

12. Alfārābī's discussion of these two concepts occurs in his **Mabādiʾ al-falsafah al-qadīmah** (Cairo: 1910), pp. 2–3.

13. As far as I can tell, Alfārābī uses the term *khabar,* which means "information" or "stating something of something else," only once in the sense of a "predicate" (**Fuṣūl**, p. 272). Alfārābī refrains from using this term in the sense of "predicate," perhaps in order to avoid using terms coined by the Arab grammarians for their own purposes and for use in grammatical contexts. In grammar, the term *khabar* indicates the predicate of a nominal clause. Alfārābī does, however, use derivatives of this term. Thus in **Ḥurūf** (p. 162: 11), *mā yukhbar bih* [by means of which a piece of information is conveyed], and also (p. 181: 12) *fī ʾl-ikhbār* [i.e., in informing or conveying a message]. And again in **Fuṣūl** (p. 273), where he uses the expression *tarkībuh tarkīb ikhbār* [the structure of which is to convey a message or be informative].

14. The translation of *taqyīd* is owed to F. Zimmermann.

15. The addition of the term *of kinds* is Zimmermann's contribution.

16. Omitting the fourth type of nondeclarative sentence, i.e., the entreaties [*taḍarruʿ*].

17. By "definition" Alfārābī means only the defining part, which in itself is an incomplete phrase.

18. I am here quoting Zimmermann's trans., in op. cit., p. 45. The text reads *takhuṣṣ,* which literally means "belongs to." Perhaps "complete phrases . . . are the domain of rhetoric [*al-khutab*] and poetics [*al-shiʿr*]" would be a more literal translation.

19. Zimmermann (op. cit., lvii, n. 2) comments on these terms: "*ishtirāṭ* and *istithnāʾ* are used by the Arab translators for Aristotle's *diorizo* and its derivatives; *taqyīd,* on the other hand, may be an import from Arab grammar."

According to Gérard Throupeau (*Lexique-index du kitab de Sībawayhi* [Paris: Klinck Sieck, 1976]), the term *taqyīd* does not appear in Sībaweih's *Al-kitāb,* the major work on Arabic grammar. The term does occur, however, in the writings of a tenth-century Arab grammarian with whom Alfārābī was probably acquainted. Ibn Fāris, in his *Al-ṣāḥibī fī fiqh al-luqhah* [Companion to the philosophy of language] (Beirūt: Muʿassasat Badrān, 1964, p. 194), analyzes this term, and one can see some similarity in meaning with Alfārābī's concept of the term *taqyīd.*

20. In **Ḥurūf**, Alfārābī uses the term *taqyīd* or derivatives thereof more frequently (cf. pp. 167: 9; 168: 5; 182: 19; 185: 18; 187: 2; 190: 7 and 9).

21. See Zimmermann (op. cit., p. 233) for the correction that must be made to the text at these points.

22. The text reads as follows: *bal ittifaq^{a} dhālik^{a} ittifāq^{an}.* A better version, however, appears in footnote 2 of that text.

23. It may also be read as *muqayyidāt.* I think both readings convey the meaning. This latter term means "those that restrict," the former "those that are restricted."

24. For the source of Alfārābī's use of the example of a wall see Zimmermann, op. cit. (p. 28, n. 2; see also Appendix p. 259, commentary on p. 28, n. 2, for an additional commentary by H. A. Wolfson). According to Wolfson, Alexander of Aphrodisias repeatedly uses this example in his commentary on the *Metaphysics*.

However, this term is also used by Sībaweih (as Zimmermann states on p. 28, n. 2) as an example of a "noun" (*Al-kitāb*, I: 12) and it could very well be that Alfārābī is adopting Sībaweih's rather than Aphrodisias' example.

25. A definitory clause is a predicate, it is *not* a complete phrase. Only when it is actually predicated of its subject, will the resulting statement be a complete phrase.

26. Hence Aristotle's conclusion in *Topics* (143^{a}1–2) that "there cannot be more than one definition of the same thing," and in *Topics* 151^{b}18 that "there is never more than one definition of the same thing."

27. Alfārābī makes clear in this passage that by *nawʿ* he means not only the *infima species*, but the *intermediate species* as well.

28. It must be noted that the second of these examples does not effectively illustrate the above definition of "essential definition."

29. See also **Ḥurūf** (pp. 186–7, par. 188).

30. I.e., an intermediate species, which is a species in relation to what is above it and a genus in relation to what is below it. (I refer to this as a "relative species.")

31. I.e., the definition of the immediate genus of that species.

32. In the case of "definition" the identity is between the definiendum and the definiens. Similarly with "description" (although here the question of identity is more difficult to establish).

33. W. V. Quine, *From a Logical Point of View* (New York: Harper & Row, 1961), p. 139.

34. See also "**Kitāb al-burhān**" [Posterior analytics], in *Al-manṭiq ʿind Alfārābī* [Alfārābī's logic], ed. Mājid Fakhrī. (Beirūt: Dār al-mashriq, 1986). [Henceforth: **Burhān**] "Let us investigate these universal [statements] alone, for they are mostly used in the sciences [ʿulūm] and because investigating the universal [statements] may include* that of the particular [statements]" (**Burhān**, 22). *Translating the word *yantazim*, which I believe should be understood in the same way as *yaḍum*.

35. I am applying here Aristotle's definition of "necessary proposition" as expressed in his *Posterior Analytics* (88^{b}32).

36. Cf. Porphyry's *Isagoge*, p. 40.

37. Aristotle, *Categories* (1^b10-15).

38. See Ackrill's commentary on the above-quoted passage from Aristotle's *Categories*.

39. For this terminology see also **Ḥurūf** (p. 181, par. 181).

40. This relates to Alfārābī's **Ḥurūf** (pp. 184–5, par. 186), where the relationship between the *mā* and the *ayy* questions are discussed.

41. Alfārābī's expression *li-baʿḍ al-ajnās* should be understood in this passage as "one genus" rather than "several genera" (another possible meaning of this expression).

42. This phrase is missing from Alfārābī's text, but it is safe to assume that it supports his intention.

43. This phrase is inferred from Alfārābī's general discussion and from his examples, but does not explicitly appear in the text.

44. In **Madkhal** (p. 127), however, Alfārābī drops the option that a combination of accidents alone can produce a description of a subject. His definition of *rasm* in **Madkhal** includes the genus of the subject under consideration as a necessary element of the formula of *rasm*.

45. I.e., the proximate genus.

46. Alfārābī's concept of *incomplete description* [*rasm nāqiṣ*] is also outlined in this passage. The only difference between complete and incomplete description is that in the latter 'R' and 'S' are not convertible. However, unlike the definition of "incomplete *ḥadd*," 'R' as an "incomplete *rasm*" need not be more general than 'S'; it may be more specific.

47. The source of this predicate, I believe, is Aristotle's *Topics* (102^a20-21), where an equivalent of 'capable of knowledge' is discussed as a "property." The expression in the Aristotelian text is 'capable of learning grammar,' but this distinction does not affect my line of argument.

48. Otherwise we will return to the same invalid situation, namely having only a combination of accidents as a "description."

49. In fact Alfārābī states this argument explicitly in **Risālah** (230): "Each species may have several descriptions, but not several definitions; rather, each species has one definition only. Similarly, each species may have several properties."

50. To borrow W. V. Quine's phrase from his discussion of "self-contradictoriness" and "analyticity" in the essay entitled "Two Dogmas of Empiricism," op. cit., p. 20.

3

The Concept of Essence in Alfārābī

The problematic issues raised at the conclusion of chapter 2, regarding the concept of "definition," will best be resolved by a thorough exploration of the related concept of "essence." This chapter on "essence" will be divided into two main sections: 1) a discussion of the Arabic question particles as they relate to "essence" and 2) a discussion of the various types of "essence" Alfārābī identifies.

We have already seen how Alfārābī links the use and the meanings of many of the interrogative particles, not only to his discussion of predicates in chapter 1 but also to his analysis of "definition" as presented in chapter 2. Let us now explore this very novel approach of Alfārābī's more thoroughly.

The Role of Question Particles in Definition

According to Alfārābī the subject of an inquiry may be either an individual or a universal. Thus when you ask "what is this thing?" the reference may be to either a particular or a universal. As Alfārābī puts it:

> The question 'what is it?' may refer to an individual or individuals or it may refer to a universal. . . . The appropriate answer that should be employed to answer the question 'what is it?' [*mā huwa?*] may be either a name for that thing [i.e., the subject of inquiry], it can be some of its individuals[1] or it can be some of the universals that are predicated of it. Our intention here, however, is to discuss that question to which the answer is provided by stating certain universals [that are predicated] of the subject of inquiry. (**Alfāẓ**, 65)

Alfārābī's intention in this passage is to *limit* his philosophical search for an answer to the question 'what is a thing?' by setting up prior parameters. He immediately excludes from his logical vista answers that involve giving examples of the thing under discussion. He also excludes answers that describe linguistic entities, such as the names of things. Alfārābī, it seems, is solely concerned with analyzing answers that describe the "essence" [*māhiyyah*] of a thing.

In the remainder of this section, we will investigate the various ways in which the Arabic *question particles* relate to the concept of "essence" in Alfārābī's logical system. From this discussion, we will proceed to a more general (but related) analysis of types of "essence" in section 2 of this chapter.

The Hal Particle—Establishing Existence

There are, Alfārābī says, certain interrogative particles that may be added to a singular noun or to an expression *functioning* as a singular noun [*aw mā kāna bi-manzilat al-mufrad*] (**Alfāẓ**, 49). These particles are employed when one intends either to inquire about the nature of a thing [*dhāt al-shayʾ*] or to understand the meaning of its name [*maʿnā ʾl-ism*] (**Alfāẓ**, 48–49). If the latter is the case, then there is no need to presuppose that "the thing" exists in order to proceed to ask about the meaning of its name.

Alfārābī is more explicit about this issue in **Ḥurūf** (pp. 170–171, par. 169):

> It may happen, however, that what he [the questioner] conceptualizes and comprehends from [stating] the name is a concept that is unknown [*ghayr maʿlūm*], whether it has [external] existence or not, such as when the concept 'elephant' is outlined to someone who has not seen an elephant, it may be the case that his assent [*taṣdīq*] regarding its existence does not come about and he will not know whether that which is thus and with these attributes exists or not. . . . All these are expressions [*aqāwīl*] that explain the names and may be called "definitions" figuratively and by way of extending the meaning of the terms. By these expressions one seeks to bring about concepts of these utterances. . . . And if it turns out that this concept has no [external] existence, then these parts that are the name's components remain only in the man's mind and whatever that expression denotes is not an essence of anything.

Thus, according to Alfārābī, one can speak of names and expressions without asking about the existence of any external entities to which they may refer. In this case the linguistic expression will have a corresponding mental concept and that need not have a corresponding reality; it is an explanation of the name only; it is a definition of the name."

According to Alfārābī one can explain, for example, the term *tamāthīl al-ḥammāmāt* [frescos in the public baths] as that which painters sketch and which come about in the soul as concepts, but they do not have a real existence.

> Thus the expressions composed in order to signify the concepts [*maʿānī*] under consideration signify things that do not exist, and much of this class of expressions are expressions signifying what is not known, whether it exists or not. The likes of these are called definitions only by way of license [*musāmaḥah*] and figuratively [*tajawwuz*]. Rather they [should be] called "expressions that explain the names" [*al-aqāwīl allatī tashraḥ al-asmāʾ*]. (**Ḥurūf**, p. 170, par. 169)

However, when inquiring about the essence of a thing one must presuppose its existence, otherwise one's inquiry will be meaningless [*la-kāna ʾl-qawlu bāṭilan*] (**Alfāẓ**, 48–49). If this type of inquiry is carried out in Arabic, then there are two ways to pose the question, either with the copulative verb or without it [*mā huwa al-shayʾ* or simply *mā al-shayʾ*]. Faced with either one of these two questions one can, according to Alfārābī, answer by providing a singular name [*ism mufrad*] of that thing, or by using a composite expression [*qawl murakkab* or *lafẓ murakkab*].[2] Either of these would constitute an appropriate answer to the question 'what is it?'. However, if a composite expression is used rather than a singular name, then the "essence" of the thing under consideration is provided.

According to Alfārābī, inquiry about a thing may be carried out in various ways, depending on the intention [*maqṣūd*] of the inquirer (**Alfāẓ**, 46). Thus, if the question is concerned with the quantity [*miqdār*] of a thing, then the person being questioned must provide the inquirer with information concerning the quantity of that thing. Similarly, when one asks about the location [*makān*] of a thing or about the time [*zamān*] of its occurrence (**Alfāẓ**, 46–47).

The question as to whether a thing exists or not, however, is in a sense the most fundamental question, for all other questions about a thing will be appropriate [*yaṣluḥ*] only once it has been established that the thing exists. It would be meaningless, for example, to ask 'what is that thing?' about a thing we do not see or a thing we are not sure exists (**Alfāẓ**, 48).

In inquiring about the existence of a thing in Arabic, one uses the term *hal.* This particle must be added to a compound expression (whether explicitly or implicitly) in order to produce a meaningful question. You cannot, for example, say 'is Zayd?' unless you have in mind some predicate for this noun, such as 'is Zayd going?' [*hal Zayd munṭaliq?*]. This particle, Alfārābī concludes, must always [*abadan*] be added to a compound expression that is itself a meaningful expression (i.e., a statement).

In **Ḥurūf** (p. 200 ff., par. 210) Alfārābī goes a step further, explaining that this particle is in fact always added to two contrary statements [*qaḍiyyatayn mutaqābilatayn*] connected to one another by a conjunction particle (such as, *am, immā,* and *aw;* all are taken by Alfārābī to mean roughly "or"): for example, *hal Zayd qā'im aw laysa bi-qā'im* [is Zayd standing up or not standing up?].

The Kayfa Particle—In Search of Qualities

Once the existence of a thing has been established, the inquiry about that thing can proceed in many different directions, such as asking about the time of a thing's occurrence [*matā,* when?] or about its location [*ayna,* where?]. However, the two most significant kinds of questions from a philosophical point of view are questions seeking to conceptualize the *essence* of a thing [*taṣawwur dhāt al-shay'*] (**Alfāẓ**, 48) and questions seeking to know the *form* [*ṣīghah*] and the *structure* [*hay'ah*] of a thing (**Alfāẓ**, 50).

In this latter case, one employs the particle *kayfa* ('how is it?' or 'what is it like?'). The answer provided in response to this type of question should contain the *kayfiyyāt* [qualities] of the thing being inquired about, Alfārābī explains, noting that the word *kayfiyyāt* is clearly derived from the question particle *kayfa* employed in posing questions about a thing's qualities.

These qualities can be, Alfārābī notes, either the *qualities of the essence of a thing* [*ṣīghat dhātih*] or *qualities external to its essence* [*wa-immā 'l-khārijah 'an dhātih*] (**Alfāẓ**, 51). Thus according to Alfārābī, when the question particle *kayfa* is used, the intention of the questioner may be to inquire about the *form of a thing's essence* or about its *external qualities*. Alfārābī, for example, considers the question 'how is Zayd?'. The possible answers ('he is good,' 'he is sick,' etc.) describe (some of) Zayd's attributes [*ṣīyagh,* pl. of *ṣīghah,* lit., form] that are external to his essence.

However, Alfārābī continues, only one of these types of questions concerns the philosopher—namely, the question regarding the form of a thing's essence—and his interest in this type of question is something that separates him from the common masses: "The forms by which the thing is affirmed [*yathbut*] [i.e., by which its essence is indicated] are unknown to the multitude. . . . It is the external attribute they are accustomed to refer to when they use the particle *kayfa*" (**Alfāẓ**, 51). For philosophers, on the other hand, the particle *kayfa* is a tool by means of which one inquires about internal as well as external properties or attributes.

Now if the answer to a question is concerned with the essence of a thing (i.e., if it describes the internal qualities of the thing), then these qualities are called *kayfiyyāt dhātiyyah* or *kayfiyyāt jawhariyyah* [essential qualities].[3] However, if the answer to the *kayfa* question provides an external description of the thing, then the qualities provided in this kind of answer are called *kayfiyyāt ʿaraḍiyyah* [accidental qualities] or *kayfiyyāt ghayr dhātiyyah* [nonessential qualities] (**Alfāẓ**, 52).

The Ayy Particle—In Search of Difference

We touched upon the issue of "essential" as opposed to "accidental qualities" in our discussion of definition [*ḥadd*] and will return to it again during the course of our discussion of *māhiyyah* in section 2 of this chapter. However, I would now like to turn to a third question particle, the particle *ayy* [which one?]. This is the question particle we use when we seek to know how a thing is distinguished from other things. As Alfārābī sees it, when one uses the particle *ayy* and asks the question *ayy shayʾ huwa* or *ayyumā huwa* ['which one is it?'] one is seeking, in Alfārābī's words, "to distinguish (a thing) from others or to know what sets it apart from other things" (ibid.).

This kind of question implies that the "universe of discourse"[4] has at least two objects, otherwise the question would be meaningless [*bāṭil*], Alfārābī observes (ibid.). Similarly, he says, when you ask 'what is it?' or 'how is it?', then you must assume that the universe of discourse has at least one object, the object about which we are asking. For if we ask 'what is man?' or 'how is Zayd?', then the question is meaningful as long as the universe has the object of inquiry in it, even if there is nothing else in that universe [*al-ʿālam*].

The particle *ayy* plays a significant role in the process of arriving at the definition of a thing, i.e., of seeking to know its essence. For example, Alfārābī says (**Madkhal**, 122–123), when the question 'what is man?' is presented and the answer provided is 'it is a certain body [*jism^{un}-mā*],' then the answer is given here in terms of some remote genus and not at all what the inquirer expects to hear, since it is too general. He must therefore proceed to ask, *ayy jism huwa* ['what kind of body?' or 'which body?'].

When the answer 'a man is a nourished body' is provided in answer to the same question, this still fails to answer the inquirer's question, since there are many nourished bodies that are not men. Thus he must ask again and again by means of the *ayy* particle until he reaches the final answer, the answer that provides the *essence* of the subject of inquiry (in this case 'man'). That is, the inquirer must continue to ask until the *definition* of this subject is provided.

This is what Alfārābī means in **Ḥurūf** (pp. 181–182, par. 183–184) where he addresses the same issue:

> If a certain thing is understood [*fuhim*^{a}], conceived [*tuṣuwwir*^{a}] and intellected [*ʿuqil*^{a}] by means of an attribute [*bi-amr*^{in}] that is common to it and to other things [i.e., predicated of it and of other things], the inquirer does not find it sufficient to understand [the thing's nature] without understanding, conceiving and intellecting what sets it apart [*bi-mā yanḥāz huwa*] from the other things with which it has that common attribute. . . . Thus we seek to conceive, intellect and understand it by means of that which sets it apart, that which makes it unique and distinguishes it from whatever else participates in that genus. When we become familiar with that thing [which sets it apart from the others], then the species [i.e., the subject of inquiry] becomes known.

Thus, he says, we come to use the particle *ayy* (**Ḥurūf**, 182 – 183, par. 184).

We have already mentioned that the question *ayy shayʾ huwa* ['what kind of a thing is it?'] is supposed to distinguish a certain thing from other things of the same genus. By this we mean (as Alfārābī explains in **Ḥurūf**, 182) that we are seeking to know the things by which our subject is set apart from its partners [*al-anwāʿ al-qāsimah lah*]. The answer to this inquiry can be formulated (just as in the case of the *kayfa* particle) in two ways:

1. *by means of its essence and by stating how the essence of this thing differs from other essences; or*
2. *by means of an "accident" [ʿaraḍ] that is external to the essence of the thing under consideration.* This *ʿaraḍ* pertains to the thing (only) and is taken as a sign to it so that it is distinguished from the other dividing species (*anwāʿ qāsimah* [lit., dividing species since they divide the genus that is predicated of all of them] that participate in that proximate genus.

An example of the first is the difference between 'wool' and 'silk.' These are different in their essences. An example of the second is the difference between the different *aḥwāl* [(external) states] of the same thing; e.g., one wool is distinguished from other wools by means of the different colors they may have.

The term *aḥwāl* mentioned above is defined in Alfārābī's **Alfāẓ** (p. 53) as follows: "Qualities [*kayfiyyāt*] that are external to a thing's essence are called '[external] states' [*aḥwāl*] when they are provided to answer the question 'what kind of thing is it?' [*ayy* question]." According to Alfārābī, an example of a thing distinguished from others by means of its external states is the difference between two men, 'Zayd' and "ᶜAmr'—the one good and the other, bad. We know for sure [*yaqīn*] that 'Zayd' does not differ from "ᶜAmr' in the same way he differs from 'wool.' (In the latter case the difference is essential.) *Aḥwāl* is, therefore, another term used by Alfārābī in reference to the external properties of a thing. Other equivalent terms are *'kayfiyyah ᶜaraḍiyyah,' "ᶜaraḍ,' 'kayfiyyah ghayr dhātiyyah,'* and *'kayfiyyah ghayr jawhariyyah.'*

The Mā Particle—In Search of Essence [Māhiyyah]

What happens when we examine the relationship between the *ayy* question ['which?'] on the one hand, and the *kayfa* question ['how?'] and the *mā* question ['what?'], on the other?

According to Alfārābī, everything that is an appropriate answer to the question 'how is it?' (*kayfa* question) is also appropriate as an answer to the questions 'which one is it?' and 'what kind of thing is it?' but not vice versa. In Alfārābī's words: "much of what is appropriate in answering the question *ayy shayʾ huwa* is not appropriate in answering the question *kayfa*" (**Alfāẓ**, 52).

As I see it, Alfārābī is arguing as follows: When you answer a 'how?' question you indicate those qualities (whether essential or not) that describe the thing under consideration and make it known. And this is precisely what one does when one is asked to draw the distinction between the object and its partners (i.e., when one replies to the *ayy* question). However, when the *ayy* question is presented, then the answerer does not necessarily indicate the absolute qualities of a thing; in some cases, the answer to this question is formed in relative terms, such as 'the one who has more money,' without implying that the object of inquiry possesses the quality of being rich. Similarly, a meaningful answer to the question *ayy shayʾ huwa* ['which thing is it?'] is 'the one that stands to the right of x,' but this is not a meaningful answer to a question of the form *kayfa huwa* ['how is it?'].

This amounts to saying that, in order to be meaningful, the *ayy* type question must be applied to a universe of at least two members since, by definition, by asking this question you are searching for the qualities that separate your object from other things that also exist. Consequently the answer can always be provided in relative terms.

A similar situation exists when the *ayy* question is compared with the *mā* question, for here also there are cases in which the answer to one question may be appropriate as an answer to the other, or as Alfārābī puts it in **Ḥurūf** (p. 183, par. 185):

> The answer used here [to answer the *ayy* question] is identical [*bi-ʿaynih*] to the answer employed to answer the question 'what is a man?'. Therefore, the answer to the question 'what kind of animal is a man?' is identical to the answer given to the question 'what is a man?'

However, there is a basic philosophical difference between the conditions under which each of these particles is used. By employing the particle *mā* one seeks to know the essence of the subject of inquiry per se and not in relationship to other things, Alfārābī says. When you use this particle, he continues, you need not think of anything other than the object with which you are concerned, and you can intellect it in itself, even if nothing else exists.

It is true that sometimes, the argument continues, there are other things beside the object of inquiry, but by asking 'what is X?' ('X' being your object of inquiry) one does not intend to receive a reply related to these other objects that are with 'X,' for this question seeks the definition of 'X' only.

It is true, Alfārābī continues, that answering the question 'what is X?' means mentioning some characteristics of the object of inquiry that distinguish it from the rest of the things, but this is only accidental [*bi-ʾl-ʿaraḍ*] and it is not the prime intention [*wa-lā ʿalā ʾl-qasd al-awwal*] of this question/answer exchange, Alfārābī concludes.

We now turn to the *mā* particle and its role in definition. In **Ḥurūf** (p. 172, par. 171) Alfārābī states that the four different usages of the question particle *mā* (described earlier, beginning in par. 166 of **Ḥurūf**) have one thing in common: by using the particle *mā* as a question particle,[5] "one seeks to know, to intellect and to conceive the essence of the subject of inquiry." But just what does it mean to know the essence of a thing?

It was mentioned at the beginning of this section that, according to Alfārābī, the answer to this question may involve either the mention of a *singular name* (i.e., the name of the thing under consideration) or the stating of an appropriate *composite expression* [*lafẓ murakkab*] (**Alfāẓ**, 49–50).

Alfārābī explains that by "composite expression" he means "some of the universals predicated [of the subject of inquiry, whether it is a universal or an individual]." He also makes clear that his main concern is to discuss this second kind of answer, involving a composite expression: "our intention here is to discuss the question 'what is it?' to the extent that the answer to it is by means of some of the universals predicated of the subject of inquiry" (**Alfāẓ**, 65). In other words, Alfārābī wants to discuss those universals that are properly used in answering the *mā huwa* question, dismissing the other two possibilities [i.e., mentioning the name of the thing or its external qualities] of answering this type of question. Not surprisingly, Alfārābī's discussion also extends to those universals appropriately used in answering *ayy* and *kayfa* questions, those that have been grouped since Porphyry under the five predicates discussed in chapter 1: genus, species, difference, property, and accident.

The Arabic question particles are a central component of Alfārābī's logical system and we shall have cause to return to them during the following discussion of types of "essence," as well as throughout later chapters of this study. Let us now move, however, to a higher level in our discussion of Alfārābī's view of "essence."

The Many Facets of Essence

In **Alfāẓ** (p. 50) Alfārābī offers a series of terms used in Arabic as virtually synonymous in reference to the phrase "the essence of a thing."

1. *Māhiyyat al-shayʾ* occurs frequently in Arabic translations of Aristotle's *Organon* and was probably introduced by the translators.[6] It is derived from the question particle *mā huwa* ['what is it?'], used in this type of inquiry.
2. *Jawhar al-shayʾ* is borrowed from Persian.[7] It is equivalent to the English terms *substance* or *being*, and both are translations of the Greek *ousia* (Aristotle, *Metaphysics*, $1038^{b}33$). According to Aristotle's doctrine, however, essence and substance are the same (see appendix I). Thus many translators use these two terms interchangeably, just as Alfārābī uses *jawhar, māhiyyah* and the other terms in this list interchangeably. *Jawhar* occurs frequently in the Arabic translations of Aristotle's *Organon*.[8]

3. *Inniyyat al-shay*ʾ is derived from the Arabic particle *inna* [it is really, truly so]. *Inna* is given by Alfārābī as an example of what he calls *al-ḥawāshī* [lit., marginalia, meaning "sentence modifiers"] (**Alfāẓ**, 45, par. 7).
4. *Ṭabīʿat al-shay*ʾ, i.e., the nature of a thing.
5. *Dhāt al-shay*ʾ is used frequently by Alfārābī in the sense of "essence." Here again, he seems to follow the translators who introduced the term.[9]
6. Alfārābī also mentions two expressions that appear to be synonyms of the above (**Alfāẓ**, 50): a) *qawl jawhar al-shay*ʾ [stating the essence of a thing] and b) *al-qawl al-dāll ʿalā mā huwa ʾl-shay*ʾ [the expression that signifies what a thing is].

These six Arabic terms, then, are employed in Alfārābī's writings to express the concept that in English is usually known as "essence." Four of these terms, however, are used more frequently by Alfārābī and his colleagues than the others: *inniyyah, jawhar, dhāt*, and *māhiyyah*. A closer examination[10] of these terms is crucial to our progress in this study.

Inniyyah *as an Essence*

According to Alfārābī, when the particle *inna* [it is really, truly so] is added to a thing, it signifies that the existence of this thing is affirmed and that its validity is firmly established, such as in the following examples: 'God is really one' and 'the world is truly finite.' Perhaps, Alfārābī says, this is the reason that the existence of a thing [*wujūd al-shay*ʾ] is called its *inniyyah*. This statement is a reference, it seems, to Aristotle's *Topics* (V, 133^b33), where the Greek *ousia* [being] was translated into Arabic as *inniyyah*.[11]

Similarly, Alfārābī's statement *wa-yusammā dhāt al-shay*ʾ *inniyatuh* is a reference to another passage from Aristotle's *Topics* (VI, 141^a31), where the Arabic translation (*Manṭiq Arisṭū*, 655) reads, *wa-dhālika anna kulla wahid*^{in} *mina ʾl-ashyāʾi innamā āniyyatuhu*[12] *wa-dhātuhu shay'*^{un} *wāḥid*. *Inniyyah*, Alfārābī says, is often used instead of *jawhar*, and there is no difference between them, but the former is used less than the latter. However, according to Alfārābī, *inniyah* is often used by scientists (**Alfāẓ**, 45).

Jawhar *as an Essence* [Māhiyyah]

Jawhar, Alfārābī says (**Ḥurūf**, 97, par. 62, and 100, par. 67), has both a popular and a philosophical meaning. *Jawhar* is used by the common people in two ways: (1) to indicate what is very precious, such as precious stones; and (2) to describe someone's qualities. When people say, for example, 'x's *jawhar* is good,' they mean, Alfārābī explains, that the ancestors or the people or the group to which 'x' belongs are distinguished and his particular character is attributed to the way he was raised and to the good example he learned from those who raised him. In the eyes of the masses, Alfārābī says, the character of 'x' (good or bad) can be acquired from the group of people to which 'x' belongs.

On the assumption that the ancestors of 'x' are his matter, the multitude concludes that if this matter is good, then 'x' himself is good, just as when a bed is produced from good wood, the bed must also be good. According to Alfārābī, the multitude's conception of *māhiyyah* is identical to its conception of *jawhar* and of *māddah* [matter]. Most people, he claims, when they say 'x's *jawhar*,' are referring to the ancestors of 'x,' whom they consider to be the matter of which 'x' is made. For them, this is what determines x's disposition, by which they mean *māhiyyah*. Similarly with swords, beds, walls, shirts, etc., the essence of each of these is, according to the popular conception, the matter from which each is produced.

Yet, Alfārābī continues, it is often the case that by saying 'x's *jawhar* is good,' the multitude refers to the individual 'x' himself as being naturally disposed to do well morally and otherwise. This disposition (whether innate or due to the environment) stands in the same relation to 'man' as the quality of 'sharpness' stands in relation to 'sword.'

Alfārābī cannot satisfactorily terminate his discussion of the popular notion of *jawhar* with this conclusion, since this conception does not agree completely with his own views on the subject, namely that a *māhiyyah* of 'x' is a combination of form and matter, rather than just the matter from which 'x' is produced. That is the reason his discussion concerning the popular view of *jawhar* ends with the following statement (**Ḥurūf**, 100: 10–12): "Some people believe[13] that the essence of a thing is in its matter only, others [believe] that it [i.e., matter] is in part of the essence [*bi-ajzā' māhiyyatih*]."[14]

This conclusion paves the way for his view that matter is only a *necessary condition* for *māhiyyah;* the question of whether it is a *sufficient condition* (as the popular conception presented by Alfārābī implies) is a question Alfārābī answers in principle by stating that matter should have a certain form in order to become a *māhiyyah*.

> It is evident that the perfect essence of a thing [*māhiyyat al-shay' al-kāmilah*] lies in its form, if this form is in an appropriate matter that supports the actions emanating from it [i.e., form]. Matter, then, is a necessary factor in the essence [of any thing]. The essence of

> a thing is, therefore, the form of certain matter that is shaped to fit that form, the existence of which is to fulfill a certain purpose [*al-kā'inah li-ghāyat*ⁱⁿ*-mā*]. (**Ḥurūf**, 99, par. 65)

'Disposition' and 'sharpness,' Alfārābī argues, are examples of the "form" [*ṣūrah*] of 'man' and 'sword,' respectively. When the form of anything [*kull shay'*] is in the appropriate matter [*māddah*], this form will be the source of all actions of that thing, Alfārābī states. This combination of form and matter is for Alfārābī the *māhiyyah* of a thing, a theme to be discussed more fully in the conclusion to this chapter.

Next, Alfārābī discusses the philosopher's conception of *jawhar* (**Ḥurūf**, 100, par. 67), briefly introduced in chapter 1 of the current work.[15]

First and above all, philosophers use *jawhar* to indicate 'this' (i.e., an individual thing) that is never 'in a subject.' But it is also used to describe "every predicate that makes the *individual material objects*[16] known, whether it is a species, a genus or a differentia, or whatever makes the essence of each species of these individual material objects known" (ibid., emphasis mine). *Jawhar* (usually translated as "substance") is, therefore, a term used for both individual material objects that cannot be 'in' a subject and for the universals that are 'said of' them.

As already discussed, Alfārābī (following Aristotle's *Categories*) calls these two applications of the term the "primary substance" and the "secondary substance," respectively. Primary substances exist independently of us, whereas secondary substances comprise the mental counterparts of the former and are ontologically posterior to them, yet Alfārābī also calls secondary substances "substance without qualification" [*jawhar ʿalā 'l-iṭlāq*]. The reason for this terminology, Alfārābī explains (**Ḥurūf**, 101, par. 68), is the (relatively) independent ontological status of the primary and secondary[17] substances, i.e., the priority they have over other things.

Yet, *jawhar* is also used to indicate whatever makes known (*mā ʿarrafa*) the essence of any thing of any category. By that Alfārābī means the special combination of universals that constitutes the essence of a thing. When this combination is intellected, the thing itself is intellected, as he explains in **Ḥurūf** (p. 101: 5). And it is in this sense that the term *jawhar* is used in Alfārābī's writings interchangeably with *māhiyyah* and with *dhāt*.

This third meaning of *jawhar* is, unlike the first two meanings, qualified and relative, for *jawhar* in this sense refers to the *māhiyyah* of a thing, and the *māhiyyah* is always a *māhiyyah* of something. This is the reason that *jawhar,* when used as a synonym for *māhiyyah* and *dhāt*, is a "relative *jawhar*" [*jawhar muḍāf*]. There is, however, a difficulty in understanding Alfārābī in this regard, as emerges from the following statement in **Ḥurūf** (p. 101: 9–12):

> The second meaning [*maʿnā*] of *jawhar* is also said to be without qualification since it is the intelligible of an individual which is not in a subject, and the intelligible of a thing is [identical with] the thing itself. However, the intelligible of a thing is that thing insofar as it is in the soul, and the thing is that intelligible insofar as it is outside the soul.

Alfārābī is presenting here his position that there is an identity between the object and its mental counterpart. He clearly states that the second type of unqualified substance, i.e., the secondary substance, is the intelligible [*maʿqūl*] of the thing. Now, we have already seen that, according to him, this can mean either the genus or the species or the differentia of the object under consideration. But does Alfārābī really mean that the identity exists between objects and their species or genus or differentia? Clearly he cannot mean that the individual 'Zayd,' for example, is identical with the species 'man' or with the genus 'animal,' particularly since he repeatedly emphasizes that the (right) *combination* of these predicates is such that "when it is intellected, the thing itself will be intellected" (**Ḥurūf**, 100–101, par. 67). It is the essence, rather than the individual predicates of which it is composed, that is the mental counterpart of the object.

If so, then (on the basis of Alfārābī's own criterion mentioned in the above-quoted passage) the formula that expresses the essence of a thing deserves the title "unqualified *jawhar*" to the same extent as do any of the secondary substances. But this is not acceptable to Alfārābī, who insists on calling it "relative and qualified *jawhar.*"

This problem can be resolved only if we insist on interpreting Alfārābī to mean by *maʿqūl al-shayʾ* [the intelligible of a thing, i.e., the mental counterpart of a thing] all the intelligibles of a thing combined, rather than the individual intelligibles of genus and that of the specific differentia, the combination of which results in the species.[18]

A similar type of problem occurs in **Ḥurūf** (pp. 104–105, par. 72–73), where a new category is added to 'what there is' and it is called "the thing that is neither said of a subject [*lā ʿalā mawḍūʿ*] nor is it a subject [*wa-lā huwa mawḍūʿ*] to any thing at all."

There is nothing in Alfārābi's scheme as presented thus far that falls under this category. It is obvious, therefore, that either there is a textual mistake in this passage or that Alfārābī is introducing a *fifth sort of being*. If he is speaking here of the primary substance in the following terms—"most deserving of all to be [called] *jawhar* is the thing the existence of which is the most perfect and the firmest"[19]—then I can venture to correct the second part of the statement under consideration, such that the whole passage would read: "The thing that is neither 'said of' a subject nor is 'in' a subject at all [*wa-lā huwa fī mawḍūᶜ aṣlan*]."[20]

This thing is of course the primary substance, i.e., the individual material objects. There is, however, another possible interpretation, namely that Alfārābī is indeed talking about a new sort of being that is "external to the categories [*wa-yakūn hādhā jawhar khārij ᶜan al-maqūlāt*] since it is neither a predicate nor a subject of anything at all" (**Ḥurūf**, 105: 4–5). That can be only *God.* God, according to this interpretation, is the firmest sort of being and the most deserving to be called a *jawhar,* even more so (with apology to Aristotle) than the primary substances themselves.

But then one can say: while it is true that 'God' is not said of anything, it is not true that it is not a subject of predication for it is perfectly meaningful to state that 'God is merciful,' and 'God is the greatest,' etc. Alfārābī's answer to this challenge would be a metaphysical, rather than a logical one: 'God,' he would probably argue, is beyond the concept of predication and does not need anything for his existence, rather everything else emanates from him. It is only by imitation that God is the subject of predication of anything.

That 'God' is beyond the concept of predication is implied by Alfārābī (ibid.) when he says that "that thing is beyond the concept of categories [*wa-yakūn hādhā jawhar^{an} khārij^{an} ᶜan al-maqūlāt*]." To paraphrase Alfārābī, as long as we do not confine ourselves to the sensible [*maḥsūs*] and to the 'this' which is neither 'in' a subject nor is it 'said of' a subject (but is a substratum and subject for everything else) then the truly absolute substance is that which is neither 'in' a subject nor a subject of anything, nor is it 'said of' a subject; namely, 'God' (**Ḥurūf**, 105, par. 4–5).

Alfārābī concludes that "substance" [*jawhar*] is used for: (a) "the ultimate subject that has no subject," i.e., the individual material objects; (b) "the essence of a thing," i.e., the universals the combination of which provides the essence of a thing; and (c) "(a thing) that has no other category as a subject nor is it a subject to any of these categories," i.e., 'God.'

Based on Alfārābī's own analyses, the correct conclusion should have been what has already been mentioned: the term *substance* is applied to the following things: 1) things that are neither 'in' a subject nor 'said of' a subject (primary substances), which is the same as category A above; 2) things that are 'said of' a subject but never 'in' a subject (secondary substances); and 3) the essence of a thing, or equivalently, the formula or combination of predicates that expresses this essence. The first two kinds of substance are also termed "substances without qualification," whereas the third kind is a relative and qualified sort of substance.

In addition, if the above explanation of the "fifth sort of being" (i.e., 'God') is what Alfārābī really means, then we must add a *fourth* application of the term *jawhar,* an application for a concept that is beyond all the categories; 'God is *jawhar.*' Moreover, it is truly the absolute *jawhar,* if we can prove that something with these qualities exists, he says (**Ḥurūf**, 105–106, par. 73–74).[21]

Dhāt *as an Essence (Māhiyyah)*

The discussion of this fifth sort of being recurs when the concept of *dhāt* is analyzed. Alfārābī (**Ḥurūf**, 106, par. 74) defines this term as follows: "It neither has a subject at all [i.e., is not 'said of' a subject] nor is it a subject to anything." This recurrence makes the second explanation of the problematic passage analyzed above all the more plausible. It seems, after all, that Alfārābī is indeed introducing a fifth sort of being. He never gives an example of it, nor does he give it a name. Most probably, then, it is the concept of 'God' to which he is referring.

Just as in the case of *jawhar,* the term *dhāt* has several applications and meanings in philosophy, one of which has been mentioned above ('God'). *Dhāt* is applied to an additional category of things, those things which are 'this' (i.e., individual objects) and 'in' a subject. *Jawhar* is never used for any of these things "neither absolutely nor relatively" (ibid.). Thus *dhāt* is used for any sort of being ranging from 'this' which is not 'said of' a subject (such as 'this spot of a certain color') to 'God.' In each of these cases the term *dhāt* is called "unqualified *dhāt.*" In this sense *dhāt* is simply a synonym for *shay'* [thing], for both terms refer to some sort of being.[22]

This use of *dhāt* is contrasted by Alfārābī with what he calls "a relative [*muḍāfah*] *dhāt*, i.e., a *dhāt* in relation to something (or in short, a *dhāt* of something). In this sense, Alfārābī says, *dhāt* can be said of the *māhiyyah* of a thing as well as of each part of which this *māhiyyah* is constituted, and "in general [it is 'said of'] whatever is [appropriately] used to answer the question—concerning anything—'what is it?'. Whether that thing is a 'this' not in a subject or a species of it, or a 'this' in a subject or a species of it" (**Ḥurūf**, 106: 12–14). In the expression '*dhāt* of x,' Alfārābī's explanation implies, the term *dhāt* can refer to any of the following: essence [*māhiyyah*], genus [*jins*], or differentia [*faṣl*] and even species [*nawᶜ*]. For it, too, can be used to answer a 'what is it?' question (when the subject of inquiry is an individual, of course).

This division of the "relative *dhāt*" is equivalent to the distinction between "essence" and "(secondary) substances" or between "essence" and "essential predicates" of which the former is composed. This distinction is, unfortunately, not pursued by Alfārābī. Rather he refers only to the "essence" when he explains (**Ḥurūf**, 106, par. 75) that "the relative *dhāt* of some thing must be different from that thing, no matter what that difference is, as long as it is a certain kind of difference" (ibid., lines 14–16).

By this means, Alfārābī wishes to draw the distinction between things ('this man,' 'that triangle,' 'the eclipse of the moon') and their essences. So that when we ask, 'what is the *dhāt* of the thing we see?' we seek more than knowledge about the individual that is the immediate subject of investigation. We are seeking the "essence" of the individual, which is more general[23] than the individual, and moreover is the real essence (rather than the individual character).

Although Alfārābī does not elaborate, one can of course claim that this principle may also be applied to the second sense of "relative *dhāt*." "Relative *dhāt*" of the second type (i.e., the secondary substances) is always a *dhāt* of the *māhiyyah* of which it is a part (and consequently, it can be considered a part of the thing of which that *māhiyyah* is a conceptual counterpart). Furthermore, as part of the *māhiyyah*, the *dhāt* is different from it. This theme is pursued several decades later by Avicenna (see appendix 2).

Alfārābī does discuss, however, one of the derivatives of *dhāt*, namely, *bi-dhātih*, which literally can mean any of the following: 'in itself,' 'by itself,' and 'in its essence' (or roughly, 'by its nature').[24] Alfārābī's discussion of this term interests us here only from one particular angle, namely that in which he describes the applicability of the term *bi-dhātih* to the subject-predicate relationships (**Ḥurūf**, 107, par. 77).

Bi-dhātih, he says, is used when the predicate is a part of the *māhiyyah* of the subject. For example, the *māhiyyah* of 'man' includes the concept 'animal.' Therefore, 'animal' is predicated *bi-dhātih* of 'man.' In this sense, *bi-dhātih* is a synonym for the above-mentioned relative term of *dhātī*, i.e., an "essential predicate."

In this kind of predication there is a necessary connection between the subject and the predicate. It is a conceptual connection since the concept that stands for the subject can be analyzed into its conceptual components and the predicate under consideration will be one of them. Thus, the concept 'man' includes the concept 'animal' and the statement 'man is an animal' is called, in modern terminology, "analytical" in the sense that its negation implies a contradiction: 'man is not an animal,' for example, is a self-contradictory statement; just as the negation of 'two is an even number' is a self-contradictory statement, since 'two' is 'even' as part of its definition and cannot be otherwise.

The second usage of *bi-dhātih* discussed by Alfārābī and concerning us here is that used when the predicate of a subject is included (conceptually) in that subject, such as in the statement 'man is capable of laughter.' The predicate of this statement is a *property* of the subject and as such it is implied by the subject, as has been explained. The property, by its nature or by its constitution, applies only to its subject and has no existence without that subject. The reason Alfārābī applies the term *bi-dhātih* to this type of predication is that by its very nature the presence of this predicate indicates that this particular subject exists, too.

The suffix pronoun attached to the term *bi-dhātih* in the first application refers to the *dhāt* of the subject and not to the predicate of that subject, for it is the definition of the subject that includes the predicate. In the second case, however, it can refer to either, but Alfārābī attributes it to the predicate, explaining that the essence of 'capable of laughter' is to be predicated of 'man.' It is by virtue of the meaning of the term that it is predicated of this subject.

There is another important difference between these two kinds of predications. The statement 'man is an animal' is not convertible while 'man is capable of laughter' is convertible, i.e., the subject and the predicate can be exchanged and the resulting statement will also be true. The latter is an identity, the former is not (although it is an identity when we replace 'animal' with 'rational animal,' which is the definition of 'man').

In the above analysis of the terms *jawhar, dhāt* and its derivatives, and their various applications, the concept *māhiyyah* itself was assumed and not discussed. The above discussion, however, has introduced to a significant extent what Alfārābī means by *māhiyyah*. This brings us to the fourth topic of this section on types of "essence," the concept of *māhiyyah*.

The Concept of Māhiyyah *in Alfārābī: A Closer Look*

A rather useful account of this concept is presented in **Ḥurūf** (p. 116: 14 ff.):

> In general *māhiyyah* is applied to whatever belongs to a thing and is correctly applied in answering the question 'what is it?' or in answering the question when the subject of inquiry is referred to by

a different sign,[25] for everything that is asked about by means of 'what is it?' [must] be known by some sign different from its *dhāt* and *mahiyyāh*, which are sought in using the particle *mā*. The answer might be provided by means of its genus, its differentia, its matter, its form or its definition. Each of these is [either] a part of its *māhiyyah* or [the whole of] its *māhiyyah*.

A further explanation of this definition of *māhiyyah* is given in Alfārābī's discussion of the particle *mā* later on in **Ḥurūf** (p. 168: 18 ff.):

> Each of those [universals] appropriately applied in answering the question 'what is it?' makes the subject of inquiry as well as its mental counterpart comprehensible [*yufhim al-shayʾ al-masʾūl ʿanh wa-yufhim maʿnāh fī ʾl-nafs*]; due to [the answer given to the *ma*-question] man conceives it [*yataṣawwaruh*] and a certain intelligible develops in his mind.

According to Alfārābī, the genus of a thing makes that thing comprehensible in a general way, since it presents it to the soul accompanied by other things. The species,[26] on the other hand, presents it to the soul in a more specific way than does the genus. The thing may also be comprehended by presenting the name of the species to which the object of inquiry belongs, Alfārābī argues. But in this case, he adds, it is comprehended [*yuʿqal*, lit., becomes intelligible][27] in a general way and without specification of its essential constituents.

The *ḥadd* [definition], however, is the most perfect way through which a thing can be comprehended, Alfārābī claims (**Ḥurūf**, 169: 2 ff.; 184: 11). The *ḥadd*, the argument continues, makes it possible to comprehend things through their essential constituents. *Ḥadd*, in other words, is the only thing (among those mentioned so far) that expresses and introduces *māhiyyah* in its most perfect way to the human intellect. *Rasm* [description], too, Alfārābī claims, can make a thing comprehensible, but only by means of its nonessential (i.e., accidental) attributes, always external to its essence.

According to the epistemological scheme Alfārābī has developed here, there are several degrees of knowledge. The clearest and most perfect of these can be achieved if the *definition* of the subject of inquiry is provided. The vaguest degree occurs when the thing is described by means of its most remote genera or by means of certain predicates very remote from its essence.

By "remote from its essence" Alfārābī probably means those separable accidents, the duration of which—in relation to the subject under consideration — is relatively very short, such as standing up or sitting down in relation to 'man.'[28]

Between these two degrees of knowledge there is a wide range of possibilities that I think Alfārābī would have agreed to present in the following (descending) order: the most perfect answer (after definition, of course) is by means of a thing's differentia, followed by that given by means of the thing's proximate genus, followed by its description per genus and property, followed by other combinations of descriptions,[29] followed by its property, followed by its inseparable (universal) accidents, etc.

It should be noted that, generally speaking though not as a rule, Alfārābī uses the term *to intellect* and its derivatives in Arabic to describe the mental act that occurs when an object is presented by means of its essential parts and above all, of course, by means of its essential definition. Thus, we often find Alfārābī associating *yuʿqal* with *dhāt*.[30] In all other cases, he uses terms like *tafhīm* [make comprehensible], and *taṣawwur* [conceptualizing, presentation]. What is behind this is the distinction between the conceptual or scientific knowledge attained by means of the essential parts of the thing, on the one hand, and a nonscientific knowledge of things, on the other. The former type of knowledge (which parallels the Greek *epistemi*) is defined by Alfārābī in the introduction to his **Mūsīqā** (p. 82): [''Knowledge [*ʿilm*] of a thing] is the act by which we become aware [*yaḥṣul ʿindanā*] that the thing exists, of the cause for its being and that in itself, the thing, cannot be different from what we have become aware of.''

In scientific knowledge, therefore, things should be known as they are, and that is exactly what Alfārābī means by their *māhiyyah* and that is precisely the kind of knowledge that can be expressed by *ḥadd*. In nonscientific knowledge, Alfārābī would argue, we have images of things or beliefs about them but not *knowledge of them*.

Essence as a Combination of Form and Matter: The Role of the *Kayfa* Particle

We have mentioned that by using the question particle *kayfa* ('how is it?' or 'what is it like?') the inquirer may be seeking to know either the essential attributes of the subject of inquiry or some of its accidental attributes. Now in **Ḥurūf** Alfārābī elaborates further on this point, adding new and important dimensions to the discussion presented in **Alfāẓ** (pp. 50–51). The *kayfa* particle, Alfārābī says (**Ḥurūf**, 194, par. 201), can be attached to singular expressions (such as 'how is Zayd?'), as well as to delimitative expressions, the referent of which is also singular (such as 'how is Zayd's body?').

Next Alfārābī moves from the domain of natural bodies to the domain of manmade bodies and asks not 'how are they?' but 'how were/are they made?'

This question, however, can refer either to a particular person and to a particular thing being produced by that person, or to the general features of a certain art and the general structure of the products of that art. The question can be, for example, 'how does 'x' build this wall?' or 'how can a wall be built?' By the former question, the inquirer intends to learn about the particular 'x' and his ability to build a wall, whether he is good or bad, fast or slow. In presenting the latter version of this question, on the other hand, the inquirer seeks to know how the wall is structured and how the pieces are put together in order to produce that wall. By presenting this latter question, Alfārābī concludes (**Ḥurūf**, 195, par. 203), what is being sought is the structure or the form of the product. The description of how this form comes about, in Alfārābī's words,

> is nothing other than describing the structuring [*iqtiṣāṣ*] of the constituents of that product and informing [*ikhbār*] about the fitting [*ilti'ām*] of its parts to each other until the product comes into being. This [product], that was structured and described, is both the structured [*mukawwanah*] *māhiyyah* and the *māhiyyah* of the thing described.

The last sentence of this passage is of special interest, since it includes a significant element. For the first time, the expression *māhiyyah mukawwanah* is introduced by Alfārābī.[31] The meaning of this expression is "produced or structured essence" and it refers specifically to a handmade production, as opposed to natural/production or to things produced by chance.[32] By using this term, Alfārābī wishes to indicate once again that essences of things (at least of manmade things) are produced and therefore each individual thing carries in it that essence of its kind. This is what he means when he writes that this structured essence is *also* (*thumma*, [lit., then]) its essence, i.e., the essence of the kind or species as expressed or actualized (to use the Aristotelian term) in a particular thing of that kind.

This explanation amounts, however, to saying that *māhiyyah* is a combination of form and matter, or as Alfārābī puts it in **Ḥurūf** (p. 196, par. 204):

> The essence of many of the man-made bodies is merely putting together and arranging the parts of these bodies, and the essence of

> many others is making them square or round and in general [the essence is] to bring about a certain form [*shakl*] in a matter appropriate [to support] that form in carrying out the action [*fiʿl*] and the benefit [*manfaʿah*] sought through that body, the essence of which is *in* that form. (emphasis mine)

The form of a sword, for example, is the essence of the *kind* of sword. It is the idea of 'sword' or it is the potential 'sword.' But producing this sword and that sword from the appropriate matter (iron rather than wax), or as Alfārābī calls it, a definite matter [*māddah muḥaṣṣalah*], is the *māhiyyah* in its actuality. This connects us to Alfārābī's idea discussed earlier that *māhiyyah* has two modes of appearance. In this case, the form is the mental component and the structuring of that form into certain definite matter is bringing about or producing the external component or the external existence of that *māhiyyah*.

Earlier in **Ḥurūf** (p. 120, par. 94) Alfārābī explained that the grammatical form *mafʿūl* (as well as *fāʿil*) indicates (more precisely, he says it is used by the multitude to indicate) both actuality and potentiality. Thus, *maḍrūb* may indicate 'one who actually has been beaten' or 'is still being beaten,' but it can also indicate 'a person who may be beaten' or 'will be beaten in the future.'

This theme is vital to our discussion, since Alfārābī is using the double meaning of the term *mukawwanah*, a term we have been discussing in precisely this way. According to this grammatical explanation, the *māhiyyah* (of nonnatural things) is both actual and potential; it is potential as a form[33] (in the mind) and it is actual when certain individual material things are produced, in accordance with this form, from appropriate matter.[34]

Yet it is the idea in the mind (not the Platonic "Form" or "Idea," but rather the form of the product) that is considered and generally referred to as *māhiyyah*. Matter, in which this form is actualized, is a secondary component in relation to the *māhiyyah*. This is what Alfārābī means by the following (**Ḥurūf**, 196: 18–21):

> The primary intention of using the *kayfa* particle is to inquire about the *māhiyyah* of a thing as its form and shape rather than as [its] matter. Matter is mentioned in the answer only as a secondary factor;[35] as an instrument and introducer [*muʿarrif*] of the form, it supports its [external] existence and its action.

Therefore, when the particle *kayfa* is used to ask about manmade products, the questioner is seeking to know the essence of these products, i.e., their form and how this form is being actualized in definite matter. This is the essence of manmade products. Yet this question-particle, Alfārābī continues (**Ḥurūf**, 197, par. 205), is used in the same manner and with the same intention when we move to the domain of natural phenomena, which he calls *ṭabīʿiyyāt*. Thus when we ask 'how is the eclipse of the moon?' we are seeking an *explanation* of this phenomenon, rather than a *description* of certain aspects of it (such as, that it happens quickly, etc.). We want to know, in other words, the essence of the thing called "eclipse" and the essence of it is knowing how this or that occurs. Just as in the case of manmade objects, in natural phenomena the essence of a phenomenon is identified by Alfārābī with the question 'how does this phenomenon come about?', i.e., with the explanation of how it happens or how it comes about or is structured [*yaltaʾim*].

Similarly, Alfārābī continues, when we use the particle *kayfa* to ask about natural bodies, such as animals. When someone asks 'how is a camel?', the appropriate answer should be the camel's shape or form [*khilqah*], which is identified by the multitude, the argument continues, with the *māhiyyah* of the camel (**Ḥurūf**, 197, par. 206).

When we ask about the species as a species of any natural kind by using the particle *kayfa,* Alfārābī argues in the same passage, the first thing that comes to mind and the immediate reaction of the answerer is to describe the form or the external structure of the subject of inquiry. Alfārābī seems to be identifying form with essence at this point. He has already mentioned that form is the primary component of the essence of any thing and matter is only a secondary component. Yet he has never before said that form is essence, as he seems to be implying here in **Ḥurūf.**

A closer examination of this new thesis will reveal, however, that this is not exactly so. What Alfārābī is attempting to explain here is the primary use of the particle *kayfa* and what people understand from that particle. Alfārābī is actually describing the *common meaning* of this particle [*al-mashhūrah ʿind al-jumhūr*]. This meaning is the primary meaning of the *kayfa* particle and is associated with the shape of things or with the way they are structured or come about. In fact, Alfārābī is saying here more than that, i.e., that the association between the *kayfa* particle and the form as the essence of a thing is subjective and does not mean necessarily that what individuals think about it is the true essence. People, Alfārābī says, respond to the *kayfa* particle according to the understanding of the answerer [*an yaqūl mā ʿindah*] (**Ḥurūf**, 197: 5) of the phenomenon or the object they are asked about. Shapes [*ṣiyagh*] and external structures [*khilaq*] of things are *epistemologically* prior [*wa-hiya ʾl-asbaq ilā ʾl-maʿārif awwalan*] to any of the other qualities those things may have (**Ḥurūf**, 198, par. 207) and therefore they are identified by the multitude with the essences of things.

Alfārābī does *not* criticize this conception—according to which 1) *māhiyyah* is the shape [*ṣīghah*] and 2) *māhiyyah* is subjective—because, Alfārābī claims, the actual *māhiyyah* of a thing is not necessarily the *māhiyyah* different people may have in mind, usually identified with the *ṣīghah* of that thing. Moreover, different people have in mind different shapes of the same thing and each answers the *kayfa* question, when it inquires about a species rather than about an individual, according to what he considers to be an essence of the subject of inquiry [*fa-innamā yujīb bi-ʾlladhī huwa ʿindah māhiyyat dhālika ʾl-shayʾ* . . .] (ibid. 198: 6).

In this passage Alfārābī is presenting a view not far from that expressed in an earlier stage of this section, namely that the major factor in identifying or separating one species from another is the thing's form, which is specific to that species. Matter, according to this conception, is secondary because it is common to all material things and therefore cannot be a sign or factor in distinguishing one thing from another. Through form alone, species are differentiated [*tataghayyar*].[36] Form, therefore, plays the role of a specific differentia, whereas matter plays the role of genus. Indeed, Alfārābī does make this link, which amounts to identification (at least, in some cases) of form and (specific) differentia (ibid.),[37] both of which are called essential qualities [*kayfiyyāt dhātiyyah*].

This term is contrasted by Alfārābī in this passage with nonessential qualities [*kayfiyyāt ghayr dhātiyyah*], usually used to answer the *kayfa* question when individuals, rather than species, are the subject of inquiry. The nonessential qualities, in other words, separate individuals from each other, rather than one species from another. The *kayfa* question can be applied, therefore, to ask about individuals, just as well as to inquire about the essential qualities of a thing, i.e., of its species. When the latter is the case, then, Alfārābī claims (ibid.), what is sought is identical with what is sought when the *mā* particle is employed.

In both cases the questioner seeks to know essential attributes of the species under consideration. In both cases, Alfārābī says, the questioner wishes to know the object in relation to itself without drawing comparisons to other existing things. In both cases, in other words, the domain of discourse can consist of the subject of inquiry alone and the inquiry will still be carried on. Thus, when we ask 'how is the eclipse of the moon?' and 'what is the eclipse of the moon?', we are seeking one and the same thing, namely to know the essence of this thing called 'eclipse of the moon.' Or when we ask 'what is a camel?' and 'how is a camel?', we are again inquiring about the essence of the species called 'camel.' Yet there is an important difference between the usage of these two particles (a difference more clearly apparent from the second example above, namely, the 'camel'). When *mā* is used, the essence expressed by means of the *ḥadd* formula is sought, whereas in using the *kayfa* particle one seeks the essence expressed in the shape or form of the subject of inquiry [*māhiyyatuh allatī hiya ṣīghatuh*]. One does not use the genus (i.e., the matter) to reply when one is asked a *kayfa* question, Alfārābī concludes (**Ḥurūf**, 199: 2–3).

Usage of the *kayfa* particle overlaps with that of other particles, both of which (the *ayy* and the *mā* particles) were discussed earlier in section 1 of this chapter. Yet there is another significant usage of the *kayfa* particle, namely, its use in inquiries about the causes of certain phenomena, such as when we ask 'how did you come to believe the sky is a sphere?'

Discussion of this usage of the *kayfa* particle, however, will be reserved for the following chapter, which will deal with definitions of a different type, the *causal* definition.

Notes to Chapter 3

1. By the expression *baʿḍ juzayʾātih* (another possible reading is *baʿḍ juzʾiyātih*) Alfārābī means "some of its individuals" or "some of its particles." The reference, I think, is to a proposition such as 'Man is Zayd and ʿAmr and Khālid,' which is one way to answer the question 'what is man?' and the answer is given by pointing to certain individuals that belong to the species that is the subject of inquiry in this case. This kind of proposition was mentioned earlier in this work in reference to the classification of propositions proposed in the beginning of Alfārābī's **Madkhal.** It was referred to as a "UI" type often used in induction [*istiqrāʾ*].

2. Alfārābī uses them interchangeably. In this passage Alfārābī seems to be very careful in distinguishing between "things" and the "words" that signify them. He says (**Alfāẓ**, 50), "one employs in his answer a thing [*amr*] which is signified by a composite expression." It is, however, the exception and not the rule that Alfārābī is so careful about this distinction.

3. The terms *dhāt* and *jawhar* are used interchangeably by Alfārābī when they mean "essence," as will be discussed further in section 2 of this chapter. Here we see yet another form expressing the identity of the two terms.

4. Alfārābī's usage of the term *al-ʿālam* [universe] in this context parallels the usage of this term in modern logic.

5. The *mā* particle may also be used as a negation particle and in many other usages that do not concern us here.

6. Mostly in the *Topics,* which was translated by Abu ʿUthman al-Dimashqi. See for example *Topics* I (103ᵇ11); V (133ᵃ1,2), VI (141ᵇ23–24). *Māhiyyah* is sometimes translated into English as "quiddity" (lit., whatness). Consult also

the article by Jozef Bielawski, "Deux périodes dans la formation de la terminologie scientifique arabe," *Rocznik Orientalistyczny,* 20 (1956), 284. See also the philosophical dictionary composed by Suhail Muhsin Afnan, *Vajeh nameh falsafi* [*Philosophical Dictionary*] (Beirūt: Dār al-mashriq, 1968). But "essence" is also used as an equivalent of this Arabic term. See, for example, the English translation of *Topics* by E. S. Forster in Aristotle's, *Posterior Analytics, Topica.*

7. Jozef Bielawski, "Deux périodes," p. 277.

8. See especially the translation of the *Topics* V (130^{b}1 ff., 130^{b}25, 131^{a} 18, 20); VI (140^{a}35, 37; 143^{a}19); VII (153^{b}30 ff.).

9. For example, (the Arabic translation of) *Topics* (146^{b}3). The most significant of these synonyms for "the essence of a thing," however, and consequently the most often used, are *māhiyyah, jawhar,* and *dhāt.* These will be further analyzed and discussed later in this section.

10. This examination will be largely based on Alfārābī's **Ḥurūf.** This book is considered to be Alfārābī's commentary on Aristotle's *Metaphysics* (see Mahdī's introduction to this work of Alfārābī, pp. 30–34).

11. In the text (*Manṭiq Arisṭū,* ed. ʿA. R. Badawī, 2: 604) the editor puts it as *aniyyah.* I think it should be *inniyyah* since it is derived from *inna.* For this issue, consult Abū Ridah's commentary on al-Kindī's philosophical collection in, al-Kindī op. cit. p. 97 ff.; Richard M. Frank, "The origin of the Arabic philosophical term *aniyyah*" in *Cahiers de Byrsa,* 6 (1956): pp. 181–201.

12. See preceding footnote.

13. In *Metaphysics* Z chapter 3, Aristotle considered "matter" as a candidate for the title *ousia* [substance]. But he immediately dropped this claim on the grounds that matter can neither be a 'this' nor 'separable.' However, Alfārābī cannot be referring to Aristotle's conception at this point since he (i.e., Alfārābī) is still talking about the popular view of the term *jawhar.*

14. Possibly a reference to Aristotle's position as analyzed throughout *Metaphysics* Z. As Alfārābī's next step is to analyze the philosophical point of view concerning the nature and definition of *jawhar,* it is not unlikely that Alfārābī in this passage *is* referring to Aristotle.

15. That presentation was based on Alfārābī's **Maqūlāt** as compared with Aristotle's *Categories.*

16. Another way of translating *al-mushār ilayh,* which I sometimes render as "this" or "the thing pointed to."

17. Alfārābī does not state clearly this priority of the secondary substances over everything else (except the primary substances, of course), but this can be implied from his principle that the thing and its intelligible are one and the same thing (a principle that will be discussed below).

18. There is always the possibility of "missing phrases" from Alfārābī's original texts. This is true particularly when **Ḥurūf** is considered. A new, more informative and more accurate manuscript has recently been found and a new edition of the text is under way. I was fortunate to have been informed by Professor Muhsin Mahdī, the manuscript's editor, of many of the changes the new manuscript introduces and I have made full use of this knowledge in my study.

19. As we have seen earlier in this work, this is Aristotle's characterization of primary substance in his *Categories* (2^a11).

20. I have added the word *fi* [in] (which incidentally appears in Manuscript M, as indicated on p. 105, n. 41 of the text) after *huwa* and eliminated the word *al-shayʾ* that occurs after *mawḍūʿ* in the original text.

21. In *Ārāʾ ahl al-madīnah al-fāḍilah* (ed. A. N. Nāder [Beirūt: Al-maṭbaʿah al-kāthūlīkiyyah, 1959], p. 40), Alfārābī refers to 'God' as the *jawhar* to which all beings owe their existence. They all emanate [*yafīḍ*] from him. (See also pp. 38–39.)

22. This general use of *dhāt* is described by al-Tahānawī in his *Kashshāf iṣṭilāḥāt al-funūn* [Dictionary of technical terms], ed. Mawlawies Muḥammad and Gholan Kaider (Beirūt: Khayyāṭ, 1966). Tahānawī says: "Whenever some thing is described by a name or by an adjective, then that thing is a *dhāt* whether it has no [external] existence such as the goat-stag [*ʿanqāʾ*] or [whether] it does exist. Existence is of two kinds: the pure existence which is the Creator's *dhāt*, and the existence that is corruptible and that is the *dhāt* of the created things."

23. In the same passage in **Ḥurūf** (p. 106, par. 75) Alfārābī uses the terms *more general* [*aʿamm*] and *more specific* [*akhaṣṣ*] to describe a similar thing. One is inclined to believe that there is a textual mistake and that Alfārābī should have used in both cases the term *aʿamm*, but this is not the case. The text is correct; for when we use the general term *thing* in the question the answer should provide a more specific [*akhaṣṣ*] description of that general 'thing' in order to specify the subject of inquiry ('man,' for example, which is more specific than 'thing' and more general [*aʿamm*] the individual man).

24. Alfārābī does, of course, use the term *dhāt* in expressions like *faṣl dhātī muqawwim*. See, for example, **Alfāẓ**, 73, and particularly **Burhān**, 28 ff., where he speaks of two kinds of essential predicates [*maḥmūlāt dhātiyyah*]: 1) definitions and their parts, and 2) essential accidents [*aʿrāḍ dhātiyyah*] "which essentially and by their nature subsist in their subjects . . . such as the existence of motion and rest in relation to natural bodies." This predicate is synonymous with inseparable accidents, introduced in chapter 1 of this study.

25. I.e., different from the general term *shayʾ* which was used in the previous question. Alfārābī simply wants to state that we can refer to the subject of inquiry by its name or any other sign that may identify that subject (for example, 'what is this animal?').

26. I think that Alfārābī could have said *faṣl* rather than *nawʿ* in this passage. However, in this respect it does not make much difference, since it is more specific to say 'Zayd is man' than to state 'Zayd is animal'; the former is more comprehensible than the latter.

27. The translation of *yuʿqal* as "becomes intelligible" is based on the fact that *maʿqūlāt* has been translated as "intelligibles" in this study.

28. In **Burhān** (p. 45), however, Alfārābī states that the least perfect conception of a thing comes about through mentioning the name of that thing, i.e., the name of its species; in his words: "The least perfect conceptions [*anqaṣ al-taṣawwurāt*] are those that come about by means of the single utterances—or whatever plays a similar role to them [*wa-mā jarā majrāhā*]—that signify the thing; the most perfect, by means of the essential definition [*al-ḥadd*]."

29. See **Ḥurūf** (p. 175), the last two lines.

30. Example, ibid. (pp. 172: 5; 173: 9; 175: 12 and 13; 184: 18).

31. I am unable to find a similar expression in the Arabic translation of Aristotle's *Metaphysics*, the work most likely to contain any expression of this sort (particularly, *Metaphysics* Z, Book 7).

32. Cf. Aristotle's *Metaphysics* (1032^{a}13–15), "of things which are generated, some are generated naturally, others artificially,* and others spontaneously." *I.e., "by art," as Richard McKeon translates the phrase in *The Basic Works of Aristotle* (New York: Random House, 1941).

33. There are five different terms used by Alfārābī to express what in English is referred to as "form." They are: *ṣīghah, hayʾah, shakl, khilqah*, and *ṣūrah.*

34. Cf. Aristotle's *Metaphysics* Z, Book 8 (especially 1033^{b} 5 ff.).

35. Literally, Alfārābī says "second intention" [*ʿalā ʾl-qaṣd al-thānī*], but it is less complicated to understand in this way.

36. This term appears in the recently discovered manuscript **Ḥurūf**, to which I have referred earlier in this study.

37. Similar to the previous footnote.

4

The Concepts of Demonstration, Division, and Classification and Their Relationship to Definition

'How?' and 'Why?' [*Kayfa* and *Lima*] Questions

In discussing the *kayfa* particle and its role in definition, Alfārābī says (**Ḥurūf**, 199: 20 ff., 200: 1 ff.):

> When we ask: 'how did the sky become a sphere?' . . . we seek to know the things the composition of which have made the sky a sphere or that have made true our belief that it is a sphere. . . . This means that the answerer must provide the "demonstration" [*burhān*] or the "syllogism" [*qiyaš*], from which it is validly implied that the sky is a sphere.

Thus, in addition to its use in inquiring about the internal and external states of a thing (chapter 3, section 1), *kayfa* therefore, is also used, according to Alfārābī, to inquire about the causes as they are (or as we know them) for the occurrence of certain phenomena. The terms *demonstration* and *syllogism* are mentioned by Alfārābī as the methods of providing an answer to this type of inquiry. This kind of inquiry presupposes the fact that the 'sky is a sphere,' for example, and that we wish to inquire 'how does it happen?' and 'how is it structured?', just as we ask 'how do plants grow?' or 'how is the wall being built?' (**Ḥurūf**, 200: 1,2).

However, when the *kayfa* particle is used to inquire about natural phenomena, what is sought are the reasons [*asbāb*, pl. of *sabab*] that have brought about these phenomena. The *structure* sought in asking about handmade objects and the *form* sought in asking about natural objects is replaced by *causes* sought when inquiry by means of the *kayfa* particle is applied to *natural phenomena*. In this sense, the 'how?' [*kayfa*] particle overlaps with the 'why?' [*lima*] particle.

The *lima* particle is classified by Alfārābī among his "marginal words" [*ḥawāshī*] (**Alfāẓ**, 53). According to Alfārābī, this particle is one of the particles added to things (or rather, to phrases signifying these things) in order to inquire about the *reasons* that have brought them about. Other particles that assume the same role, Alfārābī's argument continues, are 'what is it about?' [*mā bāl*] and 'what is the matter?' [*mā sha'n*]. These particles are appropriately attached to a thing only after that thing's existence has been established; otherwise, Alfārābī's argument continues, the question would be meaningless [*bāṭil*]. Moreover, according to Alfārābī, this family of particles must be added to a composite expression, by which Alfārābī means "a sentence, whether it is explicitly stated or implicitly understood."

In **Ḥurūf** the *lima* particle and its role in philosophical inquiry are further analyzed by Alfārābī. This particle, Alfārābī says (p. 204, par. 215), is composed of the letter *lam* and the *mā* particle (already discussed in chapter 3). Indeed, it is a short form of the *li-mādhā* particle,[1] as Alfārābī explains.

The *lima* particle is employed primarily in order to inquire about the reason for a thing's existence, whether about the absolute existence of a substance or about the existence of some thing in something else as its subject.[2]

In Alfārābī's system, the *lima* particle plays a central role in two well-known philosophical areas, namely the four Aristotelian causes[3] (the material, the formal, the efficient, and the final) and the Aristotelian theory of demonstration. Let us begin with the four Aristotelian causes.

Mādhā, Li-Mādhā, Bi-Mādhā, and *ʿAn Mādhā* Questions

There are apparently three kinds of particles used to inquire about the reasons [*asbāb*] and causes [*ʿilal,* pl. of *ʿillah*] of a thing's existence, Alfārābī says (**Ḥurūf**, 205: 1,2). These three particles are: 'why?' [*li-mādhā*], 'in what?' [*bi-mādhā*] and 'from what?' [*ʿan mādhā*].[4]

In their Arabic form, all three question-particles are combinations of the *mādhā* particle and the preposition that precedes it (in the first two cases, as a prefix).

The *lima* particle, as a preposition in Arabic, indicates direction and goal,[5] just as when we use the expression *li-ajl* which means "for the sake of" or "in order to." This is the reason Alfārābī identifies the expressions *li-mādhā wujūduh* [why does it exist?] with the expression *li-ajl mādhā wujūduh* [for what end or purpose does it exist?] (**Ḥurūf**, 206, par. 216). In both cases, he says, the *purpose* [*gharaḍ*] and the *end* [*ghāyah*] are sought. (In Aristotle's language, this means the "final cause.")

Just like the particle *mādhā* [what?], the particle *li-mādhā* [why?] is answered[6] by providing the definition [*ḥadd*] for the subject of inquiry.[7]

The basis for this statement, I believe, is the Aristotelian definition of the *final cause*, according to which the final product or final result of a thing's development is the full realization of this individual as a member of its species. When an individual reaches the final stage of its development (whether this thing is a natural object or a phenomenon or a manmade object), then it should have the form and the matter (or the differentia and the genus) it shares with other members of its species. When an individual reaches this stage of its development or production, then it has the right, so to speak, to be defined as a member of its species. Reaching the final stage of development means, in the Aristotelian scheme, that the individual is no longer *potentially* a member of its species, rather it is *actually* so.

Reaching this final stage, however, is partly due to the *final cause* that nature or man (depending on the case) wished to achieve. The activity of both nature and man was guided by that ultimate goal to bring the individual into full actualization. The final cause is, therefore, a *necessary condition* for the individual to reach its final stage of development or production. This is what Alfārābī probably means in stating that: "The essence of a thing, therefore, is one of the causes for its existence; [moreover] it is the most specific [*akhaṣṣ*] cause for this existence." (**Ḥurūf**, 205, par. 216).

The usage of the *li-mādhā* particle is also connected by Alfārābī with the meaning of the *bi-mādhā* particle [lit., of what?, from what?]. These two particles, Alfārābī says, inquire about the very same reason.

The passage that explains the relationships between these two particles, however, is obscure, and it is difficult to extract any coherent line of reasoning explaining this connection between *li-mādhā* and *bi-mādhā*. The task of understanding Alfārābī in this passage is rendered particularly difficult since his conclusion of this short passage links the *bi-mādhā* particle to the *mādhā* particle, rather than to the *li-mādhā* particle with which the discussion began.

The passage may yield some sense, however, if we adhere to the identification maintained by Alfārābī between *mādhā* and *li-mādhā*, as discussed above. If these two particles are entirely synonymous in Alfārābī's system (and there is no indication to the contrary), then we may attempt to make some sense of this troublesome passage. Given the above assumption, the pronoun *huwa* in line six of page 205 should be taken to refer to the particle *mādhā*. Line six, then, will read: "The particle 'what' overlaps [*dākhil*] with [the usage of the particle 'from what' [*bi-mādhā*] in the expression] 'from what does it exist?' when the existence of this thing is due to itself [*wa-huwa fīh*] [rather than to an external reason]."

Alfārābī is speaking here about the *efficient cause* of a thing's existence. The efficient cause [*al-fāʿil*] may be external to the thing, Alfārābī explains in the passage under consideration, implying that it is usually an external factor (especially in the domain of natural products). The existence of the day, for example, is derived from the sun, and as such the sun is an external efficient cause of the day.

Now, we can claim that when Alfārābī says the particles *li-mādhā* and *bi-mādhā* signify (or inquire about) the same reasons, he means that they both refer to the efficient cause. However, one of them—*li-mādhā* or *mādhā*—refers to an external efficient cause, whereas the other—*bi-mādhā*—refers to an internal efficient cause, just as the germ of the oak that develops to become an oak carries within it the efficient cause to become an oak tree.[8]

The last particle of this group is the *ʿan mādhā* particle, discussed briefly by Alfārābī in **Ḥurūf** (p. 206: 1–5). By the use of this particle, one inquires about both the efficient cause [*al-fāʿil*] and the *material cause* [*al-māddah*], Alfārābī says.

This statement is probably based on the fact that one of the meanings of the *ʿan* particle is synonymous with that of the *min* particle; i.e., they both denote "from."[9] In this case the question *ʿan mādhā wujūduh* will mean 'from what does it exist?', i.e., it inquires about the material cause.

The particle *ʿan* can also mean 'the result of so and so.' In this case the same Arabic question *ʿan mādhā wujūduh* (this time with the meaning, 'what is its cause?' or 'what is it the result of?') is inquiring about the immediate cause of the thing's existence, namely about the efficient cause (i.e., about the agent the initial impulse of which set the phenomenon or the development in motion).[10]

Now we turn to the second philosophical issue involving the use of the particle *lima*.

Theory of Demonstration

Let us begin with the distinction Alfārābī draws in his **Ḥurūf** (p. 212, par. 226): "It should be known that the reason for a thing's existence is not identical with the reason that led to our knowledge of its existence."

An example of this distinction is found in **Ḥurūf** (p. 213, par. 227), where Alfārābī argues as follows: when one asks 'why is this object still alive?' the answer 'because it breathes' is *not* the reason for its being alive. Our knowledge that this object breathes indicates or leads us by implication to the knowledge that this object is alive. This implication is the conclusion [*luzūm*] of a valid syllogism composed of the following two premises [*muqaddimah*, pl. *muqaddimāt*]:

1. 'x' breathes
2. whatever breathes is alive.[11]

These two premises lead necessarily to the conclusion that 'x is alive.'[12]

Providing an answer by means of a syllogism is demonstrating the conclusion, Alfārābī claims (ibid.). This type of demonstration "puts an end to all inquiries concerning this conclusion" [*wa-lam yabqa fī luzūm mā lazim mawḍiʿ masʾalah*]. If you assume premises are true, then the conclusion is validly or necessarily implied from these premises [*luzūm mā yalzam ṣaḥīḥ*]. However, if you question the truth of one of the premises, then this is another matter altogether.

For example, when you question whether or not the premise 'all things that breathe are alive' is true or not, then you must conduct a completely separate inquiry. Our knowledge that 'x is alive' was reached by necessity through a demonstration, i.e., a valid syllogism (of a special kind—see below).

According to Alfārābī, knowledge of premises may be achieved in five different ways:

1. *through an accepted premise by an individual or group of individuals* [*maqbūlah*, a postulate];
2. *through generally accepted premises* [*mashhūrah*];
3. *through empirical facts* [*maḥsūsah*];
4. *through innate ideas or the apriori* [*maʿqūlah bi-ʾl-ṭabʿ*], i.e., universal premises [*muqaddimāt kulliyyah*] that are innate in us, such as certain truths or certain knowledge [*ʿilm yaqīn*], without us being aware of how they came about (such as that 'four is an even number');[13]
5. *through a syllogism;* the premises of certain syllogisms may be the conclusions of other syllogisms, which themselves may be known in any of these five ways.

For our purposes in this study, two additional terms must be further explained:

1. *the middle term of a syllogism* [*al-ḥadd al-awsaṭ*], explained by Alfārābī in **Qiyās ṣaghīr** (p. 251), is the term that appears in both premises. The middle term is the connection [*muʾallif*, lit., the

composer] between the two premises of a syllogism.
2. *demonstration* [*burhān*], a syllogism the premises of which are necessarily true or necessarily certain, as will be discussed further below.

In **Burhān** (pp. 25 ff.) Alfārābī, explains the important term *ʿilm* [knowledge] in the following manner:

> The term "knowledge" [*ʿilm*] is used in general as we have mentioned, to describe either a judgment [*taṣdīq*] or a conception [*taṣawwur*]. Judgments are either certain [*yaqīn*] or not-certain [*laysa bi-yaqīn*]. "Certain" can be either necessary [*ḍarūrī*] or unnecessary [*ghayr ḍarūrī*].[14]

It is obvious, however, Alfārābī's description continues, that the term *knowledge* is applied to what is *certain by necessity* [*yaqīn ḍarūrī*] more often than it is applied to what is not certain or to what is certain but not by necessity (i.e., the *contingent*). Alfārābī calls the former "certain knowledge" [*ʿilm yaqīnī*]. Certain knowledge may be, according to him, of three types:

1. *Certainty of the being [wujūd] of a thing only,* i.e., the knowledge of being [*ʿilm al-wujūd*]. This is referred to by some as "knowledge that the thing is" [*ʿilm inna ʾl-shayʾ*].[15] This kind of knowledge is sought by using the particle [*hal*], discussed in Alfārābī's **Ḥurūf** (pp. 200–202, pars. 210–212; pp. 206–207, par. 218); and in **Alfāẓ** (pp. 47–48).
2. *Certainty of the reason [sabab] for the thing's being,* referred to by some as the "knowledge of why [*lima*] the thing is."
3. *Certainty of both 1) and 2) above.*

The most appropriately described as "certain knowledge," Alfārābī says, is the knowledge that combines both the certainty of the thing's being (answering the 'whether?' question) as well as its cause (answering the 'why?' question). Syllogisms composed of premises of the type "certain by necessity" can, therefore, be of three kinds. A syllogism composed of premises certain by necessity and covering[16] any of these three types is called a *demonstration* [*burhān*].

A demonstration in Alfārābī's conception is not *any* syllogism. Rather, a demonstration is a certain kind of syllogism, namely a syllogism the premises of which are necessarily true or necessarily certain, as he refers to them.[17]

Now, this corresponds to the Aristotelian definition of "demonstration" as presented in the *Posterior Analytics*,[18] according to which a demonstration is a syllogism the premises of which are true, necessary, and immediate, as is the conclusion of such a syllogism. The problem with the Aristotelian text, however, is its failure to provide a single example of a demonstration. Moreover, in the entire Aristotelian corpus, there is not a single perfect example of a demonstration,[19] a fact that has not, however, discouraged modern scholars from attempting to analyze and modify certain Aristotelian arguments in such a way as to fit Aristotle's mode for demonstrative reasoning.[20]

Alfārābī, too, attempts to use the Aristotelian examples provided in chapter 8 of Book II of the *Posterior Analytics* in order to illustrate the notion that a demonstration provides the cause of certain phenomena (such as, 'eclipse,' 'thunder') and thereby answers the question 'what is that thing?' In **Ḥurūf** (p. 206, par. 217), for example, Alfārābī explains that

> [in order to show] whether the eclipse of the moon is the absence of light on the moon or not, one uses the premise that the moon is shaded by the earth [from the sun] at the time of the interposition [*waqt al-muqābalah*]. . . . The absence of the moon's light, therefore, is in itself the moon's eclipse and is the same as when the moon is shaded from the sun [by the earth].

The above argument may be arranged as a syllogism that provides a cause and effect explanation for the phenomenon under consideration:[21]

1. Whatever has another body interposed between it and its source of light loses its light.
2. The moon has another body (i.e., the earth) between it and its source of light.

Therefore, the moon loses its light.

This syllogism is clearly of the form:

If MAP
SAM
then SAP

where:

'M' = the middle term ('to be another body interposed between something and its source of light')

'P' = the major term ('to lose one's light')
'S' = the minor term ('to be a moon')

This syllogism answers both questions: 'what is an eclipse?' and 'why does it happen?'. The interposition of the earth is the cause for this phenomenon; indeed, the phenomenon could not have occurred without this interposition taking place (whether through the earth or through any other body). If this cause (which is the middle term of the syllogism) disappears, the phenomenon will not exist. The essence of the eclipse is, therefore, identical with the cause of the eclipse. *The 'what?' and the 'why?' are one and the same thing.*

Yet, the above syllogism, although it answers both the 'what?' and the 'why?' questions is not a demonstration in the strict sense, since neither its premises nor its conclusion are necessary statements; they are all contingent statements and could be otherwise.

Luckily, however, Alfārābī is not entirely trapped in this Aristotelian shortcoming. In his **Burhān** (pp. 33–39), Alfārābī offers eight different categories of demonstrative syllogism, each including four cases or more, totalling thirty-nine cases in all.

Now, on the surface it appears as though demonstrations do indeed demonstrate what things are, i.e., they reveal the essence of things by showing that certain essential attributes belong to the subject of inquiry. That is to say, demonstrations answer the *'whether?'* (x belongs to y) [*hal*] question, or at least they seem to.

Alfārābī, however, expresses reservations concerning the effectiveness of this method as a means of revealing what the essence of a thing is.[22] Attributing this method to a certain *Kasānaqrāṭīs*,[23] Alfārābī says (**Burhān**, 52–53) that this method is able to demonstrate the essence of a thing only if we assume that things have more than one definition, an assumption rejected by many people (a reference to the peripatetics).

In order to demonstrate that 'A' is a definition of 'B,' Alfārābī explains (ibid.), it requires that the middle term of that demonstration also be a definition of 'B' (see example below). For, it is a feature of the demonstration, the argument continues, that the middle term being the cause of 'B' is prior [*aqdam*] to 'B.' This means that 'B' will have another definition (i.e., the middle term of the demonstration) that is prior to 'B' and consequently to 'A,' which is supposed to be provided by the demonstration as the definition of 'B.' Alfārābī presents the following example to illustrate this argument.

> We want to prove that 'man is a featherless biped animal.' In order to do so, Alfārābī says (ibid.), we use the following premises:

1. Every man is a rational mortal animal.
2. Every rational mortal animal is a featherless biped animal.

The middle term of this syllogism is 'to be a rational mortal animal.' And it is obvious, Alfārābī says, that we must be equipped with the knowledge that this middle term is a definition of 'man' in order to prove that 'man' has another definition, namely that 'man is a featherless biped animal.' Thus man has two definitions: the one, i.e., the middle term, is prior to the other as its cause.

Furthermore, the argument continues, if the demonstrative way is the only way to discover that the middle term is a definition of the subject under consideration ('man' in this case), then it is necessary that this subject should have a third definition (i.e., the middle term of the new demonstration). And if the latter can be validly known only by the method of demonstration, then the subject under consideration should have a fourth definition. This process may be continued *ad infinitum* [*ilā ghayr nihāyah*], Alfārābī concludes.

According to Alfārābī, therefore, a demonstration cannot demonstrate the essence of a thing, unless we assume that things have more than one definition, an assumption that will upset the entire Aristotelian metaphysical assumption that everything has only one essence and one definition. This would have far-reaching consequences for Aristotle's theory of definition.

Demonstrations, then, can prove only parts of definitions rather than the whole definition, Alfārābī argues (ibid.). You can prove, for example, that 'man is an animal' or that 'man is rational,' but you cannot prove that 'man is a rational animal' by means of demonstration, without assuming that a thing has more than one definition.

This conclusion forces Alfārābī to seek alternative avenues of acquiring definition, and his next candidates are the Platonic concept of *division*[24] and the Aristotelian notion of *classification*.

Division [*Qismah*] and Classification [*Tarkīb*] in Alfārābī's Writings

In **Alfāẓ** (p. 81, par. 36), Alfārābī presents his views concerning the Platonic method of division as follows (paraphrased):

> Given a universal 'U' and given two opposite attributes [*umūr mutaqābilah*, lit., opposite things] 'M' and 'not M,' each of which is predicated with qualification of 'U,' then the formula 'U is either M or not M' will be called a division of 'U.'

In Arabic the expression "either . . . or" may be expressed by repeating the conjunction particle *immā* twice, thus the formula in Arabic will be: *U immā M wa-immā la-M*. An example of this: 'An animal is either capable of walking [*mashshāʾ*] or not capable of walking.' This formula divides the genus 'animal,' Alfārābī says, into two complementary categories [*umūr qāsimah*]: 1) animals that are capable of walking and 2) animals that are not capable of walking. In general, this may be stated as: 1) 'U that are M' and 2) 'U that are not M.'

The very use of the expression *immā . . . immā* in Arabic indicates that the terms to which this expression is attached are mutually exclusive. Hence Alfārābī's definition of this expression in **Alfāẓ** (p. 55), which he presents as a member of a family he calls "conjunctions" [*rawābiṭ*]:

> Some [particles in this family] when added to expressions indicate that each of these expressions imply the negation of the others [*qadd taḍammana mubāʿadat al-ākhar*], an example of this is the *immā* particle. . . . That is the reason this particle is called the "conjunction that indicates separation" [*infiṣāl*].

Sentences involving the *immā . . . immā* expression are also discussed by Alfārābī in **Qiyās ṣaghīr** (pp. 258 – 260) within the general context of his discussion of the conditional syllogisms, especially in his discussion of the "disjunctives" [*sharṭī munfaṣil*].[25] The *immā . . . immā* expression as used in this context indicates, according to Alfārābī, a *conflict* [*ʿinād*] between (the two or more) elements of which the disjunctive is composed. An example of this: 'The world is either eternal or created, but the world is created; therefore, the world is not eternal' (ibid.).[26] 'Eternal' [*qadīm*] and 'created' [*muḥdath*] are conflicting terms (i.e., the statements 'x is eternal' and 'x is created' cannot both be true), Alfārābī implies.

The form 'x aw y' ['x or y'] is also used by Alfārābī to indicate conflicting or noncompatible facts or terms. An example of this (**Qiyās ṣaghīr**, 259): the statement 'Zayd is either in Iraq or in Syria' implies that 'Zayd' cannot be in Iraq and in Syria at the same time.

Alfārābī presents several versions of the *immā . . . immā* expressions in his various writings. Two of these versions appear in conjunction with the *ayy* particle (**Ḥurūf**, 190 – 192) in the following manner:

1. Example: 'which one is Zayd, the good or the bad man?' The general pattern of this is: *ayy . . . x aw y.*

2. Example: 'what sort of thing is the world, spherical or not spherical?' The general form of this in Arabic is: *ayy* . . . *x am y?*[27]

These two combinations indicate, according to Alfārābī, that an inquiry is taking place and that the inquirer knows that one of the components of either of these expressions is definitely the case, but he seeks to determine definitely [*ʿalā ʾl-taḥṣīl*] which one is the case (see discussion of the *hal* particle in chapter 5).

Let us now return to the original concept that initiated the above discussion of the particles *immā, am,* and *aw,* namely the Platonic concept of *division.*

Dividing a universal concept by a series of contrary terms, as has been described above, is known since Plato as the method of division or *dichotomy.*

This Platonic procedure offers the distinct advantage that it is always *formally valid* "since it proceeds on the principle that every class must either possess a given characteristic or not possess it."[28] Alfārābī takes this formally valid procedure and expands it much beyond what Plato describes in his writings.

The universal 'U' may, according to Alfārābī, be either a genus or a species or *any* other universal, whereas the dividing elements may be whatever can be predicated with qualification of the universal 'U' they are to divide. Moreover, Alfārābī's assertion in this passage is clear, namely, that the dividing elements need not be two in number, rather they may be *any* number, as long as they are predicated with qualification of 'U.' Furthermore, these dividing elements need not be contrary concepts ('M,' 'not M'); they may be of the other type Alfārābī discusses in **Alfāẓ** (p. 73); namely, those elements (*differentiae*) that may not be predicated of each other in any way. Let us denote these elements by: 'M_1,' 'M_2,' 'M_3,' . . . ; thus the dividing formula of 'U' will be:

'U' is either 'M_1' or 'M_2' or 'M_3' . . .

Dropping the either/or expression would result in several phrases, the number of which is equal to that of the number of the dividing elements ('M_1,' 'M_2,' . . .). In these phrases one component is always 'U' and the other is one of the dividing elements, in the following manner:

'U' which is 'M_1'
'U' which is 'M_2'
'U' which is 'M_3,' etc.

Suppose, Alfārābī argues (**Alfāẓ**, 85–86), that 'U' is a certain genus and the 'M_1,' 'M_2,' 'M_3' . . . are different specific differentiae of each of the species of that genus, then the result of this division will be the different species under that genus.

If 'U,' for example, is the genus 'animal,' and:

'M_1' denotes 'rational'
'M_2' denotes 'neighing'[29]
'M_3' denotes 'barking'[30], etc.,

then 'animal' will be divided into 'rational animal,' 'neighing animal,' 'barking animal,' etc. These expressions represent the different species of 'animal,' 'man,' 'horse,' 'dog,' etc.

This process of division could have been continued, had the results been some intermediate genus, rather than the infimae species [*anwāᶜ akhīrah*], Alfārābī argues.

Incidentally, 'U' according to Alfārābī (**Alfāẓ**, 85–86), may not only be a genus, but also an infima species, and even a property or accident. Each of these universals may be divided in the manner described above by means of the attributes predicated of it in a qualified way. This means, of course, that the dividing elements 'M_1,' 'M_2,' . . . mentioned above may be any property or accident of the universal under consideration, and not only specific differentiae. For example: 'U' may be the universal 'capable of laughter,' which is a certain property (of 'man'), and 'M_1,' 'M_2,' 'M_3' . . . may be[31] 'an engineer,' 'a physician,' 'a writer,' respectively, etc., then 'capable of laughter' may be divided into: 'capable of laughter who is an engineer,' 'capable of writing who is a physician,' etc.

Similarly, the arguments continue, a genus may be divided by means of accidental differences [*fuṣūl ᶜaraḍiyyah*] that the different species of that genus may possess. For example,[32] you may divide 'animal' by means of accidents such as: 'being black,' 'being tall,' 'being thin,' etc. This division, however, will not lead to the different species of that genus. Only division by means of the specific differentiae will divide any given genus into its different species.

Moving in the other direction is possible, too, Alfārābī says (**Alfāẓ**, 84). If we take infimae species (the specific differentiae of which are contrary)[33]—say 'dog,' 'horse,' 'man,' etc.—and substitute each of these names by its proximate genus and specific differentia (a process Alfārābī refers to as the analysis [*taḥlīl*][34] of the name by means of the definition [**Alfāẓ**, 89]), and then we drop the specific differentiae leaving only their genera, we will reach the proximate genus common to them all. In Arabic, this process is called *tarkīb*, in English, "classification."

Now, the obvious question one can pose here for Alfārābī is, What are the relationships (if any) between the methods of *qismah* and *tarkīb*, on the one hand, and the concept of *ḥadd*, on the other?

Alfārābī refrains from providing a direct answer to this question. He does say, however (**Alfāẓ**, 87), that, among other things, the method of *qismah* is useful in making things comprehensible and conceivable. He also says that among all methods used for teaching purposes, only the methods of "giving example" [*mithāl*], "induction" [*istiqrāʾ*], and "syllogism" [*qiyās*] are said to "bring about an assent" [*tūqiʿ al-taṣdīq*]. All the rest, *qismah* and *ḥadd* included, are useful in bringing about a conception [*taṣawwur*] and in facilitating the process of retention. *Qismah* is particularly helpful, Alfārābī adds (**Alfāẓ**, 92–93), in imagining things that are difficult to imagine due to some general attribute belonging to the thing under consideration and to other things (namely the proximate genus).

Plato's method of division is not advocated by Alfārābī as a tool for producing definitions because Alfārābī understood that division cannot produce definitions. As Aristotle puts it, "Division is a sort of weak deduction; for it postulates what it has to prove. . . . But at first this escaped the notice of all those who made use of it, and they attempted to persuade us of the assumption that it was possible for them to make demonstration about reality and of what some thing is."[35] In chapter 5 of Book II of the *Posterior Analytics,* Aristotle repeats his criticism of "division," adding that some (probably a reference to Plato) had taken it for granted as a method from which definitions might be deduced. Aristotle's major point in this chapter is to show that the conclusions reached by the method of division are assumed rather than deduced from any premises: "Is man an animal or inanimate? If he answers 'animal,' he has not deduced it. Again, every animal is either terrestrial or aquatic: he assumed terrestrial. And that man is on the whole—a terrestrial animal—is not necessary from what he had said, but he assumes this too" (ibid., 91^b18–22).

Alfārābī understood and endorsed (**Burhān**, 52–3) this Aristotelian criticism of division as a method of producing definitions. It is for this reason that he considered it only a useful tool to render a definition easier to imagine and to understand.[36] This, incidentally, is also Aristotle's position in chapter 13, Book 2 of his *Posterior Analytics,* where he continues to maintain that "it is necessary to postulate by dividing" (96^b35). Yet he also claims in this passage that division *may help* in the discovery of definitions (96^b26–29).

Alfārābī also dismisses *"classification"* [*tarkīb*] (which he attributes to Aristotle) as a safe way to produce definitions. In **Burhān** (p. 57) he explains the shortcomings of this method and concludes: "For this reason this method is not sufficient for everything we need in definition. However, it does make it easier for us to choose the predicates of the thing, especially where individuals and the infimae species are concerned [i.e., are the subject to be defined]."

In this chapter, we have presented a new family of particles, showing how Alfārābī clarifies their philosophical significations by linking them either to the logical theory of demonstration or to the philosophical doctrine known as the *four Aristotelian causes*. The following question particles have been discussed: *lima (li-mādhā), mādhā, bi-mādhā, ʿan mādhā, mā bāl, mā sha'n, immā, am* and *aw.* In addition, the particle *kayfa,* introduced in chapter 3, returned with a new signification that Alfārābī associates with the question particle *lima,* namely, seeking the cause of a thing.

Regardless of the fact that many questions related to the logical theories presented in this chapter must still be raised, Alfārābī's efforts in linking these logical theories with certain question particles are invaluable. The meanings these terms bear in these philosophical contexts are indeed very remote from what these same terms signify for the grammarians or in common use. This chapter, then, is a prime example of the way in which Alfārābī develops his logical lexicon in Arabic.

The following chapter will be devoted to the analysis of a new family of question particles (*hal* and *alif*) and their relation to the philosophically important term *mawjūd* [exists], which plays a significant role in Alfārābī's linguistic philosophy (chapter 6).

Notes to Chapter 4

1. It is possible that Alfārābī is considering the *mādhā* particle itself as a short form of any of the following expressions: 1) *mā hādhā* [what is this?]; 2) *mā dhākā* [what is that?]; 3) *mā ʾl-ladhī* [what is it that . . . ?]. (See **Ḥurūf**, 166, par. 167.)

2. This is, at least, my interpretation.

3. This topic is raised and discussed by Aristotle mainly in his *Physics* Book II, chapter 3.

4. In the Arabic translation of Aristotle's *Physics,* none of these particles is used. This Aristotelian work was translated by Isḥāq Ibn Ḥunayn with commentaries by Ibn al-Samaḥ, Ibn ʿAdī, Mattā Ibn Yūnis, Abū al-Faraj Ibn al-Ṭayyib (See *Aristūṭālīs, al-ṭabīʿah,* ed. ʿAbd al-Raḥmān Badawī [Cairo: Al-dār al-qawmiyyah li-l-ṭibāʿah wa-ʾl-nashr, 1964].)

5. See **Alfāẓ**, 56: 4.

6. Alfārābī uses the term *yadull*, which literally means "signifies" or "indicates."

7. This identification between the *mādhā* and *li-mādhā* particles is based on footnote 6 of **Ḥurūf**, 205.

8. In giving this example, I was guided by A. E. Taylor, *Aristotle* (New York: Dover Publication, Inc. 1955), p. 51.

9. See E. W. Lane, *Arabic-English Lexicon*, New York: Frederick Ungar Publishing Co., 1956, 5: 2163.

10. One cannot conclude discussion of these particles without mentioning that in this passage Alfārābī does not mention, implicitly or explicitly, anything about the *formal cause*, one of the four Aristotelian causes. I have no satisfactory explanation for this.

11. Alfārābī uses this example in order to explain his understanding of the particle *li-anna* [because] (**Ḥurūf**, 212–213). According to him this particle is always an answer to the *lima* question. The *li-anna* particle is always attached to the cause of the subject of inquiry. This cause can be provided by means of the middle term of the demonstration or by conjunction of the two premises of that demonstration. *Li-anna* is defined in **Alfāẓ** (56: 8) as one of the particles that indicates the reason for something that either precedes or follows this particle. This agrees with the grammarians' use of the particle. (See W. Wright, *A Grammar of the Arabic Language* [Cambridge, England: Cambridge University Press, 1975], Part Second, pp. 284–285.)

12. In **Qiyās ṣaghīr** (p. 250) Alfārābī explains the concept of syllogism:

> A syllogism [*qiyās*] is a notion [*qawl*] composed of premises [*muqaddimāt*] which are posited [to be true] and which, when combined, result in a different thing from the given premises, essentially [*bi-dhātihā*] and not by accident. Whatever comes to be known by a syllogism is called a conclusion [*natījah* or *radf*].

A commentary on the terms *bi-dhātihā* and *radf*, which appear in this definition, is required. The term *bi-dhātih* literally means "in itself." But as we have seen in chapter 3, this term in Alfārābī's system means, something we would today call "analytical truth," such that the conclusion is already included in this composition, exactly in the same way that the concept 'animal,' for example, is included in that of 'man.'

The term *radf* is not often used in this logical sense. In Ibn Manẓūr's *Lisān al-ʿarab* (Cairo: Al-dār al-miṣriyyah li-l-taʾlīf wa-ʾl-tarjamah, 1966), this term is defined as follows: "Radf is whatever follows [*tabiʿa*] a thing. Anything that follows another thing is called its follower [*radfah*]."

We have met a derivative of *radf* in chapter 1, section 3 of this study. There we met *yurdaf* which was used by Alfārābī to mean "followed by."

13. In **Burhān** (p. 23) Alfārābī calls these premises "first principles" [*al-mabādi' al-uwal* or *al-muqaddimāt al-uwal al-tabī'[iyy]ah li-l-insān*, i.e., the first natural premises man has or possesses]. Alfārābī explains that these principles come about naturally and we become certain of them "without realizing whence and how we achieve them, nor did we ever feel we were ignorant of them or desired to know them or sought them at any time at all; rather we find that our souls have been innated with them since our creation, as if they were instinctive [*gharīzī*] and that we cannot be without them."

14. This parallels Aristotle's distinction between "knowledge" and "opinion." The latter is the case but can be otherwise, the former is necessary and cannot be otherwise. See Aristotle, *Posterior Analytics,* Book I, chapter 33.

15. See **Alfāẓ**, 45.

16. Literally, "informs."

17. By necessary (and therefore true) premises, Alfārābī means all the following: 1) axioms [*mabādi' ūlā*] which are innate truths [*al-ma'ārif allatī bi-'l-ṭab'*] (**Mūsīqā**, 96); 2) postulates [*muqaddimāt waḍ'iyyah*] (**Burhān**, 27); 3) definitions or parts of definitions (genera and essential differences).

18. *Posterior Analytics,* 71^{b}15 ff., 72^{a}15–24. See also 74^{b}15–17.

19. See J. Barnes, "Aristotle's Theory of Demonstration" in eds. J. Barnes, M. Schofield, R. Sorabji, *Articles on Aristotle* (London: Duckworth, 1975–79), vol. 1: 66.

20. This form is traditionally known as the *Barbara* mood (after the first mood of the first figure), but only with necessary premises and a necessary conclusion, i.e., a modal syllogism.

Example, Sir David Ross in *Aristotle* (p. 50) claims that "the demonstration of the attribute as necessarily following from some cause requires only verbal alteration to provide its definition." In this passage, Ross analyzes the 'eclipse of the moon' given in Aristotle's *Posterior Analytics* (93^{a}36).

Incidentally, Alfārābī argues similarly in his **Burhān** (p. 47). The example he gives there is: how do we demonstrate the existence of thunder? If we want to prove this, Alfārābī says, we explain that 'thunder' is a voice coming from the clouds, then we change the order of this definition so that it becomes demonstrable: There is a sound in the clouds, etc.

21. Ibid., p. 51.

22. Aristotle rejects this method as a method of demonstrating essences (*Posterior Analytics,* Book II, chapters 1–7). In chapter 8 of this work, Aristotle shows, however, some flexibility on this issue, but the chapter may be read in different ways and there is no clear-cut position in Aristotle regarding this issue.

23. Most probably Alfārābī is referring to *Xenocrates,* whose arguments concerning demonstrations of definitions are presented (and rejected) by Aristotle in his *Posterior Analytics,* Book II, chapter 4.

24. This method is discussed in several of Plato's dialogs: "Phaedrus," "Philebus," and particularly in the "Sophist."

25. Compare Alfārābī's views on this subject with those of Galen, a fair account of which can be found in Kneale and Kneale, op. cit., pp. 182–3. For the origin of this term, as well as that of *sharṭī muttaṣil* [conjunctive] see Zimmermann op. cit., p. 47, n. 4.

26. The first premise of this argument has the logical form 'pvq' (i.e., 'p or q,' which is equivalent to '-p q' (i.e., 'if not p then q'), which in turn is equivalent to 'q p' (i.e., if not q then p). This logical equivalence makes it clear why the sentences of the form *immā . . . immā* are considered by Alfārābī as conditionals [*sharṭī*]. Incidentally, 'p' and 'q' (or the concepts they represent) must be related, otherwise the argument will not be valid.

27. Alfārābī and a number of Arab grammarians do not distinguish between expressions containing *immā* and those containing *aw;* they use them interchangeably. Cf. Wright, *A Grammar of the Arabic Language* (Cambridge, England: Cambridge University Press, 1975) Part 2, p. 293. According to a tenth-century grammarian, there is a difference between these expressions. Rummānī, in his *Kitāb maᶜānī ʾl-ḥurūf* (ed. ᶜAbd al-Fattāḥ Ismāᶜīl Shalabī [Cairo: Dār nahḍat miṣr li-l-ṭabᶜ wa-ʾl-nashr, 1973], p. 130), describes this distinction in the following manner: When we use the *immā . . . immā* expression it indicates that it is certain that one of the factors in this expression is true (and the other is false), but there is a doubt as to which one is true. When one uses the form "*. . . aw . . . ,*" however, the argument continues, the doubt occurs to the person after pronouncing the first part of the sentence. In the former case, you begin with the knowledge that you are in doubt and you build your argument on that factor. In the latter case, you begin with certainty, but it later occurs to you that this might not be the case. Sībaweih op. cit., (vol. 3: 169) makes a similar statement about the *am* particle: When you ask, 'is Zayd or ᶜAmr with you?', he says, you assume that one of them is with the person to whom the question is directed, but your knowledge is not definite [*ᶜilmuka qad istawa fīhimā*]. And in discussing the *aw* particle, Sībaweih says (vol. 3: 179): "When you ask, 'Did you meet Zayd or [*aw*] ᶜAmr or [*aw*] Khālid?' it is like asking 'Do you have [in your company] any of those?', since you really do not assume [when you ask the question] that any of them is with you."

Alfārābī, as mentioned above, ignores these distinctions.

28. Quoted from L. S. Stebbing, *A Modern Introduction to Logic* (New York: The Humanities Press, 1933), pp. 435–436.

29. This example is provided in Porphyry's *Isagoge*, p. 48, as a property of 'horse' and is also often used by Alfārābī as a property of 'horse' (see, for example, Alfārābī's **Madkhal**, 125).

30. This is my example; Alfārābī's list stops at the second example.

31. Here I have taken the liberty of extending Alfārābī's example of **Alfāẓ** (p. 86), which is confined to division by *dichotomy*.

32. Not in Alfārābī's text. I am supplementing this text with an example of mine.

33. This condition is necessary in order to guarantee that this process will lead only to one highest genus. This condition amounts to saying that the infimae species with which we begin this process should be of the same category. For example, they should all be of the category of substance or all from the category of quality, etc. Otherwise this process will lead nowhere.

34. In **Alfāẓ** (p. 90) Alfārābī says that some people call this process of substitution *qismah* and others call it *taḥlīl*.

35. Aristotle, *Prior Analytics*, $46^{a}32$–7.

36. Cf. Avicenna's criticism of the method of division. Avicenna's views on this issue may be found in *Al-shifā*ʾ, *al-manṭiq, 4: al-qiyās*, ed. Saʿid Zayid (Cairo: Al-hayʾah al-ʿāmmah li-shuʾūn al-maṭābiʿ al-amīrriyyah, 1964), pp. 455–9.

5

The Term *Mawjūd* in Nonlogical Contexts

A key term Alfārābī employs in analyzing the subject-predicate relationship is that of *mawjūd,* the most common meanings of which in English are: "is" [to be],[1] "exists," "subsists," and "is present."

Mawjūd parallels both the English "is" and the present participle of the Greek verb *to be* (*on*/*ontos*), from which the term *ontology* is derived. *Mawjūd* is related to *wujūd* [existence] in the same way that "is" is related to "being." *Wujūd* and "being" play a central role in Arabic and English, respectively, in metaphysical doctrines, just as *mawjūd* and "is" play a central role in logical theories. Yet, the terms *wujūd* and *mawjūd,* as well as the roles assigned to them by the Arab philosophers and the translators of Greek philosophy into Arabic, have not been adequately studied.

Our purpose in this chapter is to explore the meanings and roles of *mawjūd* in nonlogical contexts. The logical roles of this term will be investigated in our final chapter in the context of the discussion related to the concept of "copula."

Typically, Alfārābī links his analysis of this term and the various roles it plays in a sentence to question particles—in this case, *hal* and *alif,* both of which in the common language mean "whether" (in indirect speech) or "isn't so and so the case?" Let us begin with these question particles, as presented in Alfārābī's system.

The Question Particles *Hal* and *Alif*

The question particle *hal* was mentioned earlier (chapter 4, section 3) in conjunction with our discussion of another question particle, the *lima* [why?] particle. There we suggested that by using the question particle *hal,* one seeks to know about a thing's existence or about a thing being the case or not. A brief characterization of this particle was also offered in chapter 1.

Like the *lima* particle, Alfārābī explains, the *hal* particle may be used in a meaningful way only if added to a composite expression (**Al-**

fāẓ, 47). By "composite expression," Alfārābī means a complete sentence that is either explicitly stated or of which only parts are stated, with other parts referred to implicitly by the speaker [*qā'il*] as well as by the listener [*sāmiʿ*] (**Ḥurūf**, 201, par. 210).

Furthermore, in **Ḥurūf** (p. 200: 16–17) Alfārābī states that it is generally accepted [*fī 'l-mashhūr wa-bādī' al-ra'y*] that this particle should always [*abad*[an]] be attached to two statements opposed to each other in some sort of opposition [*qaḍiyyatayn mutaqābilatayn . . . ʿalā ayy ḍarb kāna taqābuluhumā*] and connected by one of the disjunctive particles [*aḥad ḥurūf al-infiṣāl*], such as *aw, am,* and *immā.* The examples given by Alfārābī to illustrate this point are:

1. 'Is Zayd standing up or is he not?'
2. 'Is the sky spherical or is it not?'
3. 'Is he blind or is he capable of seeing?'
4. 'Is Zayd the son of ʿAmr or is he the son of ʿUmar?'

It is clear from these examples that "opposition" [*taqābul*], as employed here by Alfārābī, does not mean only formal opposition. Rather, Alfārābī is considering here also opposition between the contents of sentences.

From Aristotle (*De Interpretatione,* chapter 6 ff.) we know there are *three kinds of opposition* between parts of statements: *contradiction, contrary, and subcontrary.* In each of these types of opposition, it is assumed that the subject and the predicate of one of the sentences of an opposite pair should be the same as the subject and the predicate of the other sentence in the pair.

This, at least, is how Alfārābī understands Aristotle.[2] (**ʿIbārah**, 62–3):

> The conditions of opposition between affirmation and negation] are: the affirmation and negation should be about one and the same thing; the mode [*al-jihah*] should be one and the same; and whatever stipulation is made in the affirmation [*al-ījāb*] should be made in the negation [*al-salb*], regardless of whether this stipulation is about the subject or about the predicate.

Of the four examples given above, only the first and second are composed of opposing statements in this strict sense, i.e., in the formal sense. Both the third and the fourth are composed of two statements that are in opposition or conflict only due to our knowledge of their content. The *form* of each of these pairs does not indicate an opposition or a conflict or, as Alfārābī puts it in his discussion of the indefinite statements (ʿ**Ibārah**, 68): "The statement 'it is not day' is only a negation of the day's presence. This expression does not indicate [in itself] the presence of the night, rather the presence of the night follows [*lāzim*] from the negation of the day."

So, opposition for Alfārābī means in this context both *formal* and *material* opposition, the latter suggesting that the opposition between two sentences is due to their content, rather than their form.

In the previous chapter, we met two examples of material opposition borrowed from Alfārābī's **Qiyās ṣaghīr** (p. 259) in order to explain the *immā* and the *aw* particles and their role in disjunctive arguments [*sharṭī munfaṣil*]. One of the examples ran as follows: "The world is either eternal or created, but it is created; therefore the world is *not* eternal." In a footnote, it was pointed out that in disjunctive arguments the 'p' and the 'q' (or rather, the statements they represent), must be related (in some way) in order to guarantee that this specific argument is valid. What was meant then by "in some way" should now become more clear.

There is nothing formally conflicting or opposing about the terms *eternal* and *created*. The conflict between these two terms (and consequently between the statements 'the world is eternal,' and 'the world is created') is a material conflict that depends on the meaning of these terms in a given language. Similarly, the Arabic terms *aʿmā* [blind] and *baṣīr* [capable of seeing] (in the third example above) conflict due to their *meaning* in Arabic. There is nothing in the *form* of these terms to imply that they are in any kind of opposition, nor is there anything related to the form of the sentences 'he is blind' and 'he is capable of seeing' that might indicate an opposition of any kind between these two sentences (or rather, between the statements they represent).[3]

These two sentences conflict due to the *meaning* of the terms of which they are composed, and not due to their *logical form*.

We have seen that, according to Alfārābī, the particle *hal* is always attached to two opposing statements. Alfārābī also says (**Ḥurūf**, 201, par. 211) that the particle *hal* is employed when the inquirer knows for sure that one of the statements to which the particle is attached is true or that it is accepted and admitted by the answerer (especially in dialectical debates).[4] By using the particle *hal*, the argument continues, the inquirer seeks to know definitely [*ʿalā ʾl-taḥṣīl*] which of the two statements is the true one, or which is accepted and admitted by the answerer.

It is obvious that in stating these rules concerning the particle *hal* (or *alif*) Alfārābī is relying on the logical law known as the "excluded middle," the general form of which is 'either p is true or p is not true' where 'p' represents a gap into which a declarative sentence may be inserted.[5] This law, however, does not serve Alfārābī's purposes entirely. For, two statements may be *a priori* assumed to be of the form 'p and not p' only if we assume that every kind of opposition is a contradiction. But this is not the case. There are two more types of logical opposition: contrary and subcontrary, and there is also the nonlogical or material type of opposition, namely opposition that depends on meaning rather than on form. Subcontrary statements (such as 'some men are smokers' and 'some men are not smokers'), for example, may both be true at the same time, and contrary statements (such as 'all men are smokers' and 'all men are not smokers') may both be false at the same time, thus preventing us from assuming *a priori* that one of the sentences involved is true (and the other, false).[6]

This distinction between the various types of opposition is important as long as we speak of universal statements, i.e., those statements the subjects of which are universals. In the case of a particular statement, i.e., a statement the subject of which is one individual, we are reduced to two types of opposition: contradiction and material opposition. This is probably why the entire set of Alfārābī's examples in this regard is composed of particular sentences (representing particular statements). However, he neglects to state explicitly the following qualification in describing the *hal* particle: it is always attached to two *particular* contrary statements.

Alfārābī's discussion of the *hal* particle is a typical example of his adherence to the philosophical meanings and usage of terms, even when this necessitates disregarding what Arab grammarians and philologists have to say. Alfārābī's main concern, with respect to the *hal* and *alif* particles, for example, is to investigate questions related to "existence" in its various forms and modes. This is not something that overly concerned the grammarians of that period.

A brief comparison of Alfārābī's views on *hal* and *alif* with those of the eighth-century grammarian Sībaweih should underscore the significant differences between their respective approaches.

Alfārābī claims, as we have seen, that the *alif* particle—when used as a question particle—is a synonym of the *hal* particle [*taqūm*[7] *maqām 'hal'*] (**Ḥurūf**, 202, par. 213). In both cases, Alfārābī's discussion implies, the inquirer knows for sure that one of the opposite statements to which he attaches either of these particles is true and the other, false, although he does not know which is true and which, false.[8]

The question of the existence of something in something (a quality in a substance) as opposed to the question of the absolute existence of individuals ('Zayd,' 'the sun,' etc.) is precisely what characterizes Alfārābī's definition of the question particles *hal* and *alif*. According to Alfārābī, when we question whether 'x exists' or whether 'x exists in y,' we always assume (whether we say so or not) that 'x either exists or does not exist' and that 'x exists in y or does not exist in y.' It is the way these particles are used, then, in philosophical contexts that suggests their meanings to him. This is the reason that according to him the *hal* and the *alif* particles are synonymous; what determines their synonymity is the fact that their *roles in philosophical contexts* is one and the same.

Philosophical inquiry, while playing a major role in Alfārābī's systematic treatment of the question particles, does not enter at all into the grammarians' treatment of these same particles. The grammarians, though primarily concerned with the syntactical features of the particles, often discuss their semantical features as well. However, philosophical issues such as the explicit or implicit opposition between two statements do not even occur to them.

Sībaweih, for example, in his *Al-kitāb*,[9] discusses the *hal* particle in relation to other particles. Like Alfārābī he stresses the similarity in meaning between this particle and the *alif* particle. Unlike Alfārābī, however, the grammarian Sībaweih maintains that, despite a basic similarity, there is a definite distinction in their meanings. When one uses the *hal* particle in posing the question 'are you beating Zayd?,' one does not assume that the act of beating Zayd is taking place; one is simply seeking knowledge about whether it is happening or not. When one asks the same question using the particle *alif*, on the other hand, one is actually *assuming* [*taddaᶜī*] that the act of beating Zayd is taking place and simply wondering why.[10]

For Alfārābī, use of either of the particles assumes there is some type of opposition between two statements, an *a priori* assumption ('either x or not x') and always true (i.e., requiring no empirical verification). For the grammarians, however, the inquirer makes a more or less conscious choice of one over the other particle, indicating when he chooses *alif* that he has prior empirical knowledge related to the subject matter of the event being inquired about.

Hal and its Uses in the Syllogistic Arts

The question particle *hal*, Alfārābī says (**Ḥurūf**, 206, par. 218) is a general question, used in all the syllogistic arts [*al-ṣanāʾiᶜ al-qiyāsiyyah*]. However, the argument continues, the usages, the types of opposition to which this particle is attached, and the purposes of inquiry sought by use of this particle differ from one art to another. It is the uses of the *hal* particle in the demonstrative sciences (such as mathematics and physics) that are of principal interest to us at present.

In the demonstrative sciences, the *hal* particle is attached to two contrary statements [*qawlayn mutaḍāddayn*][11] (ibid.). In this case, the *hal*[12] is a demonstrative question [*su'āl burhānī*] (**Ḥurūf**, 226: 13).[13] In dialectics [*jadal*] the *hal* particle is attached only to contradictory statements [*yuqran bi-'l-mutanāqiḍayn*] (**Ḥurūf**, 206: 19–20). In this case it is a dialectical question [*su'āl jadalī*] (**Ḥurūf**, 226: 13–14).

The principles of these sciences, Alfārābī says (**Ḥurūf**, 209, par. 221), have been established (through or with the help of dialectical conversations)[14] and have become certain truths, as is evident in the science of mathematics [*taʿālīm*]. In these sciences, the argument continues, the use of the question particles emerges not from the need to establish principles for these sciences, but rather in order to acquire knowledge that has been proven and demonstrated. According to Alfārābī, when we use the *mā* particle, for example, we seek to conceive and understand what is already known (to someone other than the inquirer). Similarly, when we use the *hal* or *lima* particles in any of the demonstrative sciences, we seek to become acquainted with the *demonstration* that provides certain knowledge of a thing's existence or of the cause of its existence.

The motive for using the question particles in the demonstrative sciences, Alfārābī seems to argue, is a lack of knowledge of the facts and principles on the part of the learner and inquirer, rather than a doubting of the validity of these facts and principles (as is the case in dialectics and sophistics). In the demonstrative sciences, lack of knowledge, rather than dispute and disagreement, is what initiates the use of the question particles.

This distinction between the uses and roles of the *hal* particle in the sciences versus its use in other disciplines is significant. For, the *purpose* of its use in science is different from the purpose of its use in dialectics. In the case of dialectics, we begin and end our inquiry with the *hal* particle (**Ḥurūf**, 207: 4–10). No further inquiry is involved beyond the knowledge of whether a thing is or is not so. In the case of science, using the *hal* particle is only a first stage in the inquiry about a thing. Once we obtain an answer to the *hal* question, we proceed to ask 'what is that thing?', 'how is that thing?' and 'why is that thing?'.

When we ask, for example, whether a certain geometrical property exists in a triangle or not, we seek in fact more than a 'yes' or 'no' answer. Raising this question amounts to asking about a general rule or principle that exists (or does not exist) in the entire species ('triangle,' in this case). We are asking, then, about the essence or about a certain essential property of that species. The use of the *mā* particle (and possibly other particles), is therefore *implicit* in the use of the *hal* particle (in mathematical inquiries, at least). Similarly, when we ask about a natural phenomenon using the *hal* particle. In this case, Alfārābī seems to argue, we are in effect asking about the causes for the occurrence or nonoccurrence of a certain phenomenon, i.e., we are implicitly employing the *hal* particle as a *lima* particle.

The idea that there is an overlap in meaning between the various particles used in the demonstrative sciences, becomes clearer still when we examine the various meanings of the term *mawjūd* and its relationship to the *hal* particle as presented by Alfārābī.

Mawjūd and the Concept of Truth

The particle *hal*, Alfārābī says (**Ḥurūf**, 213, par. 228), enjoys a number of different applications in the sciences. The most obvious of these is the inquiry about the absolute existence of things, such as 'nature,' 'void,' etc. In such cases, the *hal* particle is attached to a statement [*qaḍiyyah*] in which the term *exists* [*mawjūd*] is a predicate [*maḥmūl*] of the subject of inquiry.[15]

Here the term *exists*, Alfārābī explains, means a correspondence [*muṭābaqah*] between a concept and a thing that exists outside the mind. Hence, when we ask, 'does x exist?', we seek to know whether the concept we acquired through the term 'x' has an external counterpart or not. In this application, therefore, the term *mawjūd* means *external existence* (the *internal existence*, i.e., the concept, is not doubted, since the very question assumes it exists and that we are seeking to know only whether it has an external counterpart or not). This brings us to one of the central questions of the philosophy of logic, namely *the concept of truth*.

According to Alfārābī, *māhiyyah* as we by now know, is the combination of form and matter or of the proximate genus and the differentia of the definiendum, *always* in this order; genus must be the first element of the definition (**Alfāẓ**, 80). This latter combination itself is called the *ḥadd* [essential definition] of the thing. And we have seen that when the *ḥadd* of a thing is presented to the mind, then the thing itself, i.e., its *māhiyyah*, is comprehended and consequently acquires its mental existence. This mode of existence is contrasted by Alfārābī with the external existence of things (**Ḥurūf**, 117–119), to which he usually refers by means of the phrase *munḥāz bi-māhiyyat*^{in}*-mā khārij al-nafs*, which literally means, "that which is set apart outside the mind by (or due to) a certain essence." For convenience sake, however, I will continue to refer to the concept in its shorter form: "external existence." Similarly, Alfārābī sometimes refers to the internal or mental existence as *munḥāz bi-māhiyyat^{in}-mā mutaṣawwarah* [that which is separated due to a conceived essence]. I will refer to this only as "mental existence."

According to Alfārābī, there is no mutual implication between these two modes of existence. The external existence of things is independent of our conception [*taṣawwur*] of them or lack thereof (**Ḥurūf**, 117: 22–23; 121: 20–23), and vice versa:

> Things may have only mental existence [*māhiyyah mutaṣawwarah*] but no external existence . . . an example of this is the void [*khalā'*], which has a certain essence. For, we may ask, 'what is a void?' and the answer will be in accordance with what a 'void' is. This answer will be an expository expression for its name, and what exposes the name is a certain essence, although it has no external existence. (**Ḥurūf**, 118: 4–9)

This was earlier (chapter 3, section 1) referred to as nominal definition, but in this case it is also an "empty concept"; a certain concept or *māhiyyah* existing without a corresponding entity in the external world. This distinction between two modes of existence leads Alfārābī to his definition of the concepts of truth and falsity (**Ḥurūf**, 117–18, par. 91):

> It is evident that whatever is true has an external existence, and whatever has an external existence is more general[16] than what is true. For, whatever has an external existence becomes true only when it becomes conceived by the mind. It had its external existence before it was conceived yet it is not considered true, since the meaning of "the true" [*al-ṣādiq*] is the identity between the conception and what exists outside the mind. The concept becomes true[17] when it is compared with what exists outside the mind, and similarly when the concept becomes false. To "be true" per se is in relation to what has an external existence.[18]

By the phrase "similarly" for "when the concept becomes false," Alfārābī means that in this case there is no correspondence between the concept that forms in the mind and the object of that concept (or that "referent," to use Zimmermann's terminology). The assumption is that both the object and the concept exist, but there is no correspondence between them, i.e., the concept we have does not fit reality. The concepts "true" and "false" are applicable, according to Alfārābī, only when there is an act of comparison between the mental existence (concept) and the external existence (object). These are, therefore, relative terms. By saying *ṣādiq* [is true] one means, Alfārābī would argue, that the concept is true of an object, i.e., it fits it. Accordingly, when there is no external existence for a certain concept we may have, it is appropriate to apply either of these terms to the concept. One can at most say that this is an *empty concept* or that the concepts of "true" and "false" are not applicable to concepts that do not correspond to external entities. Alfārābī does indeed move in this direction in his **ʿIbārah** (pp. 26–28).

> Concepts [*maʿqūlāt*][19] that are neither true [*lā taṣduq*] nor false [*lā takdhib*] are single [*mufradah*]. . . . There are three kinds of single expressions: nouns, verbs and particles. By themselves all are like concepts without combination and separation, e.g., 'man' or 'whiteness' both being nouns, one the name of a substance, the other the name of an accident, if no stipulation is made with [such an expression], which could serve as predicate or subject, then it is neither true [*ḥaqq*] nor false [*bāṭil*].[20]
>
> Some single expressions signify images in the soul that are not founded on anything existing outside, like 'goat-stag' [*ʿanzayyil*] and 'sphinx' [*ʿanqāʾmughrib*][21] and some signify images founded on something existing outside. But no single expression is true or false, no matter whether it signifies an image founded on something existing outside the soul or an image not founded on anything existing outside. For those that signify something founded on something existing outside are not true as long as it is not stated that they are founded on something existent. Nor are those signifying something not founded on anything existent false, unless it is additionally stated that they are [not] founded on anything existent, or rather, that they signify something [not] founded on anything existent.

In light of all this, it is surprising to see Alfārābī giving the concept *khalāʾ* [void] as an example of his definition of "falsity" in the above-quoted passage of **Ḥurūf** (p. 118: 4–9). And it is equally surprising to find him consistent in calling what has no external existence "false." Such is the case in **Ḥurūf** (p. 121, par. 95), where he discusses the term *nonexistence*, i.e., when he considers the cases to which this term may be applied. "Falsity" is used, he says, for whatever has no external existence. And that means, he explains: 1) there is neither a mental existence nor an external existence; and 2) there is a mental existence but not a corresponding external one. The latter case is identical, he says, (**Ḥurūf**, 121: 10–11) with being false [*kādhib*]: "being false may be described as that which does not exist [*ghayr mawjūd*]."

It is most likely that Alfārābī is *not* speaking of the classical correspondence theory of truth, as sketched in his **ʿIbārah** (see quotation above), but rather about a derivative meaning of this concept.

We do find a derivative or secondary meaning of "truth" in Book V of Aristotle's *Metaphysics* (1024^b 19 ff.), where Aristotle speaks of "being false" in the following sense: "In the sense that the false facts are beings but appear by nature to be either not such as they are or *what does not exist, as for example, a sketch or a dream.*" (Emphasis mine) Most probably Alfārābī is referring to this derivative definition of falsity, which identifies "being false" with "not existing." It is the statement 'void does not exist' that Alfārābī probably has in mind when he attributes falsity to the concept of 'void.'[22]

Finally, the concept *kādhib*, Alfārābī says, is not the same as the concept "untrue." Rather, the latter is broader than the former, since it applies not only to the former, but also to the cases where no "essence" at all is involved. In other words, whereas the concept of "being false" applies only to the second category above, the concept "untrue" [*ghayr ṣādiq*] applies to both categories, i.e., it applies whenever no essence at all is involved. What is "false" may be comprehended, conceived, or imagined, and always has an essence; one may always inquire about it by means of "what is it?" and a full answer can be given. For example, when you ask "what is a 'void?' " [*khalāʾ*], whoever has a concept of this term will tell you it is 'a place that can never have anything in it,' or a similar answer that fits whatever concept the answerer has. According to Alfārābī, the extension of the predicate "being false" is, therefore, a subclass of "being not true."

The distinction between external and mental existence and the analysis of these concepts offered by Alfārābī make clear that *māhiyyah* for him is not merely a mental concept. Rather, it is in the things themselves. Thus we find him stating time and again that things are set apart in the external world due to their *māhiyyah*. The mind, in other words, does not create the *māhiyyah* of things that have an external existence; it merely conceives them. This is a theme touched upon earlier (chapter 3, section 5), when Alfārābī's concept of *māhiyyah* as a combination of form and matter was described and linked to the *kayfa* particle.

A major focus of our analysis in the previous five chapters has been the exploration of the logical meanings of the following particles: *mā, kayfa, ayy, am, immā, aw, lima, mādhā, bi-mādhā, li-mādhā, ʿan mādhā, hal, alif,* and *a-laysa* (discussed in a footnote). We have also investigated the *inna* particle and its application in Alfārābī's philosophy. These particles were linked to logical theories and issues and their meanings in logical contexts, clarified.

In addition to the terms discussed thus far, a number of other terms are analyzed by Alfārābī, though from a somewhat different angle, namely from a logico-linguistic point of view. Terms such as *mawjūd* and its derivatives play significant roles not only in metaphysical doctrines (as discussed in this chapter), but also in linguistic analysis.

Our emphasis in the remainder of this study will shift from the analysis of logical theories and their particular manifestation in the Arabic language to analysis of the Arabic language itself, from a logical point of view. During the first five chapters, the Arabic language served Alfārābī (and us) in a sense as a metalanguage, that is, a particular natural language through which a variety of philosophical issues were discussed. From this point on, Arabic will become an object language, a language whose very *structure* becomes the focus of logical analysis.

Let us turn now to Alfārābī's Linguistic Philosophy, beginning with a discussion of the verb system in Arabic.

Notes to Chapter 5

1. In philosophical usages.

2. Aristotle says in *De Interpretatione* (17ᵃ34): "I speak of statements as opposite when they affirm and deny the same thing of the same thing, not homonymously."

3. Alfārābī uses the logical term *qaḍiyyatān,* which is more appropriately translated as two statements rather than two sentences.

4. Consult **Ḥurūf** (pp. 206–207, par. 218–219).

5. Kneale and Kneale, op. cit., p. 47.

6. Alfārābī does not explicitly state that the other must be false, but it is clear that this is his intention, especially in light of his explanation that the purpose of using the *hal* particle is to learn *which* one is true.

7. It should read *yaqūm* rather than *taqūm*.

8. In *Maʿānī ʾl-ḥurūf,* p. 102, Rummānī attaches the meaning of "already" [*qadd*] to the particle *hal,* a meaning Alfārābī ignores altogether. (This meaning is apparently based on Sībaweih's *Al-kitāb.*)

9. Sībaweih, op. cit., vol. 3: 175 ff.

10. This is close to but not identical with the meaning of the *a-laysa* particle in Alfārābī's system (**Ḥurūf**, 202: 2–10). *A-laysa* is another question particle composed of the *alif* (which gives the composite form its question force) and the negation particle *laysa*. *A-laysa* may be roughly rendered into the English as: "Isn't it the case that . . . ?' Alfārābī maintains that when one uses this particle, one attaches it to *one* of the opposite statements, viz., the one known or assumed to be true. By using *a-laysa,* one seeks approval or acknowledgement from one's opponent. For the origin of the term *ays,* from which its negation *laysa* is derived, cf. Abū Rīdah's analysis in Al-kindī, op. cit., p. 182.

11. The reason is that in science *universal* statements are used and these may be of two types. 'Every x is y' or 'no x is y.' Traditionally, the first is called a statement of the 'A' type (affirmative universal), whereas the second is of the 'E' type (universal negative). The only type of opposition possible between 'A' and 'E' statements is *contrary.*

12. There is no explicit mention of the *hal* particle in this passage, but it is certain that *hal* is one of the particles Alfārābī has in mind in this general discussion of the use of the particles.

13. Here Alfārābī uses the term *falsafah* [philosophy] to refer to the demonstrative sciences. Earlier in **Ḥurūf** (p. 213, par. 228) he uses the term *ʿulūm* [sciences] for the demonstrative disciplines.

14. This indicates the positive role Alfārābī attaches to dialectics.

15. When Alfārābī says that the *hal* particle is attached to a (single) statement, he assumes it to be understood that an opposite of this statement is always implicit. When we ask 'is it x?', we are really asking 'is it x or is it not x?'

16. *Aʿamm,* in the sense of "being broader in scope."

17. Literally, Alfārābī says *yaḥṣul al-ṣidq fī ʾl-mutaṣawwar,* which should be translated as "the truth comes to be in what is conceived," but then it would be very difficult to translate the whole phrase. Similarly with the phrase *yaḥṣul al-kadhib fī ʾl-mutaṣawwar,* which literally means "the falsity occurs to it," but which I have translated as "becomes false."

18. See also **Ḥurūf** (pp. 121–122, par. 95): "what has an external existence cannot be said 'to be true' unless it is conceived."

19. Usually I render *maʿqūlāt* as "intelligibles," but I am here striving to be consistent with the term I have been using in this context.

20. See **Alfāẓ** (p. 79), where Alfārābī uses this term to indicate an inquiry about a subject, the existence of which has not been affirmed. Note his use of the terminology. The terms *ḥaqq* and *bāṭil* are most often used in other disciplines, such as religion and ethics. But Alfārābī seems to apply them in logic as synonymous with *ṣidq* and *kadhib*, respectively (or in our case, *ṣādiq* and *khādhib,* i.e., the [active] participle).

21. Alfārābī mentions these two terms again in **Burhān** (p. 80) in conjunction with two other terms he considers of the same category, namely *al-khalā'* [void] and *lā-nihāyah* [infinity]. For the source of the term *ʿanqā' mughrib,* see Zimmermann, op. cit., p. 15, n. 4.

22. The first example given by Alfārābī in **Ḥurūf** (p. 118: 6) for this derivative concept of falsity is most probably borrowed from Aristotle's *Metaphysics* (1024ᵇ20): "The diagonal [of a square] is commensurable with the side." In Averroes' text *Tafsīr mā baʿd al-ṭabīʿah* (ed. Maurice Bouyges [Beirūt: Dār al-mashriq, 1938–48]) the *translation* of this Aristotelian example is: *Khaṭṭ al-quṭur musāwī li-khaṭṭ al-ḍilʿ* (vol. 2: 684.) Alfārābī, however, uses the term *mushārik* [commensurable] rather than *musāwī* [equal]. Alfārābī uses *mushārik* each time he gives this example. (See, for example, **Burhān**, 61.) Both terms, however, convey the message. This is probably why Averroes, in his commentary on this passage (vol. 2: 686), uses both terms interchangeably.

6

Alfārābī's Linguistic Philosophy

The Arabic Verb System versus Aristotelian Logic

According to the Arab grammarians, the Arabic verb system is based on two temporal forms: a form that designates a finished or *perfected* act [*māḍī*], and one that designates an act currently in progress [*kā'in lam yanqaṭi*ᶜ] or one that will take place in the future. This latter form is called the "imperfect" tense [*muḍāri*ᶜ].[1]

In Arabic, the present tense does not have a verb form that expresses it without a future connotation, because the imperfect tense [*muḍāri*ᶜ] expresses both present and future times. Thus, if one wishes to express the idea that someone 'is walking now at this moment,' there is no way to say it in Arabic without using a nonverbal term (an adverb of time) that specifically states the time of the action under consideration ("now" [*al-ān*], for example).

Alfārābī attempts to show that the grammarians' conception of time is too narrow, thereby not only disregarding basic Aristotelian principles, but also going against objective reality itself. Alfārābī's explanation for the concept of "now" is based on two Aristotelian definitions, one that roughly parallels the grammarians' concept and a second that goes beyond that to develop an alternative concept necessary for the analysis and discussion of logical principles.

The first view of the "now" concept is found in Aristotle's *Physics* (VI, chapter 3), where the Greek philosopher argues that the "now" is a *limit or boundary;* it is not part of time, any more than the points are parts of a line.[2] Evidently, this is the view held by the grammarians (whether aware of the Aristotelian definition or not) in their staunch defense of the lack of a verb form in Arabic that explicitly indicates the present tense. Witness the following description by one of Alfārābī's contemporaries:

> As for the present tense [*fi*ᶜ*l al-ḥāl*] it is [the verb] which comes about while the speaker speaks and [therefore] it is neither in the

domain of the past and the discontinued, nor is it in the domain of the expected future time. [The present tense] takes place in the past time and in the beginning of the future time. The present tense is in fact, therefore, the future tense.[3]

Alfārābī points out, however, that this concept of "now," which virtually does away with the present tense, is not that employed by Aristotle and the philosophers when they deal with grammatical tenses. There exists also an alternative definition of "now," according to which *the present is the source* and the other two tenses (past and future) are merely derivatives. As Aristotle puts it in *De Interpretatione* (16^b16): "Similarly, 'recovered' and 'will recover' are not verbs, but inflexions of verbs. They differ from the verb in that it additionally signifies the present time, and they, the time outside the present."

This view of the "now" as an omnitemporal present tense—consisting of the past and the future, as well as the present tense—is important for the expression of logical relations that are *tenseless or timeless*. Interpreting the present tense or the "now" in this omnitemporal way allows Aristotle to avoid the strictly timeless predication, i.e., the eternal, "bound up with the Platonic metaphysics of the realm of timeless forms, which he had abandoned."[4]

It is on the basis of this omnitemporal Aristotelian conception of time that Alfārābī attacks the grammarians, whom he accuses of going against truth itself in this particular issue (ʿ**Ibārah**, 40). He believes that this scientific conception of time offers a much better basis for understanding the concept of the verb, covering many more cases of the verb and of linguistic and logical relations than the previous concept of the "now" had been able to cover.

Without the introduction of Greek logic into the medieval Arab world, this controversy between philosophers and grammarians over the nature of the "now" in Arabic might never have arisen. However, once introduced to Greek logic, the Arab logicians found the Arabic language inadequate for certain logical tasks posed by Aristotle, their highest authority in logical matters.

Aristotelian logic is a predicative logic. Regardless of the grammatical structure of any given sentence, the logical *form* of that sentence should always fit the schema: *S is P,* where 'S' is the subject and 'P' is the predicate.

This logic aims at a uniform rewriting of all sentences, regardless of whether the time in which the subject and the predicate coincide is in the past or the present or the future. This logic, furthermore, does not distinguish between the active and passive forms of the verb (i.e., between the sentences 'John loves Mary' or 'Mary is [being] loved by John'). Nor does it distinguish between the forms 'John runs' and 'John is running.'[5]

In fact, Aristotelian logic is based on the assumption that every finite verb or active verb form may be rewritten as a combination of the copula "is" and a participle. This is one of the basic "logical" principles Alfārābī has in mind when he maintains that the *rābiṭah* [lit., connector] is necessary for logical and theoretical investigations (**Ḥurūf**, 112:3).

In Greek[6] (and in most Indo-European languages), for example, the transformation from 'John walks' into 'John is walking' (S is P) does not present a logical problem. In Arabic, however, the situation is different. Although the language does have a past-tense copula, the copula is simply not expressed when a sentence is cast in the present tense. Thus, *Zayd yamshī* [Zayd walks] may be transformed into *Zayd māshī* [Zayd (is) walking], but this new sentence does not include a verb, only the participle *māshī*. The sentence is, therefore, unsuited for the standard logical structure 'S is P' and contradicts Aristotle's explicit principle that: "Every affirmation will contain either a noun and a verb or an indefinite name and a verb. *Without a verb there will be no affirmation or negation.*" (Emphasis mine)[7]

Caught between rigid Aristotelian principles on the one hand (such as, that a sentence must have a verb and that the copula is a necessary language element) and the Arabic language on the other hand (which, in the present time frame, allows predication without a copulative verb), Alfārābī finds himself embroiled in one of the most significant controversies in Arabic logic: the theory of the copula. It is through his work in this area, which lies somewhere between philosophy and language,[8] that Alfārābī develops his linguistic philosophy.

Yet the question of the copula is, in a sense, only a symptom of a larger problem, namely the Arabic verb system and its perhaps limited ability to cope within certain philosophical parameters previously established by the Greeks. So zealous is Alfārābī in following Aristotle's logical lead, that he even seems to propose major changes in the Arabic language to help him manage more effectively (in Arabic) with the "universal" issues he is investigating. Such proposals, suggesting modification of the Arabic language for philosophical purposes, of course, exposed Alfārābī and the other Arab logicians to criticism from the Arab grammarians, who resisted any such changes as foreign and unnecessary invasions of their language.

In this chapter we will examine precisely those aspects of the Arabic language that pose problems from a logical point of view, as well as Alfārābī's recommendations for resolving them. The problems Alfārābī sets himself to resolve as a philosopher *of* (and *in*) the Arabic language are in fact all related to the concept of the "verb," to which Alfārābī refers by the term *kalimah* [**Risālah**, 270].[9] These general topics may be summarized as follows:

1. the dual nature of every Arabic verb: predicative and copulative;
2. "lack" of a present tense copula in Arabic;
3. "lack" of an exclusively present tense in Arabic;
4. formation of nonverbal sentences in Arabic;
5. transformation of Arabic sentences from the form 'S Verb' into 'S is Participle';
6. the relationship between the verbal noun [*maṣdar*] and the verb in Arabic;
7. the logico-linguistic concept of *mithāl awwal* [prototype].

All of these closely interrelated topics will be covered throughout this chapter, which will be structured as follows: Sections 2 through 5 will deal with various aspects of tense and the copula; section 6, with Alfārābī's views on language acquisition; section 7, with the concept of *mithāl awwal;* and section 8 with the abstract nouns in Arabic.

The Dual Character of Arabic Verbs: The Existential Verb as Copula

Alfārābī divides the Arabic particles [*ḥurūf*] into five categories, developed in accordance with Greek grammatical doctrines. Alfārābī says he was prompted to use the Greek model, because the Arab grammarians had not yet produced a similar classification, preferring instead to refer to all particles under the general name of *ḥurūf*,[10] without further distinction.

The *rawābiṭ* [lit., connectors] comprise one of the five classes of particles Alfārābī presents in **Alfāẓ** (p. 42). Now, the term *rābiṭah* as used in Alfārābī's **Alfāẓ** classification describes only *conjunctions* that serve to connect sentences with each other. None of the eight types of *rawābiṭ* (pl. of *rābiṭah*) is or can be used to connect parts of a sentence with one another. None, in other words, may be considered a *copulative conjunction*, if by that we understand a term (or terms) that serves as a link between the subject and the predicate of a sentence. In **Ḥurūf** (p. 112: 3), however, Alfārābī speaks of *rābiṭah* in another context—

namely, as a connector functioning *within* a sentence, connecting the subject with the predicate, a type of connector commonly referred to as a "copula."

In traditional grammar, a verb is said to be performing a copulative function when it connects a subject and a predicate. According to Alfārābī, if the predicate of a sentence is a verb, then it acts as a predicate and a copula simultaneously (**ʿIbārah**, 33). In his view, therefore, *every verb has both a copulative and an assertive or predicative side.*

Most verbs merely have the ability to connect *themselves* with the subject. A few verbs, however, are able to *connect things with each other without themselves being part of the connection*. As such they are *rawābiṭ* [copulas; lit., connectors] only. These are the *existential verbs,* which can exhibit their copulative side without simultaneously serving a predicative function.

The grammarians divide the verbs into two categories—*fiʿl (māḍī) nāqiṣ* [(semi) past tense verbs] and all the rest. Under the category *fiʿl (māḍī) nāqiṣ*, the grammarians include such verbs as *kāna* [was] and *ṣāra* [became], verbs used with the subject in the nominative case and the predicate in the accusative case. In a sense, Alfārābī too divides the verbs into two categories, with his division almost paralleling that of the grammarians, but his rationale for doing so is completely different. Let us now examine one of Alfārābī's existential verbs [*yūjad*] in action, along with the related *mawjūd* and *wujūd*.

On page 90 of **Al-thamarah al-marḍiyyah** [Philosophical papers],[11] in answer to the question as to whether the statement 'man exists' has a predicate or not [*'al-insān mawjūd,' hal hiya dhāt maḥmūl am lā?*], Alfārābī maintains there are two points of view on this matter, each in its own way, correct:

> Some say this statement contains no predicate and some say it does contain a predicate. In my view, both of these propositions are correct, each in its own way. For, when a natural scientist, who is concerned with things [per se], investigates this kind of statement, [he will conclude] that it has no predicate, because the existence of a thing is nothing other than the thing itself. [From a natural scientist's point of view,] a predicate ought to be an attribute [*maʿnā*], the existence of which in a thing can be affirmed or denied.[12] From this point of view the statement [i.e., 'man exists'] does not have a predicate.
>
> When a logician investigates it [the same statement], however, [he will conclude] that it is composed of two words that are

its parts and that it is capable of being true or false. From this point of view, the statement does contain a predicate. Both positions are, therefore, correct, each in a certain way.

From a logical point of view, therefore, the term *exists* in the sentence 'man exists,' plays, according to Alfārābī, the same (predicative) role that *white* plays in the sentence 'man is white,' *animal* in the sentence 'man is an animal,' and *walks* in the sentence 'Zayd walks.' In another sense, however, these three sentences represent three different types of relationship between the subject and the predicate.

We by now know that, according to Alfārābī, the predicate 'white' in the sentence 'man is white' is an accidental predicate of 'man.' 'White' is a quality of certain individuals of the species 'man,' rather than an attribute belonging to the entire species, and only to it, all the time. Alfārābī calls this latter type of attribute an *essential predicate* or *essential attribute,* as 'animal,' for example, in the sentence 'man is an animal' is an essential predicate of 'man.' But is 'exists' in 'man exists' an *accidental* or an *essential attribute?*

Alfārābī addresses this issue in another letter published in the same work. In **Thamarah** (p. 66) he says that the "existence" of a thing is neither identical with that thing's essence, nor is it a part of its essence. According to this source, "existence" [*wujūd, huwiyyah*][13] is one of the inseparable accidents of the thing [*min jumalt al-ᶜawāriḍ al-lāzimah*]. "Existence," the argument continues, does not belong to the constituting elements of a thing [*laysa min jumlat al-muqawwimāt*], nor does it belong to the predicates implied by the essence of a thing.[14]

The second and the more important aspect of *wujūd* [being] from our point of view, is the meaning and use of the related terms *mawjūd* and *yūjad.* These terms function in a manner equivalent to that of the English copulative *is* in such inquiries as 'whether in every triangle the sum of the angles *is* equal [*mawjūd . . . musāwiyah*] to two right angles,' or 'whether every man *is* [*mawjud*] an animal.' In such cases, Alfārābī says (**Ḥurūf**, 214, par. 230), the term *mawjūd* is serving as an "existential verb" [*kalimah wujūdiyyah*] that connects the subject and the predicate, thus forming a "predicative sentence" [*qaḍiyyah ḥamliyyah*].

The use of the *hal* particle in combination with a predicative sentence of this sort, Alfārābī's argument continues, may have two purposes: 1) to learn *whether a statement is true or false* (by means of the correspondence theory, i.e., by comparing the concept with the external world), or 2) to learn *whether the connection between the subject and the predicate of the sentence is necessary or accidental*.

The relationships between the subject and the predicate in a sentence may be examined by asking whether the subject (or more accurately, whether what the subject stands for) is constituted by the predicate of the sentence under consideration, i.e., whether the predicate of that sentence is the essence (or part of it) of that subject. If the result of the inquiry is positive, the argument continues, then the constitution [*qiwām*] of the subject and consequently its cause or causes become known.

According to Alfārābī, the subject-predicate relationship may also be examined by asking whether the subject implies the predicate by necessity [*yūjib*], such as when we ask 'whether in every triangle the sum of the angles is equal to two right angles.' Asking this question is in fact asking whether the concept 'triangle' (i.e., the subject of the above-mentioned example) necessarily implies the attribute expressed by the predicate.

If a demonstration can be provided to show a conceptual connection between the subject and the predicate of a sentence, then we know that that predicate is implied by the subject. This does not mean, however, that the predicate is the essence or part of the essence of the subject. A property, for example, is necessarily implied by its subject; yet it is not a part of the essence of that subject.

It is reasonable to assume that the distinction Alfārābī is attempting to make in this passage of **Ḥurūf** (pp. 214–215) is between a necessary predicate that is part of the essence [*dhātī*] and one that is not part of the essence [*ḍarūrī*] (i.e., a property, a description and an inseparable accident).[15]

Now, if we demonstrate that the connection between the subject and the predicate is a necessary one, then the demonstration will not only be an answer to the *hal* question but also to the *lima* question, on the grounds that in science every demonstration provides the cause or causes of the thing demonstrated.

This is probably what Alfārābī means when he says (**Ḥurūf**, 216, par. 234) that the *hal* particle—when used to inquire about statements, the truth of which have been established[16]—contains [*yaḍumm*][17] these two (a reference to the *lima* and *mā* particles).

Moreover, since in geometry, Alfārābī explains, forms (i.e., the figures) are the basis of every geometrical proof, then the particle *kayfa* is also implied when we use *hal* in geometry.[18] For we have shown that, according to Alfārābī, one inquires about the form of a thing by using the *kayfa* particle.

The main meanings and uses of the *hal* particle in the sciences as conceived by Alfārābī were discussed in section 1 of the previous chapter. In this section we have employed the *hal* particle in an analysis of the relationships between subject and predicate, thereby initiating a discussion of "predication" in Alfārābī's system, which will be continued in the following section.

Filling a "Gap" in Predication: The Pronoun *Huwa* as Copula

It was mentioned earlier in this chapter that according to Alfārābī the sentence 'Zayd exists' makes perfect sense from the logician's point of view, since "every one [of the existential verbs] may itself be a predicate [*khabar*]" (**Fuṣūl**, 272). In that sense, the existential verbs [*al-kalim al-wujūdiyyah*][19] function as a *predicative term*, just like any other verb.

From Alfārābī's point of view, then, it is perfectly proper to say *Zayd kāna* [lit., Zayd was], when by this we intend to say 'Zayd was born' or 'Zayd became a creature.' It is equally appropriate to say *Zayd wujida* [lit., Zayd existed], when we mean to say 'Zayd was found' or 'Zayd came into being.' In these cases *kāna* and *wujida* function like any other verb.

The difference between existential verbs and regular verbs, however, lies in the role they can play as copulative terms, i.e., when they appear in a sentence *to indicate that something exists in some thing* or, in general, *to indicate a connection [irṭibāt] between the predicate [khabar] and the subject [al-mukhbar ʿanh]* of that sentence.

To be sure, according to Alfārābī, *all* verbs have this copulative property. Sometimes they exercise this copulative power simultaneously with their predicative power, as in 'Zayd runs.' Other times they simply link the subject to the predicate, as in 'Zayd is a man.' The former occurs when the subject is a noun and the predicate is a verb;[20] the latter case, when both the subject and the predicate are nouns.[21] From the total class of verbs, however, only an *existential verb* may function in this latter (purely copulative) manner.

In addition to existential verbs, however, Alfārābī explains that separate *pronouns*, too, may be employed to link the subject with a predicate in a sentence (**Ḥurūf**, 112, par. 83).[22]

The separate pronoun *huwa* [he][23] acquired its copulative meaning when Arab philosophers searched for a parallel to the Persian word *hast* and the Greek *estin*, both of which (in their respective languages) play the copulative role the verb "is" plays in English. The Arab translators of Greek texts, Alfārābī says (**Ḥurūf**, 112, par. 83), were forced to invent such a connector because "it is necessary for the theoretical sciences and [particularly] for logic."

The injection of the copula into the Arabic sentence is, therefore, a necessity in Alfārābī's view, a necessity imposed by the rules of logic, which is to say, by the rules of thought. This is an indication that for Alfārābī the presence of a copula is a structural matter in any language, rather than a peculiarity of one language or another. Alfārābī not only approves of the introduction of the copula to the Arabic language (by the translators of Greek philosophy into Arabic); he takes this linguistic development several steps further by assuming that it is absolutely necessary to fill the gap that logic has exposed, so to speak, in the Arabic language. After all, there is a parallelism between the laws of grammar and the laws of logic, or as Alfārābī puts it in **Iḥṣāʾ** (p. 68): "For every rule the laws of grammar provide in relation to utterances, there is a counterpart [in the text, *naẓāʾiruhā*, 'their counterparts'] that logic provides in relation to the intelligibles."

The theory that there is a correspondence or parallelism between language and thought is a major theme in Alfārābī's philosophy of language, with significant implications for his linguistic philosophy.

There are certain features common to all natural languages, Alfārābī maintains. These features exist in all languages not by accident, but because all languages are an external manifestation of one and the same thing: the realm of intelligibles which is universal. The presumed universality of the intelligibles provides the opportunity for Alfārābī to explain why logicians do and should investigate languages: "Logicians investigate expressions per se insofar as they are related to thought [*maʿqūlāt*, lit., intelligible]" (ʿ**Ibārah**, 24).

We will examine later exactly what Alfārābī means by relationships between the domain of language and the domain of thought, when we discuss his views related to language acquisition in section 6 of this chapter. Meanwhile, however, we can state that Alfārābī defends the idea that, just as the intelligibles correspond to and mirror the external world, language mirrors the intelligibles, with one major difference: the former correspondence is natural [*bi-ʾl-ṭabʿ*], whereas the latter is by convention [*waḍʿ*] and legislation [*sharʿ sādhij*] (ʿ**Ibārah**, 27).

Since the rules that govern particular languages are conventional, they can be changed and even violated [**Ḥurūf**, 81, par. 36]. But just what are the conditions under which the rules and structures of a given language can or should be changed?

For Alfārābī, it seems that the laws of formal logic are a sufficient justification for changing the rules of a given language. Although he concedes that every natural language has its own particular features, which are not universal (**Iḥṣāʾ**, 76–77), it is clear that for Alfārābī the laws of logic dominate all structures of any language, and therefore, languages cannot be incompatible with the formal rules of logic. The position of the copula in the Arabic language is for Alfārābī a case in point.

The copula (or lack of it) in any language is, as we shall see, a major philosophical issue as well as a significant linguistic feature. Alfārābī's extensive analysis of the copula and its place in the Arabic language is intended to accommodate specific questions that are both philosophical and linguistic. One of these questions is whether the Arabic language can express the *timeless statements* characteristic of logic and of other theoretical disciplines.

The Elusive Present Tense and Other Anomalies of the Arabic Verb System

As we have seen, Alfārābī claims that, according to Aristotle and the natural scientists, the concept "now" indicates "the end of the past and the beginning of the future, which is something indivisible" (ʿ**Ibārah**, 40). Alfārābī turns to *Categories* 5ᵃ7 for this alternative Aristotelian view of time: "Time also and place are of this kind. For present time[24] joins on to both past time and future time."

For the common man (including the grammarians) the concept "now," however, means something quite different. When most people say, for example, 'I did now' or 'I shall do now,' they mean, Alfārābī explains, "not the end of past time and the beginning of the future, rather they mean the time close to the end of past time and the beginning of the future" (ibid.). Nonphilosophers are not aware of the scientific definition of time, Alfārābī maintains, whereas Aristotle and the natural philosophers use both the scientific and the nonscientific definitions of the concept "now."

According to Alfārābī, the present tense as defined in this scientific way may be either long or short (ʿ**Ibārah**, 41). This enables us to express not only past and future actions, but also actions occurring at this moment and ongoing actions, such as when we say 'he lives now.' By this we mean that that individual's existence as an animal extends with the progression of the present time, which represents at once an end (of the past) and a beginning (of the future).

Obviously, Alfārābī is suggesting a reform of the Arabic verb system, modeled on a concept borrowed from Greek language via logic. By suggesting adoption of the omnitemporal view of the present, Alfārābī is in fact suggesting the establishment of new foundations for the Arabic language. He wishes to introduce a novel approach based on a concept different from, if not diametrically opposed to, the lines along which the Arabic verb system had naturally developed, namely, that actions take place either in the past or in the future and that the present tense per se does not exist.

In accordance with this view, past and future are swallowed up in an omnitemporal present, which Alfārābī feels is a better frame of reference for expressing reality. How different this view is from that of the grammarians, like Zajjājī, who in a sense believe rather that the present tense is engulfed by the past and the future, a view diametrically opposed to Alfārābī's philosophical concept of the present tense!

Despite Alfārābī's protestations to the contrary, the grammarians were not unaware of this concept of time Alfārābī is embracing as the optimum basis for understanding the verb system. In fact, Alfārābī's conception is not contradicted by Sībaweih's description of the verbs, in which Sībaweih speaks very clearly of three tenses: "As for the verbs . . . they are constructed [to describe] what has past, what will be but did not occur yet, and what is in progress without interruption."[25] This definition distinguishes among three different physical times and consequently among three tenses, indicating clearly that Sībaweih was aware of all three. Sībaweih's awareness of the three potential tenses is possibly due to his Persian origin, which exposed him to the three-tense Indo-European structure.[26] This awareness did not lead him, however, to Alfārābī's position, probably because of Sībaweih's belief in a natural, rather than a conventional development of language.

Alfārābī seems to ignore the strong correlation that exists between the natural development of a language and the perception that the native speakers of that language have. Alfārābī, for example, does not take into consideration the possibility that the natural development of a language is a factor in determining how the people who speak it *perceive* time. It is not inconceivable to think of a language that considers time to be one dimensional or four dimensional. In fact, if we can imagine creatures who adopt logical and mathematical structures as their only language, their concept of time would be one dimensional or perhaps they would develop no awareness of time whatsoever. The natural development of a language and its internal structure may well determine whether there are two or more time references. A philosophical doctrine that ignores this fact risks imposing an artificial structure on the natural language. This is most probably the trend the tenth-century grammarians were fighting so bitterly against and what al-Sīrāfī meant by charging that the logicians were "building a language within a language."[27]

When al-Sīrāfī attacks the logicians, his target is most probably issues of this sort, regarding which the logicians' analysis is neither universal nor objective. Rather, the logicians' proposals to modify the Arabic language are based on conventions in a certain culture and a certain language or family of languages (in this case Greek), the rules of which do not necessarily agree with the rules of other languages.

There is no reason to assume that al-Sīrāfī was directing his criticism at logic as a whole, denying it as a valid system of reasoning, both universal and objective. It is more likely that his criticism is directed against such elements of logic as these—the requirements, for example, that every sentence must have a verb, or that there must be a present tense copula. Al-Sīrāfī rightly identifies these elements with the rules and features of the Greek language, something the Arab logicians are unreasonably attempting to impose on the Arabic language in the name of "universality."

Alfārābī's conception of the language as a conventional thing, probably encouraged him to extremes in suggesting such reforms in the Arabic language. In ʿ**Ibārah** (p. 27) and **Ḥurūf** (p. 81) Alfārābī repeats his claim that expressions are coined by man in order to signify the intelligibles. These utterances are not natural otherwise they would be universal, just as the intelligibles are universal. The relationships between the utterances and the intelligibles, therefore, have an artificial side, since they are coined by convention [*waḍ*ʿ] and by legislation [*shar*ʿ], just as the rules of conduct in society are conventional. If so, then we can change these utterances and the rules that govern them whenever a need arises.

It is not surprising, therefore, to see that the changes in the Arabic verb system that Alfārābī is recommending are perceived by him as the right thing to do for the sake of the Arabic language, which must be "logical," he would probably argue. Alfārābī genuinely believes that language is an artificial thing and that those who determine its rules can make mistakes, which should be corrected in accordance with the rules of logic. This is a mechanistic attitude toward language which ignores the fact that language is an important factor in forming these intelligibles, upon whose universality Alfārābī insists so strongly.

Let us move now to examine the same problem (lack of an exclusively present tense in Arabic) from another point of view, namely from the point of view of the Kūfian School of grammar, the major representative of which is al-Farrāʾ (d. 822).

The Elusive Present Tense Continued: The *Kūfian* View

The Kūfian School of grammar introduced the concept of *fiʿl dāʾim* [roughly: a continuous verb] in order to describe a very similar idea to that of the omnitemporal present. According to followers of this school a *fi*ʿ*l dā*ʾ*im* "is a general and continuous time that indicates neither past [*maḍī*] nor present [*ḥāliyyah*] nor future [*istiqbāliyyah*]."[28]

That which is a *fi*ʿ*il dā*ʾ*im* for the Kūfian School is called in Baṣrian terminology *ism fā*ʿ*il* [verbal adjective], the general form of which is *fā*ʿ*il*, such as *māshī* [walking] and *qā*ʾ*im* [standing up]. This form comes very close to the English participle, which is hardly a verb when it stands by itself without a helping verb such as 'is,' 'was,' etc.

Both Alfārābī and al-Sīrāfī's Baṣrian School reject the concept of *fi*ʿ*l dā*ʾ*im* as a third category of the verb on the grounds that it is not even a verb. Thus, al-Sīrāfī, in his commentary on Sībaweih's *Al-kitāb*.[29] Al-Sīrāfī says that what the Kūfians call *dā*ʾ*im* is in fact the *ḥāl* [present participle], and it is wrong to call it a verb since it behaves like a noun in all respects.

Al-Sīrāfī mentions two syntactical features of the noun, claiming that both apply to terms like *qā*ʾ*im* [standing up] and *ḍārib* [beating], which means that this form must be a noun. "Furthermore," al-Sīrāfī's argument continues, "that which is called *dā*ʾ*im* is neither a verb of the past tense nor is it a verb of the future tense, rather it is a present tense which does not last because it has the meaning of 'now,' i.e., the meeting point of the past and the future which does not last, whereas the meaning of the *dā*ʾ*im* is that which lasts and stays."

This last argument against the Kūfian concept is reminiscent of Zajjājī and Ibn Fāris, who argue against the very same idea aimed at introducing a present form to the Arabic verb system. This is evidence of the strong resistance among the grammarians (at least those of the Baṣrian School) to such a notion.

Alfārābī, too, rejects this notion but on different grounds. He says (ʿ**Ibārah**, 41) that "others believe that derived nouns are the uninflected verbs, and they signify that a thing is taking place in the present time." Alfārābī, doubtless, is referring here to the Kūfian concept of *fi*ʿ*l dā*ʾ*im*.

"Uninflected verb" [*kalim ghayr muṣarrafah*] is an Aristotelian term that appears in *De Interpretatione* (16^b16–19), the purpose of which is to classify the verbs into two categories: the "uninflected" (which represents the present) and the "inflected" (which express either past or future events). In this passage, Aristotle considers the uninflected verbs to be the most deserving of the title of "verb," with the inflected only derivatives of it.

Referring to the form *fā*ʿ*il* (the Kūfian candidate for expressing present tense) as "derivative nouns" [*asmā*ʾ *mushtaqqah*], Alfārābī claims that the formation [*bunyah*] and the shape [*shakl*] of the "derivative nouns" does not indicate any time reference, except perhaps in an accidental way, just as the prototype nouns [*mithāl awwal*] (ʿ**Ibārah**, 41). The evidence that Alfārābī provides for his claim is the following (ibid.):

> If derived nouns are verbs by essence and formation, they would also have the signification of the copula. There would be no need for them to be connected, when predicated, by an existential verb being explicitly articulated or implicitly understood. But we find they are not connected with a subject unless an existential verb is manifestly expressed or tacitly supplied in the mind. Examples are *Zayd yūjad ʿādil* [Zayd is just] and *Zayd yūjad māshī* [Zayd is walking]. If [on the other hand] we explicitly express the copula with a predicated verb, it would be nonsensical and redundant, as in *Zayd yūjad yāmshī* [Zayd is walks], etc.

Although Alfārābī's reason for rejecting this concept of the Kūfian School is based on grammatical considerations, it is obvious that his ultimate goal is to make the Arabic language fit the previously mentioned Aristotelian criterion that every sentence should have a verb. Alfārābī is probably right in saying that the active participle [*ism al-fāʿil*], which he calls a derivative noun [*ism mushtaqq*] is not a verb. Most grammarians would agree with him that both active and passive participles [*asmāʾ al-fāʿil* and *asmāʾ al-mafʿūl*, respectively] are adjectives which are derived from verbs,[30] rather than verbs as such.[31]

Yet, the criterion Alfārābī uses to examine the validity of the Kūfian position is in itself unclear and requires some clarification. His suggestion that the copula be used in order to distinguish sound from non-sound sentences, is hardly convincing.

The introduction of an existential verb like *yūjad* to a sentence such as *Zayd māshī*, in order to connect its subject with its predicate, would produce an awkward, artificial and virtually meaningless sentence. What is worse, this artificial connector would not even achieve its purpose. In a sentence like *Zayd ṭawīl* [Zayd is tall], if one explicitly inserts a term such as *yūjad* in order to connect the noun [subject] 'Zayd' with the adjective [predicate] 'tall' we would produce something equivalent to 'Zayd exists tall.' One must wonder how it is possible for Alfārābī to present his students and readers with this structure, hoping they will accept the imposition of Greek principles on the Arabic language. It is hard to imagine that Alfārābī is willing to go to such lengths for the sake of Aristotle's principles. Fortunately, there is a solution to this awkward situation.

What Alfārābī seems to be saying is the following: the logical structure of the language, any language, must have a connector that links the subject and the predicate (or the noun and its adjective). Whenever he discusses the question of the copula, Alfārābī adheres to terminology such as the following:

1. "either explicitly manifested or implicit in the mind" [*muẓharah fī 'l-lafẓ aw muḍmarah fī 'l-nafs*] (ʿ**Ibārah**, 41);
2. "explicitly stated ... or thought of" [*yuṣarraḥ maʿahā ... tuḍmar*] (ibid.);
3. "Arabs do not use the existential verb explicitly [*muṣarraḥ bihā*] in referring to present tense [relations], rather they think of it implicitly" (**Fuṣūl**, 272);
4. "in Arabic, on the other hand, where in sentences with nominal predicates the existential verb is tacitly understood" (ʿ**Ibārah**, 103);
5. "in each statement the idea of an existential connection [*wujūd rābiṭ*][32] exists, either potentially [*bi-'l-quwwah*] ... or actually [*bi-'l-fiʿl*]" (**Ḥurūf**, 127, par. 103).

This is a clear indication that Alfārābī is thinking of two different levels of language. Any language must have a certain *logical structure*[33] that corresponds to reality and to thought. This logical structure is manifest in certain languages and is implicit in other languages. The present-tense copula, for instance, is not in the grammatical structure of Semitic languages (or of other languages such as Russian) but, Alfārābī seems to argue, it is in the logical structure of all languages. It is, therefore, immaterial whether it is expressed by a specific term in a given language or not.

Zayd māshī in Arabic, Alfārābī would argue, does indeed correspond to the structure 'S is P,' despite the fact that the Arabic language does not explicitly mention what stands for "is." Whereas "is" is an explicit sign of the English language to express the idea of a link between the subject and a predicate, this idea is *built into* the Arabic language and into every other language that does not have an explicit sign for it.

Alfārābī's assumption that all languages correspond to a fixed logical or conceptual structure that mirrors reality in a natural way [*bi-'l-ṭabʿ*] (ʿ**Ibārah**, 27) was bound to lead him to the conclusion that all languages correspond to each other. Whatever structure a given language may possess, all other languages must have a parallel construction. This is because, according to Alfārābī, all languages express no more and no less than the fixed structures (namely thought), which in turn reflect reality.

The copula is not a linguistic feature that pertains to some languages but not to others; rather it is a structural device by which all languages are capable of expressing logical relations that exist in the mind. The fact that the Arabic language does not manifest a connector that corresponds to the Greek *estin* or the Persian *hast* (**Ḥurūf**, 112, par. 83) may be easily remedied by coining a term to be used whenever the phenomenon of the copula occurs, i.e., whenever we want to express the two basic logical relations that something is 'said of' something or that something is 'in' something (**ʿIbārah**, 33).

Thus, the Arab translators began to cast about for different terms to express these logical relations, simply in order to bring to the surface whatever existed in the logical structure of the language, any language. This is most likely what Alfārābī means, when he presents structures like *Zayd yūjad ʿādil,* which translates as 'Zayd exists just,' but which really corresponds to 'Zayd is just.' When we say *'S yūjad P'* in Arabic, we express tenseless relationships between 'S' and 'P' just as when we say 'S is P' in English, which is meant to express the tenseless logical relationship.

In fact, if we adhere to the literal meaning of *yūjad*, it would mean 'will be in existence,' since it is a verb that has a future tense form, just as the English "is" would imply that this relation between 'S' and 'P' that the formula 'S is P' is supposed to express is temporal and that it is taking place at this moment, if we understand it literally. But this of course is not what is meant in using "is" to express logical relations. The relations expressed in the formula 'S is P' are omnitemporal and, therefore, neither the English "is" nor the Arabic *yūjad* are meant to express a tense, when used as copulative expressions.

This situation is very similar to Alfārābī's conception of the verb as a necessary element in every statement. And this is no accident. Alfārābī's analysis of the concept of the copula is primarily directed to a solution of the problem of the lack of a present (continuous) tense in the Arabic verb system. The copula, in Alfārābī's system, represents the idea of a timeless *verb,* despite the fact that a pronoun [*huwa*] and a noun [*mawjūd*] are used as copulas. These are only linguistic conventions, Alfārābī would argue.

Alfārābī's analysis of the language takes for granted that every statement (but not every sentence) contains a verb and that in the surface structure, that is, in the various natural languages, this may or may not have an explicit expression.

In **ʿIbārah** (p. 33), Alfārābī explains that whether the predicate of a sentence is a noun or a verb, it is always the case that "it is the verb which signifies that the predicate is linked to the subject." This indicates that Alfārābī is assuming—just as Aristotle taught in *De Interpretatione* 19^b12—that every statement must have a verb, even if that verb is not explicitly mentioned.

But Alfārābī is not merely following Aristotle in this regard. Rather, in trying to show that this is also applicable to languages, whose grammatical structure do not manifest the logical structure, Alfārābī is attempting to generalize the above Aristotelian principle to all languages.

According to Alfārābī, all languages have both existential verbs (which signify the three tenses) and a derivative noun (i.e., a participle), derived from the verbal noun [*maṣdar*] of these existential verbs. This derivative noun indicates (by convention) a timeless connection between a subject and its predicate. In Arabic the term chosen for this purpose, the argument continues, is the participle *mawjūd* (ibid., 46).[34] Since this term is not a verb (even in Alfārābī's own system), however, this casts serious doubt on Alfārābī's willingness to accept Aristotle's thesis that every sentence must have a verb. Consequently, we must reexamine our own thesis concerning Alfārābī's conception of the two levels of languages, the logical and the grammatical.

Alfārābī is aware of this difficulty, the source of which seems to be the Arabic translators of Aristotle's works, who were forced to find an Arabic term for the Greek *estin* and *on* and the Persian *ast* and *hast* (**Ḥurūf**, 112–113, par. 83). In order to overcome this difficulty, Alfārābī resorts to a new interpretation of the above-mentioned Aristotelian thesis expressed in *De Interpretatione* 19^b12 ("without a verb there will be no affirmation or negation").

Now he explains that by using the term *kalimah* (i.e., a verb) (**ʿIbārah**, 47) Aristotle means either: 1) any significant expression or 2) an expression that signifies existence [*wujūd*] and is employed as a third component[35] connecting a predicate with a subject, or 3) "The third meaning is the one defined after the noun," by which Alfārābī means the technical definition of the "verb" as presented in Aristotle's *De Interpretatione* (16^b6), according to which a verb signifies not only a subject but also a time.

The first Fārābian interpretation of the Aristotelian conception of the noun as a term that includes all the significant terms (i.e., verbs and nouns) is not baseless. In *De Interpretatione* (16^b19), Aristotle says: "When uttered just by itself a verb is a name and signifies something . . . but it does not yet signify whether or not."[36]

Nevertheless, our interpretation of Alfārābī as "placing the logical point of view before grammatical conventions"[37] should not be affected by the new Fārābian interpretation of the term *kalimah* as a significant term in general (i.e., either noun or a verb) and not just a verb, as the technical definition of this term implies.[38]

The most significant aspect to consider in Alfārābī's position on the copula is his conviction that all languages must be able to express the logical formula: 'S is P' where 'is' is a linguistic symbol meant to express either that 'P' is said of 'S' or that 'P' is in 'S.' The meaning of this symbol depends, therefore, entirely on the logical relations that exist (or do not exist) between the subject and the predicate of the particular statement.

The Copula as a Timeless Connector

The relationship between the subject and the predicate of a sentence such as 1) "The author of *1984* is George Orwell," or 2) "Every man is an animal," is expressed by a symbol of the English language, "is," which as a verb carries with it a time reference. Yet, when "is" is used in statements of identity (category 1 above), or in statements that are always true (category 2 above), it is considered a *timeless verb*, otherwise it would not express the relationships between the subject and the predicate as they exist in reality or as we perceive them.

In this use of the English term "is," it is hardly significant to classify this term as a verb, since this would carry with it the related concept of time, *not* a factor in the predication suggested above. The term *timeless connector* is, I believe, a better description of "is" in the two sentences above and in every sentence intended to express conceptual relationships between the subject and the predicate of a sentence.

Viewing the copula as a "timeless connector" rather than a verb (automatically implying time reference) helps Alfārābī overcome the difficulties involved in accommodating the Arabic language to the Aristotelian theories. Alfārābī seems satisfied with the choice of the noun *mawjūd* to play the role of a timeless connector in the Arabic language. He even goes so far as to state that in all languages there is a noun that plays this role:

> We find the same situation in all languages. We find that in all of them there are existential verbs which signify the present, future, and past times. We also find a noun derived from the verbal noun [*maṣdar*] of the existential verb, which, like other derived nouns, does not signify a time and is employed as a connector in statements [*qaḍāyā*] whose predicates are nouns. This noun is represented by the term *mawjūd* in Arabic, *estin* and *on* in Greek, and by *ast* and *hast* in Persian, and similarly in other languages. (ʿ**Ibārah**, 46)

Whether Alfārābī is right or wrong in referring to the Greek term *estin* and to the Persian terms *ast* and *hast* as nouns is immaterial in the context of our inquiry.[39]

Certain terms in each language play the role of a timeless connector or, to use Alfārābī's own words, a connector that indicates no definite time [*rawābiṭ min ghayr an yudall bihā ʿalā zamān muḥaṣṣal*] (ibid.). In some languages, these terms are verbs (i.e., used as verbs in other contexts), in others they are nouns (i.e., used as nouns in other contexts), and in still others they are pronouns (i.e., used as pronouns in other contexts). In all languages, however, Alfārābī would argue, the term chosen to play the role of a timeless connector is abstracted from its original meaning and used in a special way, namely to express that a certain predicate is either 'said of' the subject or 'in' that subject.

As far as the Arabic language is concerned, the verb *yūjad* [to be] might have been chosen to play the role of a timeless connector and indeed it is perfectly acceptable to use it, even in mathematical statements (where the relations are of the highest logical order) such as when we say: "The diagonal is [*yūjad*] different from the side" (ʿ**Ibārah**, 47).

However, when used as a connector, the argument continues, one should know that the relationships expressed by this term between the subject and the predicate are not confined only to the future (as the original meaning of the Arabic form indicates). Rather it should be understood that these relationships will exist in the future, without thereby implying that it was not the case in the past or that it is not the case now. In fact, Alfārābī continues, if we assert [*ḥakamnā*] that it is true in one time rather than another, this (logical) statement becomes a false statement.

As long as we bear in mind the meaning we assign to a term as a timeless connector, it is perfectly all right to use any term for this role, be it a verb, a noun, or a pronoun. In Arabic, the noun *mawjūd* and the pronoun *huwa* may be used interchangeably, since both express the same thing (**Ḥurūf**, 112–114, par. 83, 86). And it is most probable that Alfārābī would suggest the verb *yūjad* as a third synonym, given that we can overcome the time factor its structure implies. These terms should be understood simply as rendering the copulative *hast* or *estin*, no more and no less. We should neither think of *huwa* as a pronoun, nor contemplate the derivative character of *mawjūd*, nor think of the time reference associated with the verb *yūjad* when we use these terms as copulas.

The term *huwa* according to Alfārābī should be treated as a noun[40] rather than as a particle [*adāt*] (**Ḥurūf**, 115, par. 86).[41] The term *mawjūd*, on the other hand

> is [supposed to be understood as] employed in the sense of a prototype [*mithāl awwal*][42] which signifies neither a subject nor a passive participle [*mafʿūl*]. . . . In Arabic [this term] is employed to sig-

nify whatever is signified by the Persian term *hast* or by the Greek *estin* [when either of these is used as a copula]. (**Ḥurūf**, 113–114, par. 84)

This description concerning the copulative term *mawjūd* is repeated almost literally several times in **Ḥurūf** (pp. 113–115) with an emphasis on the conventional meaning the term has when playing the copulative role in a sentence. Alfārābī's repeated warnings that we should not associate this meaning of *mawjūd* with the term *wujūd* (from which the former is derived) is an indication of his awareness that the choice of the term as a timeless connector does involve certain problems and can, therefore, be very misleading [*mughalliṭah jidan*] (ibid., 114, par. 86).

This is the reason some people (meaning some translators), Alfārābī explains (ibid.), prefer to use the term *huwa* rather than *mawjūd* as a copula in the Arabic language. The former term is free from certain problems associated with the latter, the use of which as a copula brings up the idea that something exists in something (which is true in some cases, and false in other cases). It also brings to the mind the basic meaning of the root *wjd* which indicates an action of a human being on another human being or of a human being on an object (x found y). The term *mawjūd* as a passive participle is also associated with an indefinite subject and an indefinite object (just like *maḍrūb* [beaten], which indicates an indefinite agent who carries out the act of beating and a receiver or an object that is the target of this beating). It is a common feature of verbs and of derivative nouns (i.e., participles) that they both indicate an indefinite subject, Alfārābī says in his **Bārī armīniyās** (pp. 38, 52) as well as in **Fuṣūl** (p. 271).

The term *mawjūd,* when used as a copula, should be free or abstracted [*mujarradah*] from all these connotations, just like every other term people choose to signify something different from its original signification. This is a principle Alfārābī emphasizes in **Ḥurūf** (pp. 71–72, par. 21). In this passage, Alfārābī speaks in general of the "acquired signification" of terms, indicating that due to the conventional nature of languages, it is often the case that certain terms are made [*yujʿal*] to mean something different from their original signification. In such cases, the argument continues, we should disregard the original signification and treat the terms under consideration not as derivatives that owe their meaning to what they are derived from, but rather as terms abstracted [*mujarradah*] from that original meaning and standing for something different from (and not necessarily closely related to) that original meaning.[43]

The term *huwa* is neither a derivative noun nor a verb and therefore is free of any connotation that a noun or a verb may have when used as a copula. This is, according to Alfārābī, an advantage that certain people (meaning the translators) recognized in using *huwa* as a copula, rather than *mawjūd*.

Yet, the use of the term *huwa* as a copula entails, according to Alfārābī, one problem. Since it is neither a noun nor a verb, then no abstract terms may be derived from it in the way we derive *insāniyyah* [humanity] from *insān* [man] or *rujūliyyah* [manhood] from *rajul* [man], Alfārābī notes (**Ḥurūf**, 114, par. 86). He therefore concludes that this is precisely the reason some people have avoided using this term, turning instead to *mawjūd*.

Alfārābī's final thought on this issue is that he personally "thinks that one may use either of these terms" (ibid.). If we add to this his analysis of *yūjad* in **ʿIbārah**, we can guess that he would probably say that, if we are careful enough, we may use any of these three terms for the copula.

However, one may ask, is there logically no real difference between these terms when used as a copula? If they all mean the same thing, why do we need all three?

The question is justified, particularly in light of the fact that Alfārābī's explanation of the use of *huwa* as a copula is hardly convincing, especially since the abstract noun *huwiyyah* [being] had already been coined and used by the translators of Aristotle's works long before Alfārābī's time. And there is no doubt Alfārābī knew of it.

Alfārābī does not seem to assign different meanings or roles to *huwa* and *mawjūd* (as copulas). These two terms are used synonymously in his logical discussions. Thus, in his commentary on Aristotle's *Prior Analytics* [**Kitāb al-qiyās**],[44] Alfārābī uses these terms interchangeably, whenever he describes the formulation of a syllogism. We find him even using both terms in two different premises of the same syllogism (ibid., 23). When he discusses the fourth mood of the first figure, for example, Alfārābī uses both terms: *huwa* for the first premise, *mawjūd* as a copula in the second premise, and yet a third term (*laysa* [it is not the case that]) as a copula in the conclusion.

Moreover, it is generally true that when Alfārābī transfers from the technical language of logic ('A is in B,' 'A is included in B,' etc.), i.e., when he moves away from symbolism towards the ordinary language, he usually drops the copula altogether. Thus, we do not find traces of the copula (as a technical term) in his **Qiyās ṣaghīr**, where he discusses the theory of the syllogism in ordinary language meant to be understood by the Muslim community at large.

Even in **Qiyās**, a highly technical work, Alfārābī uses the copula only in his technical discussions. Whenever he provides examples to illustrate these syllogistic structures, he drops the copula and uses nontechnical language, much more natural from an Arab point of view. It is true that in **Ḥurūf** (p. 214, par. 230) Alfārābī uses examples such as 'man is [*mawjūd*] *ḥayawān*,' etc.,[45] with the explicit copula, but in these cases the idea is not to change the course or the manner of the Arabic language, but rather to manifest the use of the term *mawjūd* as a timeless connector between the subject and the predicate.

On the whole, however, the term *mawjūd* predominates in Alfārābī's technical language, although this is due to historical, rather than logical, reasons. Alfārābī was strongly influenced by the translators of Aristotle's *Prior Analytics* and *Posterior Analytics*. In the Arabic version of these works, the term *mawjūd* as a copula predominates, probably because the translators were very faithful to Aristotle's original. G. Patzig makes the following observation about this original Greek text:[46] "In the systematic exposition of his syllogism, Aristotle never constructs propositions of the form 'S is P' ('A estin B'), but always writes the 'A belongs to B'. . . . The 'A belongs to no B' or the 'A belongs to some B,' etc."

Patzig then goes on to wonder, with Alexander of Aphrodisias (c. A.D. 200), why Aristotle had to adhere to such artificial language, entirely unnatural for ordinary speakers of Greek.

Aphrodisias, according to Patzig,[47] has three answers to this question, only the second of which is both comprehensible and true. There is no need for us, however, to go into detail regarding this extremely interesting discussion of Aphrodisias, but I do find Patzig's conjecture toward the end of that discussion illuminating.

> I offer here the hesitant conjecture that the tendency which has continually reappeared in the history of logic, not least in more recent times, of conceiving a judgement as an equation, or even as an expression of identity, derives a good deal, if not all, of its force from the purely conventional wording of the schema 'S is P.'[48]

This should be understood as a *justification* and praise of Aristotle's use of artificial connectors. According to both Aphrodisias and Patzig, Aristotle thereby tried to make the distinction between the subject and the predicate clearer, especially given that in Greek "in the normal formulation 'A is B,' both the linked terms are in the nominative case so that to distinguish subject from predicate we depend upon the conventional order of the terms in the proposition, a convention which, in Greek as in English, is sometimes violated."[49]

In Arabic, too, the subject and the predicate in the normal formulation are in the nominative case. This is not, however, as far as I can see, a major problem in Arabic. Still, there is an important element of

Patzig's analysis that may be applied to the copula in the Arabic language. When we use *huwa* as a copula, the formulation 'S *huwa* P' is conceived (or can easily be interpreted as) an equation or an identity, regardless of whether this equation or identity exists or not between 'S' and 'P.'

This "identity" meaning of *huwa*[50] is what makes the use of *mawjūd* preferable. Perhaps both the translators and Alfārābī were conscious of this fact in adhering to the term *mawjūd*.

Our observation concerning the lack of copula in Alfārābī's ordinary language is additional and important evidence that Alfārābī was trying to show that although the copula does exist in the logical structure of all languages, it need not be manifested in every sentence in all languages. Alfārābī himself provides logical examples without the copula. He uses it most frequently in technical discussions, in order to exhibit the logical structure of a proposition. Alfārābī is well aware that the ordinary use of languages does not always manifest this logical structure of propositions.

We now move to another aspect of Alfārābī's philosophy of language, an aspect associated with epistemological inquiry and in which Alfārābī introduces his significant term of *mithāl awwal* [prototype].

Language Acquisition

The three Arabic terms *mushār ilayh* [lit., this thing that can be pointed to], *maᶜqūl* [intelligible], and *maqūlah* [category] correspond to three different levels in Alfārābī's epistemological scheme. The first of these represents the realm of sensible objects, the second that of thought, and the third the realm of language. The *maᶜqūlāt* [pl. of *maᶜqūl*] are the mental counterparts we acquire from our encounters with the external world. For Alfārābī, the process of *concept acquisition* is natural and universal (common to all people and all languages) (ᶜ**Ibārah**, 27). The process of *naming,* however, is a process Alfārābī considers entirely conventional and dependent upon human consensus.

According to Alfārābī, the development of language is related to an epistemological process initiated by man's encounters with the "sensible material objects." In Alfārābī's terminology, the sensible material object is called "the thing that can be pointed to" [*al-mushār ilayh*]. For convenience sake, however, we will refer to it as the "this" or the "material object."

The first stage of comprehension [*al-idrāk bi-ˀl-ḥiss*][51] begins, according to Alfārābī's **Ḥurūf** (p. 72, par. 23),[52] with the individual material objects, which have certain properties (such as 'this thing is a man and it is white and it is tall'). Thus we form the *first intelligible* [*awwal maʿqūl*][53] (ibid., 64, par. 6), a concept acquired directly through sense perception.[54] During this stage, we acquire concepts such as 'man,' 'white,' and 'tall,' each of which depicts a single material object (ibid., 73, par. 23): "Each of these first intelligibles [*awwal al-maʿqūlāt*] represents [*yanṭawī fīh*] only one object. The result of this is that we [acquire only one concept] of 'man' of 'white' and of 'tall,' thus distinguishing the categories [*maqūlāt*][55] from one another."

This passage brings us to Alfārābī's description of the "categories" (ibid., 62, par. 4), where he states that the expression signifying each of these primary concepts (or first intelligibles) is called a "category" [*maqūlah*]. Some of these expressions answer the question 'what is the thing?' (for example, the term *man* indicates the essence of this and of that individual) and therefore belong in the *category of essence;* others (such as *tall* and *short*) are terms used to answer the question 'how are they?' [*kayfa* question] and therefore belong in the *category of quality;* and so on.

According to Aristotle, there are ten classes of "categories" or expressions that describe all the possible states of any given individual: its essence, its place, its quantity, its quality, etc. Each of these terms, Alfārābī insists, refers to one of the first intelligibles, and not to the external objects represented by these intelligibles. Language, then, in Alfārābī's view, describes the realm of intelligibles and not (directly) the external world.

Alfārābī usually refers to the first intelligibles developed through interaction with the external world as *maʿqūlāt uwal,* although he also uses the term *maʿqūl*^{u} *maḥsūs*^{in} (**Ḥurūf**, 64, par. 6), which literally means "the intelligible of a sensible object," i.e., the intelligible that comes about due to an encounter with a certain sensible object. We will refer to this stage, which ends with the acquisition of first order intelligibles,[56] as the "first stage."

During the second and third stages of Alfārābī's epistemological scheme, the external world is removed from the discussion and the process is confined to the dimensions of thought and language exclusively. The primary intelligibles acquired during the first stage become the *objects* from which the mind abstracts new intelligibles, which may be called "second intelligibles" [*maʿqūlāt thawānī*] (Ibid., 64, par. 7). During this stage, the mind abstracts the concept 'white,' for example, from the particular cases of 'white' with which it became familiar during the first stage. A similar process occurs with other concepts, such as 'tall' and 'man,' each of which is referred to as a *first order intelligible* (or first order concept) on the thought level and as a *category* on the language level.

Due to a certain faculty (lit. action) of the mind [*fiʿl khāṣṣ*], Alfārābī says (ibid., 74, par. 25), first order intelligibles become the objects for a new set of objects, entirely detached from the external world, which in some way describe the first order intelligibles and the relationships between them. For example, the statement 'man is a species that is predicated of many individuals' is a description of a first order intelligible. This description is itself an intelligible, but it is an intelligible detached from the external world and abstracted from first order intelligibles only. In short, it is *an intelligible of an intelligible* (or a concept of a concept) and as such it is a *second order intelligible* (or a second order concept) [*maʿqūlāt thawānī*]. As Alfārābī puts it in "**Risālah fī ʾl-ʿaql**":[57]

> When the actual intelligibles are acquired, they become among the existing things and should be considered as such.
>
> And since all existing things [*mawjūdāt*] may be intellected and become forms . . . then the intelligibles are actual intelligibles (which is the same as actual intellect) and can also be intellected.[58] . . . A certain [new] intelligible becomes the form of this actual intellect.

In this passage, Alfārābī calls the level of second order concepts a "second intellect."

In Alfārābī's view, the mind abstracts new concepts from the second order concepts, thus creating a third order level of concepts. In fact, the argument continues, the mind is capable of abstracting (and does abstract) from every given level of concepts a new level of concepts, one level higher than the previous. This process may be repeated ad infinitum (**Ḥurūf**, 65, par. 8) and "nothing is impossible or absurd about that," Alfārābī says in **ʿIbārah** (p. 45: 27).

This infinite chain of connectors is only one example of the "infinite chain of intelligibles" (or more precisely, the "chain of infinite levels of intelligibles") Alfārābī is trying to describe in **Ḥurūf**[59] and to which he refers, as we have seen, in **ʿIbārah**. According to him, this infinite chain of concepts is neither absurd nor can any argument be proposed to refute it [*la ḥujjah talḥaq*] (**Ḥurūf**, 65, par. 10.). Nor should it imply that this model requires the knowledge of infinite intelligibles of each category [ibid., 66] because, in Alfārābī's words: "Since all the elements of this infinite [chain] are of the same kind [*min nawʿ wāḥid*], then the state of one of them is the state of all the rest. . . . Therefore, there is no difference between the states the first order concepts have and those the second order concepts have" (ibid., 65, par. 9).

It should be noted that the states of first order concepts are, according to Alfārābī (ibid., 67, par. 7), concepts of the second order. And states of the second order concepts are third order concepts, etc. In the above quotation, then, Alfārābī is speaking of similarity, indeed *identity*, between second order concepts and what follows from them, i.e., every level of concepts except the first order concepts. This is significant for Alfārābī's theory of language, as we shall see.

Alfārābī distinguishes clearly between terms that refer only to terms (including themselves) and terms that are the names of first or second order intelligibles.[60] As will be discussed below, the similarity between the various levels of concepts is compared by Alfārābī (ibid., par. 9) with the grammatical term *rafᶜ* [putting (a word) in the nominative case], which applies to utterances of the first order (such as 'man' and 'white'), as well as to utterances of the second order (such as the expression *rafᶜ* itself). Since the term *rafᶜ* itself refers to words and not objects, then it must be what we refer to in modern terminology as a term of the *metalanguage* rather than of the object language. In general, the things to which terms of the metalanguage refer are always themselves "terms." In this sense, we may classify metalanguage terms as "second order terms," or "third order terms,"[61] etc., but *never* as "first order terms."

Now to Alfārābī's example. The example Alfārābī presents in order to illustrate the similarity between concepts (of the same object) of any order (if that order is greater than one), is the grammatical term *rafᶜ*, which we have just explained is of the type that may never be a first order term, according to Alfārābī. The grammatical act of 'putting (a word) in the nominative case' [*rafᶜ*] applies in the same way to the term '*Zayd*' (a first order term, since it refers to a sensible material object, 'man') and to a term such as *bayāḍ* [whiteness][62] (a term of the second order). Both are treated equally, as far as grammatical terminology is concerned. Thus in the sentence *Zaydᵘⁿ huwa insān* [Zayd is a man] the term '*Zayd*' is in the nominative, just as the term *bayāḍ* is in the nominative case in the sentence *al-bayāḍᵘ huwa lawn* [whiteness is a color].

Similarly, we may speak of the term *rafᶜ* itself and refer to it as a term that occupies a certain position in a sentence (such as '*al-rafᶜᵘ* is a grammatical term'), the subject of which is the term *al-rafᶜ*, which happens to be a term of the second order in the sense explained above. But by placing the term *al-rafᶜ* in the subject position, we simultaneously classify it, in accordance with the rules of the Arabic language, as being in the nominative case, which in Arabic will be called *rafᶜ al-rafᶜ*, i.e., the term *rafᶜ* itself will be treated like any other term occupying the subject position in a well-composed Arabic sentence.

Rafᶜ al-rafᶜ, therefore, makes as much sense as the phrase *rafᶜ al-bayāḍ*. In the phrase *rafᶜ al-rafᶜ* the object of the grammatical operation we call *rafᶜ* is a term that happens to be *al-rafᶜ*, and since *rafᶜ* is a second order term, then all the terms that refer to it as an object are one level higher. This means that the first *rafᶜ* in the above phrase is a third order term. Similarly we can speak of a fourth order term *rafᶜ* in the phrase *rafᶜ rafᶜ al-rafᶜ*. The first term in this phrase refers to a term (the second term in the phrase under consideration), which is a third order term, as we have seen.

This process can obviously be repeated ad infinitum, yet essentially there is no difference between the grammatical meaning of *rafᶜ*, whether it is in the second, third, or one millionth order. All refer to and describe the same grammatical act.

Illuminating as it is, however, this example should not and cannot be taken literally when the "chain of concepts"[63] is discussed. Whereas the expression *rafᶜ al-rafᶜ* makes sense, as we have seen, the expression 'man of man,' for example, makes no sense whatsoever. Nor can the above example illustrate the meaning of a phrase such as "genus of genus,' which while it makes perfect sense, should not be viewed as being modeled on the paradigm *rafᶜ al-rafᶜ*. Still, although it should be considered as no more than an analogy, the example of *rafᶜ* does help one grasp the idea Alfārābī is trying to advance concerning the states of intelligibles. What, then, is Alfārābī trying to say?

In order to answer this question let us begin with Alfārābī's example in **Ḥurūf** (p. 66, par. 10) regarding the concepts 'genus' and 'genus of genus.' Whereas the phrases *rafᶜ* and *rafᶜ al-rafᶜ* do mean the same thing, as we have seen, these concepts 'genus' and 'genus of genus' obviously do not refer to the same thing and are not identical in any way. It furthermore goes without saying that Alfārābī could not possibly have meant that these expressions refer to the same thing. The genus of 'man' for example, is 'animal,' whereas the 'genus of the genus of man' is 'nourished body.'

The latter expression ('nourished body') is of a higher order than the former ('animal'), just as *rafᶜ al-rafᶜ* is of a higher order than *rafᶜ*. However, in the case of 'genus' and 'genus of genus,' the similarity between the concepts and the concepts about these concepts (to which Alfārābī refers as *lawāḥiq* or *aḥwāl*) is *analytical* or *conceptual*. Once we know the concept 'man,' for example, every other concept related to it is conceptually included in it. Thus the analysis of 'man' will lead to the related concepts of 'animal,' 'rational,' 'nourished,' etc., all of which are concepts about the concept 'man.' This is probably what Alfārābī means by using the example of 'genus' and 'genus of genus' to demonstrate that knowledge of the former leads analytically to knowledge of the latter. As he puts it in **Ḥurūf** (p. 65, par. 9):

> Knowing one of these concepts, therefore, amounts to the knowledge [*maʿrifah*] of all of them, whether they are finite or not, just as the knowledge of the concept [*maʿnā*] 'man' . . . amounts to the knowledge of whatever may be called 'man' or is [conceptually] related to 'man,' whether these things are finite in number or infinite.

This brings us back full circle to Alfārābī's notion of "definition." What Alfārābī is in fact saying here is that the "definition" (the formula of the essence) of any concept is identical with the concept itself, a fact we express by saying, for example, 'man is a rational animal,' where the term *is* is a sign of *identity.*

This *vertical predication,* in which the essential predicates of a concept are mentioned in a certain order, is no more than explicitly rewriting everything already included in the concept under consideration, Alfārābī would argue.[64] Thus the concept 'man' analytically implies each of its genera: 'animal,' 'capable of moving itself,' 'nourished body,' 'body,' and anything else that can be added to this vertical order.

Given that, according to Alfārābī, there is a parallelism or even a correspondence between thought (concepts) and language (terms), the next step of our inquiry follows naturally. We must examine the ideas outlined above from the point of view of *language.*

The Concept of *Mithāl Awwal* in Alfārābī's System

In a sense, the Aristotelian division of 'what there is' into ten categories may be viewed as a distinction between the category of substance on the one hand and the rest of the categories (all of which may be considered as attributes of the individual material objects), on the other hand.

Every single one of these nonsubstance categories represents an attribute of the primary substance, and as such they are described by Aristotle as "things that are 'in' a subject but not 'said of' a subject."[65] To put this in other words, the material objects have or possess these attributes.

Alfārābī relies on this philosophical distinction in order to advance the following important linguistic distinction: In the case of the *category of substance,* the terms that express species and genera are (mostly) prototypes [*mithāl awwal*], which is to say, *they are terms from which no verbs are derived* [*lā taṣrīf lahā*], whereas the nonsubstantive categories are signified by both derivatives and prototypal names (**Ḥurūf**, 74, par. 26).

Since words, according to Alfārābī, signify intelligibles rather than external objects, we must speak of the domain of intelligibles, the realm of thought.

In the mind, the first order intelligibles mirror particular material objects: 'this man,' 'this white,' 'this tall,' etc. The first of these intelligibles signifies a primary substance ('man') and, therefore, the term that signifies it ought to be, in Alfārābī's view, a prototypal from which no verbs can be derived. The other two intelligibles ('white,' 'tall') represent qualities a subject, and therefore each of them ought to be signified by derivatives or by[66] prototypal names.

The key to understanding these statements is to clarify Alfārābī's use of the term *mithāl awwal.*

The term *mithāl awwal,* which has been rendered (following Zimmermann's suggestion)[67] as "prototype," has no counterpart among the Arab grammarians' terminology. We must therefore try to comprehend it from Alfārābī's own examples and from the sparse explanation he provides in several passages of **Ḥurūf** and one of **Iḥṣā**ʾ (p. 60).

In **Ḥurūf** (p. 74, par. 25), Alfārābī offers the example of *ḍarb* [beating] (classified by the grammarians as a *maṣdar* [verbal noun, infinitive]) as an example of *mithāl awwal* from which are derived all the related terms (such as *ḍārib* [the one who is beating], *yaḍrub* [he beats], *ḍarab* [he beat], *sa-yaḍrub* [he will beat], and *maḍrūb* [beaten]).

In paragraph 27 on page 75 of **Ḥurūf**, on the other hand, Alfārābī defines "the non-declinable utterances" in the following manner: "Non-declinable [*lā tuṣarraf*] utterances, are utterances from which no verbs [*kalim*] can be derived." And in paragraph 82 on page 111 of **Ḥurūf** (lines 15–16), Alfārābī creates the misleading impression that because the term *insān*, for example, is a *mithāl awwal* it is a nondeclinable term, i.e., no verb can be derived from it: "*Insan* ['man'], which is a prototype, in Arabic has neither a verbal noun nor can it be declined." In fact, it is a general feature of all languages, Alfārābī says (ibid.), that certain utterances are prototypal and "have neither verbal nouns [*maṣādir*] nor can they be declined." How can such statements be reconciled with Alfārābī's example of *ḍarb,* which is both a *mithāl awwal* and declinable?

In order to understand this point, I would like to advance the following guidelines based on Alfārābī's examples:

1. Every verbal noun is a *mithāl awwal,* but not every *mithāl awwal* is a verbal noun.
2. Despite misleading statements by Alfārābī to the contrary, *mithāl awwal* should not be identified with nondeclinable terms. (This conclusion follows easily from Point 1 above.)

3. The last quotation from **Ḥurūf** above should be understood as follows: *insān is a mithāl awwal* that happens to be a nondeclinable term, rather than a *mithāl awwal* and *therefore* a nondeclinable term.

Mithāl awwal in Alfārābī's system is, I believe, a technical term describing the intelligibles resulting from the second stage in his epistemological system. It is associated with the second order intelligibles, such as 'man' [*insān*], 'tallness' [*ṭūl*], 'whiteness' [*bayāḍ*], 'courage' [*shajāʿah*], and 'beating' [*ḍarb*].

All these intelligibles are abstracted by a special faculty of the mind from the first level intelligibles. Thus, from the term *abyaḍ* [white] we get *bayāḍ* [whiteness], which as Alfārābī explains, "signifies the same intelligible [signified by *abyaḍ*], but [unlike *abyaḍ*] this intelligible is abstracted from any subject. Similarly with the intelligibles 'courage' [*shajāʿah*] and 'articulation' [*faṣāḥah*]" (**Fuṣūl**, 271).

Unlike *abyaḍ*, which signifies both an intelligible and a subject, *bayāḍ* (one level higher than *abyaḍ*) signifies only the idea of 'whiteness.' Similarly with the notions of 'blackness,' 'courage,' 'tallness,' etc., all of which are second order intelligibles abstracted [*muntazaʿah*] (**Ḥurūf**, 77, par. 31) from the first order intelligibles.

According to Alfārābī, however, this epistemological priority of, for example, *abyaḍ* over *bayāḍ* does not imply a logical or a linguistic priority. Once again, however, we face an extremely difficult task in reconstructing fragments of Alfārābī's arguments.[68] Let us first present some of Alfārābī's basic terminology relevant to this issue. The following references are from **Ḥurūf** (p. 73, par. 24):

a. The notions [*maʿānī*] 'whiteness,' 'tallness,' 'sitting up,' 'standing up,' etc. . . . are all abstracted [*tuntazaʿ*] or separated [*yufrad*] by the mind.
b. This act of abstraction is a mental act, completely separated from the sense perception and belonging to the mind alone [*wa-hādhā shayʾ yakhuṣṣ al-ʿaql wa-yanfarid bih dūn al-ḥiss*].
c. In this paragraph, Alfārābī uses the Arabic term *asbaq ilā ʾl-maʿrifah* to describe the priority of these intelligibles over the things from which they are abstracted. The use of the term *maʿrifah* [knowledge] implies that Alfārābī is speaking of a priority from an epistemological point of view, but every other statement by Alfārābī indicates that he really means the *logical priority*[69] (rather than the epistemological or chronological priority) of these abstract intelligibles, from which they are

seemingly derived. This will become clear when we present Alfārābī's argument in support of this logical priority (see below).

d. The logical priority of the second order over the first order intelligibles paves the way for Alfārābī's position regarding the utterances that signify these intelligibles. According to him, the logical priority of the second order intelligibles over the first order intelligibles implies a priority of the *second order utterances* (that signify them) over first order utterances: "the utterances that signify the [second order intelligibles] are prior [*aqdam*][70] because they are separated from the particular material objects [*mushār ilayh*] and therefore are simpler [*absaṭ*] and not composed with other things" [lines 12–14].
e. The utterances that signify first order intelligibles signify something else beyond the intelligible itself: they signify the concrete or the particular things.[71] As such, these utterances are posterior to [*muta'akhirrah*] and derived from [*ma'khūdhah*] the former, i.e., from the second order utterances.

Now we turn to examine the argument Alfārābī presents in support of his claim that second order intelligibles are logically prior to first order intelligibles. I will describe this argument simply in three different stages.

1. Things in the external world are not separated from their qualities (**Ḥurūf**, 76, par. 29) nor can we conceive of a quality like 'white' without implicitly referring to a subject that *has* this quality.
2. One cannot speak or know that things are composed of two (or more) things without assuming that each of these things exist in separation [*'alā ḥiyālih*] (ibid., 73, par. 25).[72] Only after the things become known separately, are they recomposed by the mind to reflect the structure of things as they are in the external world.
3. The intelligible *abyaḍ*, for example, which is a first order intelligible, cannot be known without its subject (ibid., 75, par. 26). The intelligible *abyaḍ*, like any first order intelligible, implies a subject that in fact is implicitly or potentially [*bi-'l-quwwah*] mentioned by the very shape of the first order term that signifies it, namely *abyaḍ*.

   But in order to know that this or that quality is different from the subject to which they are attached, we must assume their separate or abstract existence, that is, an existence without a particular subject involved; this existence can only be in the mind.

4. The conclusion from the previous three steps of the argument is the following: Since the source of our knowledge of things in their noncomposite state, that is, in separation from each other, is neither the external world nor the first order intelligibles (ibid., 76, par. 29), then it must be the second order intelligibles, which signify things in their simple noncomposite form. This argument may be summarized as follows: The simpler must exist before the compound and must be known before it, otherwise there is no way of knowing that there are different things from which the compound is composed. Thus, logically speaking, the intelligibles 'whiteness' and 'stone,' for example, must be known to us in order that we be able to talk about a 'white stone.'

In this sense, there is a priority of the second order over the first order intelligibles. This priority is a *logical* one in the sense explained above.

If so, then the argument appears to be a circular one,[73] for if the second order intelligibles are abstracted from first order intelligibles, it seems obvious that the former are *posterior not prior* to the latter. How can Alfārābī, then, claim that the second order intelligibles are the source from which the first order intelligibles are derived?

It is true, Alfārābī would argue, that at a certain stage of life (perhaps childhood) we acquire knowledge of particular things known, for example, as 'white things.' From this we develop the concept of 'whiteness,' which is not associated with any particular 'white thing' we ever saw. From that stage on, we can be isolated in the darkest possible room and still be able to think of a 'white book' and a 'white horse' and a 'white man,' none of which we ever saw before. In this case we will be *deriving* from the concept of 'whiteness' particular cases of 'white things' without necessarily having seen these particular things that we compose in our minds.

How can we have composed these things without having them separated in our minds? We have never seen a 'green horse,' yet we can think of it. And we certainly could not have reached this composition without having the concepts of 'being a horse' and of 'green' in separation. Each of these concepts were acquired by encountering different particular horses and different particular spots of green things.

Equipped with the principle that terms are produced [*uḥdithat*] after the things have been intellected and that the terms refer to intelligibles rather than to things (**Ḥurūf**, 75, par. 25), a principle he attributes to the "ancients," Alfārābī now moves to a description of the linguistic evolution in light of the above-described distinction between first and second order intelligibles.

According to Alfārābī, the linguistic entities that signify second order intelligibles are prior to those entities that signify first order intelligibles (**Ḥurūf**, 73, par. 24). First order terms, in other words, are posterior and derived [*muta'akhkhirah, ma'khūdhah*] (ibid.) from second order terms. In this sense, second order terms are a *mithāl awwal*, i.e., a source from which all first order terms are derived.[74]

This is, in my view, the meaning of *mithāl awwal* in Alfārābī's system: *any term that signifies a second order intelligible is a mithāl awwal* [prototype]. It may be either a declinable term such as *ḍarb* [beating] (which the Arab grammarians refer to as *ism fiʿl* [verbal noun]) or a nondeclinable term such as *insān*, from which no verb can be derived.

There are two major differences between Alfārābī's *mithāl awwal* and the grammarians' *maṣdar:*

a. Alfārābī's use of *mithāl awwal* is broader than the grammarians' use of *maṣdar.* According to Alfārābī's philosophy, all first intelligibles (and therefore all first order terms), and not just verbs, are derived from second order intelligibles. Thus 'black' (both as a concept and as a term), for example, is derived from 'blackness,' just as 'beats' is derived from 'beating.' For the grammarians, however, the issue is confined to the relationships between the verbs and the *maṣādir.*
b. The second difference has to do with the suffix . . . *iyyah*, which indicates abstraction. This will become clearer below when we discuss the abstract nouns in Arabic, a discussion to be presented in the final section of this chapter.

The view, according to which the *maṣādir,* as a subclass of *mithāl awwal*, are prior to the verbs (and to the participles) can be seen as a philosophical defense of the Baṣrian School of grammar. According to the Baṣrian grammarians, the *maṣdar* is the origin from which verbs are derived, rather than the other way around, as the Kūfian School maintained.[75]

This interpretation of Alfārābī's theory of language explains Alfārābī's statement (**Ḥurūf**, 74, par. 26), according to which nonsubstantive categories are signified by either derivatives or by prototypal names. The derivative *abyaḍ,* for example, signifies the same idea that the term *bayaḍ* (which is a prototype) signifies. The only difference is that the derivative signifies an additional thing, namely a subject that has this quality. This difference between a prototype and a derivative, Alfārābī says (**Fuṣūl**, 271), is the reason "many of the ancients"[76] considered the derivatives among the verbs, with this being particularly true of the participles derived from actions and motions (such as *mashī* [the noun 'walking'] from which the participle *māshī* is derived) and with which the element of time is usually associated [*injarr al-zamān maʿah fī ʾl-dhihn*] (ibid.).

There is a further observation to be made at this point. First order substantive intelligibles (i.e., intelligibles that signify primary substances in the mind) are signified by the same terms that signify the second order intelligibles. This is the reason that Alfārābī (**Ḥurūf**, 75, par. 27) offers the following examples for first order and second order intelligibles: the first order intelligibles include 'man' and 'white'; the second order intelligibles include 'man' and 'whiteness.'

The inclusion of 'man' in both categories is no accident, rather there is a philosophical basis for this apparent discrepancy.

Already in the first stage of the process we referred to as concept acquisition, the term *man* as a primary substance is conceived in separation from its qualities. According to the Aristotelians, first substances (as discussed in chapter 1) have an independent existence and do not need other things for their existence, whereas the nonsubstantive categories are all related to the primary substances in one way or another and, without the primary substances, have no existence.

This philosophical doctrine is mirrored in the language level in the following manner: nonsubstantive categories are known to the mind in a state of nonseparation from the primary substances of which they are attributes. This is the reason *abyaḍ, ṭawīl*, etc., by their very shapes imply subjects.[77]

However, since we cannot know that things are composed of other things unless we assume they exist in a state of separation, and since this state of separation does not exist in the external world, we must conclude that this separation takes place in the mind, which abstracts qualities from their subject, thus forming a new level of intelligibles abstracted from any sensible thing, i.e., from subjects to which they supposedly owe their existence. Thus the intelligible *bayāḍ* [whiteness] is signified by the term *bayāḍ* which does not imply a subject.

In the case of primary substances, Alfārābī says, the mind conceives them in their abstracted form, i.e., without their qualities. The mind, in other words, conceives the essence of the primary substances. Like the names given to the attributes, the names given to primary substances entail a subject. The subject in the latter case, however, is identical with the intelligible itself that the term is supposed to signify. Thus the term *insān*, for example, implies a subject (this or that individual human being) identical with the intelligible this term signifies. *Insān*, therefore, is similar to both *abyaḍ* and *bayāḍ*. Like *abyaḍ*, the term *insān* is associated with a subject, and like *bayāḍ* it is abstracted from everything that is not its essence. This is most probably what Alfārābī means in the obscure passage in paragraph 33 of **Ḥurūf** (p. 78: 21–23)

> This is the case of every [expression] that defines the essence of primary substances.[78] Every [expression of this sort] is composed of two components: one is that represented by *bayāḍ* and that in which the *bayāḍ* subsists. The totality of [these components] is the *abyaḍ;* an example of that is 'man.'

Both *bayāḍ* and *insān* are considered by Alfārābī as *mithāl awwal.* However, *insān* and any term signifying a species of primary substance signifies not only the meaning of the term, but also a subject identical with the meaning of that term. This is a general rule that holds in most cases, Alfārābī maintains (ibid., 74, par. 26): "Species and the genera of the category that signifies the primary substance are prototypal names, which in most cases [*aktharuhā*] are non-declinable."[79]

Not only the term *man,* which represents the species, but also its genus (or rather, its immediate genus) *animal* is a nondeclinable prototype term. Similarly with *horse, donkey, fish,* etc., which represent different species and are indeed nondeclinable terms, i.e., terms from which no verb can be derived.

In some cases, Alfārābī says (ibid.), the form [*shakl*] of a term is that of a derivative, but the meaning is not derivative (namely, it is a prototype that signifies a species or a genus of a primary substance). An example of this is the term *ḥayy* [alive], which looks like a derivative but in fact, Alfārābī argues, has the meaning of *ḥayawān* [animal]. In **ʿIbārah** (pp. 34–35), Alfārābī further elaborates on this point:

> Names of secondary substances[80] are clearly not to be verbalized at all, since they are not used derivatively, nor [do they] signify any subject whatever. Someone may ask about the word *ḥayy* [alive], a noun used to signify the same as *ḥayawān* [animal], a secondary substance, despite being a derived noun. Moreover, *yaḥyā* [lives] [signifies the same even though it] is a verb. How has 'animal' come to be the substance of something named by a derived noun? And how has it come to be signified by a verb? If this is so, then there is a substance that has a subject, since a derived noun always signifies a subject. Similarly if *yaḥyā* is a verb, it too signi-

fies a subject: it always signifies being predicated of something else. The answer is that *ḥayy* is of a derivative shape, and that this derivative shape may be shared by notions with a derived name and such with an underived name.[81]

We must understand these terms in their nonderivative meaning in some cases and in their derivative meaning in other cases, depending on the context, Alfārābī seems to suggest. Elsewhere (**Ḥurūf**, 71, par. 20) Alfārābī explains that the opposite is also true: the shape of certain terms is prototypal and yet their meaning is derivative, such as when we say 'man is *karam*.' The shape of the term *karam* ['nobility'] is prototypal [*shakluh shakl mithāl awwal*], but the meaning intended in this sentence is not that 'man is nobility' but rather that 'man is *karīm*' (i.e., man is generous; *karīm* is a derivative of the prototype *karam*).[82]

There is one final point to be made in this regard. Whereas terms indicating species and genera are usually prototypal and undeclinable, the terms signifying the essential differences [*fuṣūl muqawwimah*] (i.e., the second element of the formula that expresses the essence, the *ḥadd*) are all signified by derivative nouns, Alfārābī says (**Ḥurūf**, 74, par. 26).

This may be philosophically justified on the grounds that every essential difference refers to a subject, which is not necessarily identical with the idea it represents. Thus 'rational,' which is the essential difference of 'man,' indicates that something is rational. Being a 'rational animal' is not implied by the term *rational*, only 'something rational' is implied by it,[83] just as the term *abyaḍ* implies that some thing is 'white,' but we do not know what. It is only in combination with a genus such as 'animal' that the term *rational* signifies some specific thing ('man' in this case) and not merely some thing.

There are also terms that are verbal nouns [*maṣādir*] in form and yet in a certain context they carry the meaning of the derivative *mafʿūl*. The verbal noun *khalq* [creation], for example, means 'created' in a sentence such as *khalq allāh* [God's creation], Alfārābī argues.[84]

There still remains one further issue related to Alfārābī's linguistic philosophy to be discussed in this work. This is the issue of the abstract nouns, which has a direct link to issues dealt with earlier in this chapter. Alfārābī's logical and ontological interest in the term *huwa* [is] and the related abstract noun *huwiyyah* [being] led him to a general linguistic analysis of the process through which abstract nouns ending in *-iyyah* are formed. This topic will be dealt with in the final section of this chapter.[85]

Abstract Nouns of the Form '. . . *iyyah*'

W. Wright describes the formation of these nouns: "The feminine of the relative adjective serves in Arabic as a noun to denote the abstract idea of the thing, as distinguished from the concrete thing itself, e.g., *ilāhiyyah* [divine nature], *insāniyyah* [humanity]."[86]

"Relative adjectives" [*al-asmāʾ al-mansūbah* or *al-nisbah*] are formed by adding the termination *-iyy* to the words from which they are derived and denote the fact that a person or thing belongs with or is connected there (in respect to origin, family, birth, sect, trade, etc.).[87]

According to Wright, therefore, Arabic abstract nouns of the form *-iyyah* are morphologically derived from relative adjectives. He does not explain, however, the significance, if any, of this derivation on the semantical status of these forms.

Others believe that the form *-iyyah* in Arabic "was copied from Syriac, which in turn adopted it from the Greek *-iā*, the common suffix denoting an abstraction."[88]

Still others believe that the inclination of the Arabs to form abstract nouns of the form *-iyyah* is likely to have been influenced by Pahlawi and Persian.[89] The holder of this opinion bases his assumption on the observation that there are far more abstractions in the writings of philosophers of Persian origin than in those of philosophers of Arabic origin. He also observes that in Persian the mere addition of the suffix *-i* makes a perfectly good abstraction out of almost any word in the language. This last observation is supported by Alfārābī, who in **Ḥurūf** (p. 111, par. 82) illustrates this linguistic feature of the Persian language by means of the terms *hast* [to be] and *mardam* [man], each of which becomes an abstract noun through the simple addition of the Persian suffix *-i*.

Alfārābī's examples in this respect, however, are meant only as an analogy, rather than a claim that the Arabic language modeled itself in this respect on the Persian language or on any other language for that matter. Nor does Alfārābī suggest anywhere in his writings that the suffix *-iyyah*, used in Arabic for the formation of abstract nouns, is borrowed by the translators or the philosophers. There was nothing to prevent him from saying this, had he thought it was the case. And just as he did in the case of the copula, he might have argued in this case, too, that the ending *-iyyah* in the Arabic language was borrowed from or modeled on Persian or Greek.

The prephilosophic Arabic included a few terms with the suffix *-iyyah*. Thus, we find the following terms in the *Qurʾān:*

1. *jāhiliyyah,* in: *Āl-ʿimrān* (154), *Al-māʾidah* (59), *Al-aḥzāb* (33), and *Al-fatḥ* (26);
2. *zabāniyyah,* in: *Al-ʿalaq* (18);
3. *rahbāniyyah,* in: *Al-ḥadīd* (26).

There is no reason, therefore, to believe that the translators of Greek philosophy into Arabic had to borrow the suffix *-iyyah* from some other language. It is true that this suffix was applied, during the translation period and thereafter, to many more terms (such as to *ays* thus creating *aysiyyah* [being], to *kam* thus creating *kamiyyah* [quantity], to *huwa* thus creating *huwiyyah* [being], to *inna* thus creating *inniyyah* [nature (of a thing)], etc. But the translators and subsequently the Arab philosophers had no need to go beyond the Arabic language in order to find this suffix with which to produce abstract nouns. All they did was broaden the scope of its application. The only new element introduced was the idea that this suffix might be applied to terms that were not nouns, such as *huwa* (a pronoun), *kayfa* and *mā* (question particles) and even to semiverbs such as *inna* and *ays*. This linguistic neologism was discussed by Alfārābī and two centuries later by Averroes in his *Tafsīr mā baʿd al-ṭabīʿah* [Commentary on Aristotle's metaphysics]. Both philosophers discussed this issue in relation to the term *huwiyyah,* derived from the pronoun *huwa* in order to render the Greek *ousia* [being].

Alfārābī (**Ḥurūf**, 112, par. 83) states that *-iyyah* is the form of the *maṣdar* of certain nouns that are both nondeclinable and prototypal [*fa-inna hādhā ʾl-shakl fī ʾl-ʿarabiyyah huwa shakl maṣdr kull ism kan mithāl awwal wa-lam yakun lah taṣrīf*], such as *insāniyyah* [humanity], which is the abstract noun of the nondeclinable prototype *insān*. This is a somewhat surprising statement, since *maṣdar,* as we have come to know it thus far, generally refers to the "infinitive" or "verbal noun," and how can a noun such as *insāniyyah* be an infinitive? However, given that another (more essential) meaning of the term *maṣdar* is "source," the statement begins to make sense.

In Alfārābī's view, although we arrive at the abstract concepts (which are second order concepts) during a (chronologically) later stage in the language acquisition process, these forms are nevertheless *ontologically prior* to the first order concepts. It is in this sense, then, that the form *insāniyyah* can be considered a "source" [*maṣdar*] for the term *insān,* just as the second order concept *ṭūl* is ontologically prior, in Alfārābī's view, to the particular *ṭawīl,* although we first become acquainted with the latter and later abstract to the former.

Therefore, Alfārābī can state (as he does in **Ḥurūf**) that when the suffix *-iyyah* is added to *substantive nouns* (both nondeclinable and prototypal) it produces a *maṣdar.* The examples given by Alfārābī to illustrate this point are: *insān* [man] from which *insāniyyah* [humanity] is derived; *ḥimār* [donkey] from which *ḥimāriyyah* [donkeyness] is derived; and *rajul* [man] from which *rujūliyyah* [manhood] is derived. Alfārābī seems to take the liberty of identifying "abstract nouns" with *maṣādir* because this serves his purpose. Having once been coined, the "abstract nouns," as second order terms that correspond to second order concepts, become "sources" [*maṣādir*] from which every thing else (linguistically speaking) is derived.

This is, incidentally, the second difference mentioned in the previous section of this chapter between a *mithāl awwal* and a *maṣdar.* Certain *maṣādir* are therefore derived from the *mithāl awwal* when this *mithāl awwal* is of the nondeclinable type. This is a pattern according to which, Alfārābī explains (ibid., 112, par. 83), the term *huwiyyah* [being] was created, despite the fact that this pattern was originally developed to apply only to nondeclinable prototypal nouns, i.e., to substantive nouns.

Averroes, as mentioned above, also addresses this question in his *Tafsīr mā baᶜd al-ṭabīᶜah* (vol. 2, p. 557). In essence, he repeats Alfārābī's explanation that *huwiyyah* was derived from the pronoun *huwa* following the pattern of deriving (abstract) nouns from nouns. It is unusual for the Arabic language to derive a noun from a pronoun and Averroes explains that it was done in order to replace the term *mawjūd*, which was used (mainly in the *Posterior Analytics*) by the translators.[90]

It is clear that Averroes, like Alfārābī before him, speaks of this pattern of derivation as a natural phenomenon in the Arabic language. Neither of them suggests that it is modeled on other languages.

Notes to Chapter 6

1. Sībaweih's definition of the verb is formulated in his *Al-kitāb* (vol. 1, p. 12). Arab grammarians (especially of the Baṣrian School) defend this division of the verb into two temporal forms based on the physical notion of time. See, for example, Zajjājī in his *Al-īḍāḥ fī ᶜilal al-naḥw* [Clarifications concerning the causes in syntax] (ed. Māzin Mubārak [Cairo: Maktabat dār al-ᶜurūbah, 1959] pp. 86–87); or Ibn Fāris in his *Al-sāḥibī fī fiqh al-lughah* [Semantic studies] (ed. Muṣṭafa ʾl-shuwaymī [Beirūt: Muʾassasat badrān, 1963] pp. 85–86). Both of these grammarians are contemporaries of Alfārābī. "Al-Zajjājī," is a nickname given to Abū ʾl-Qāsim Ibn Isḥāq, because he was a follower and defender of the views of another grammarian of that period, al-Zajjāj (d. 923).

In Sībaweih's terminology, the term *muḍāriᶜ*, designating the imperfect tense, means "resembling" (i.e., resembling the noun), since the verbal forms of the imperfect tense have virtually the same endings as the nouns (Versteegh, op. cit., p. 78). This resemblance is described in Sībaweih's *Al-kitāb* (vol. 1, p. 14).

2. Ackrill, ibid. Ackrill, however, was wrong in citing *Physics* IV, chapter 2 as the source of this definition.

3. Al-Zajjājī, op. cit., p. 87.

4. Kneale and Kneale, op. cit., p. 45.

5. To paraphrase a statement on a related topic by Charles H. Kahn in his article "On the Theory of the Verb 'To Be,' " in Milton K. Munitz, ed., *Logic and Ontology* (New York: New York University Press, 1973), p. 12.

6. In Greek Dion *peripatei* [Dion walks] is considered as equivalent to Dion *esti peripaton* [Dion is walking]. See Versteegh, op. cit., p. 73.

7. Aristotle, *De Interpretatione*, chapter 10 (19^b 11–12).

8. To paraphrase Kahn, op. cit., pp. 1–2.

9. The Arab grammarians call the "verb" *fiʿl*.

10. Elsewhere Alfārābī uses the term *adawāt* [lit., instruments] to describe all words that have no signification of their own. *Adawāt* is a term used by the Kūfian School of grammar, whereas *ḥurūf al-maʿānī* (or *allatī jāʾat li-maʿānī*) is the term used by the Baṣrian School. The latter represents an interpretation of Sībaweih's controversial phrase *ḥarf jāʾa li-maʿnā laysa bi-ʾsm wa-lā fiʿil* [roughly, a particle that provides a meaning [within a sentence] but is neither a noun nor a verb], referring to the particles, his third category of the parts of speech.

Thus, the Baṣrian al-Zajjājī, op. cit., p. 54: "The definition of the particles which the grammarians seek is the following: a particle is [that part of speech] which signifies meaning in something else [*fī ghayrih*], such as 'from' [*min*], 'to' [*ilā*] and 'then' [*thumma*] and similar things." See also Ibn Fāris, op. cit., p. 86.

Essentially, both these terms — *ḥurūf* and *adawāt* — refer to a part of speech that is neither a verb nor a noun. There are some differences in the analysis of this part of speech by the two schools of grammar, but they should not concern us here, particularly since Alfārābī is using the two terms interchangeably.

11. Alfārābī, **Al-thamarah al-marḍiyyah** [*Alfārābī's philosophische Abhandlungen*], ed. Friedrich Dieterici (Leiden: E. J. Brill, 1890). [Henceforth: **Thamarah**]

12. This sentence, as it stands in the text, is very difficult to understand, although Alfārābī's intention is clear. I have assumed that if we insert the word *yumkin* after the term *maʿnā* the meaning of the sentence will become much clearer.

13. These two terms are synonymous for Alfārābī, or at least they play the same role in his theory of predication, as we shall see later in this chapter.

14. I.e., it is not a property of a thing. Alfārābī here presents the relationship between a thing and what follows from it as a causal relationship, saying that 'A' cannot follow from 'B' unless 'B' exists.

15. This distinction between *dhātī* and *dārūrī* is another form of Alfārābī's distinction between the different meanings of the term *bi-dhātih*, presented in chapter 3. This is probably what Alfārābī means when he says in **Burhān** (p. 25) that not every necessary is essential (but, every essential is necessary).

16. I.e., after the first purpose of using the *hal* particle has been achieved, namely, after we acquire knowledge that the statement under consideration is true, we proceed to use the particle *hal* again in order to know about the cause.

17. Rather than *yantaẓim*, as it reads in the text.

18. In this passage, Alfārābī speaks about mathematics in general, but I think geometry is what he has in mind in this case.

19. Other than the term *yūjad* (and its derivatives, such as *mawjūd*), Alfārābī also considers the verb *kāna* and what are known in Arabic as its sisters to be "existential verbs" (**Fuṣūl**, 272; **Ḥurūf**, 113, par. 83).

20. Verbs are never subjects; they can only be predicates. This feature of the verb is mentioned by philosophers as well as Arab grammarians as one way of defining the difference between a noun and a verb. Cf. 1) Aristotle, *De Interpretatione*, 16ª19 – 16ᵇ8; 2) Ibn al-Sarrāj, *al-Muwjaz fī ʾl-naḥw*, ed. al-Shuwaymī/Damirjī (Beirūt: Muʾassasat badrān li-l-ṭibāʿah wa-ʾl-nashr, 1965), p. 4; 3) Fakhr al-Dīn al-Rāzī, *Mafātīḥ al-ghayb* (Cairo: Boulaq, 1872), vol. I: 25; 4) Alfārābī: **Fuṣūl**, p. 272.

21. Adjectives, in the grammarians' sense, are also included under the designation "noun." According to the Arab grammarians, adjectives do not constitute a separate part of speech. They are, rather, a subclass of the noun. This was made clear already by Sībaweih, who divided speech into three major parts: *ism*, *fiʿl*, and *ḥarf jāʾa li-maʿnā*.

22. Pronouns are considered among the subclass Alfārābī calls *khawālif*, which he defines as follows: "Any pronominal suffix [*ḥarf muʿjam*] or any utterance that signifies a name not explicitly stated . . . " (**Alfāẓ**, 44).

It is worth mentioning that in his classification of particles in **Alfāẓ**, Alfārābī does not mention the existential verbs or the pronouns among the *rawābiṭ* [lit., connectors]. This should be taken as an indication that in this classification Alfārābī is speaking of *inter*sentence connectors, rather than *intra*sentence connectors.

23. This is the most frequently used pronoun in this context. Indeed, it is the only one I have encountered, but I see no reason for not considering other (third-person) pronouns as suitable *intrasentence connectors*.

24. According to Ackrill in *Aristotle's Categories and De Interpretatione*, p. 39, literally, "the now time."

25. Sībaweih, *Al-kitāb*, I: 12.

26. See Versteegh, op. cit., pp. 77–78.

27. *Imtāʿ*, p. 122.

28. Madhī Makhzūmī, *Madrasat al-kūfah wa-manhajuhā fī dirāsat al-lughah wa-ʾl-naḥw* (Baghdād: Maṭbaʿat dār al-maʿrifah, 1955), p. 279.

29. Recorded by the editor of Zajjājī's *Īḍāḥ* p. 86.

30. The *nomen agentis* [active participle] and *nomina patientis* [passive participle] "are *verbal adjectives*, i.e., adjectives derived from verbs, and nearly correspond in nature and signification to what in English are called *participles*." (Wright, *A Grammar of the Arabic Language*, part second, Sec. 230, p. 131).

31. This is probably why Alfārābī refers to them as "derivative nouns" [*asmāʾ mushtaqqah*]. Remember that the grammarians, as well as Alfārābī, consider adjectives a subclass of nouns, rather than an independent part of speech.

32. A strange combination of words. The meaning, however, is clear.

33. There is a certain resemblance between Alfārābī's ideas in this regard and those of contemporary linguist Noam Chomsky, originator of the theory of "generational transformational grammar." In the passages cited, Alfārābī is clearly differentiating between an implicit and an explicit level of language, which is to say, between a *deep* structure and a *surface* structure. However, there is no mention in Alfārābī of "transformations" to be made in moving from the deep to the surface level.

34. The term *mawjūd* in its copulative meaning appears mostly in the translation of Aristotle's *Prior Analytics*, where the theory of the syllogism is put forth.

35. This word order, according to which an existential verb occurs in the third position, is true of Greek sentences but, as Alfārābī himself points out (ʿ**Ibārah**, 105), is not appropriate in Arabic.

36. By this Aristotle probably wishes to indicate that the verb *runs*, for example, does signify something (i.e., running), but *not* that that thing is taking place; only when added to a subject name (or a pronoun that signifies a name) is the *assertive* (and the copulative) role of the verb exhibited.

This amounts to saying that, according to Aristotle, a verb becomes an *actual* verb only in a sentence, viz., when it performs its predicative role; otherwise it is only *potentially* a verb.

See Ackrill's analysis in Aristotle, *Categories and De Interpretatione*, p. 121–122.

37. These are the words of Helmut Gätje, who reached this conclusion in his article, "Die Gliederung der sprachlichen Zeichen nach al-Fārābī," *Der Islam*, 47 (1971):9.

38. The role of a term in a sentence is of considerable importance for Aristotle's classification of the parts of speech. Verbs, for example, can only be predicates (*De Interpretatione* $16^{b}8$). It seems also that Aristotle was not far from stating the converse: that every predicate is a verb. Thus in *De Interpretatione* $16^{a}14$ he uses the term *white* as an example of a verb.

Greek grammarians, too, referred to verbs as names in general, because every significant word for them was considered a noun. For further details on this issue, consult Zimmermann, op. cit., p. 101, n. 5.

39. See Zimmermann's criticism of Alfārābī's view on this issue (op. cit., p. 38, n. 4 and 6).

40. Perhaps Alfārābī means a "noun" in the broad sense of the word, as explained earlier in this section.

41. In his classification of the particles, Alfārābī considers the pronouns among the *khawālif* (**Alfāẓ**, 44). The term *adāt* is apparently the Kūfian term corresponding to the Baṣrian term *al-ḥurūf allatī jāʾat li-maʿnā* [particles that provide meaning (within the context of a sentence)]. Alfārābī seems to be using these terms interchangeably.

42. See below concerning the meaning of this term in Alfārābī's writings.

43. By "original meaning" of a term, I mean "the meaning originally assigned to a term."

44. Alfārābī, "**Kitāb al-qiyās**" ["Prior Analytics"] in *Al-manṭiq ʿind Alfārābī*, vol. 2, ed. Rafīq al-ʿAjam (Beirūt: Dār al-mashriq, 1986). [Henceforth: **Qiyās**]

45. More precisely, Alfārābī presents these examples in order to exemplify one of the meanings of the *hal* particle. This example appears in the text as follows: 'is every man an animal?' [*hal kull insān mawjūd ḥayawān?*].

46. Guenther Patzig, *Aristotle's Theory of The Syllogism* (Dordrecht-Holland: Reidel Publishing Company, 1968), pp. 9–15. See also page 58, where Patzig mentions the term, "Be in . . . as in a whole."

The Arab translators of these Aristotelian works usually use the term *mawjūd* and occasionally the term *maqūl ʿalā* ['predicated of' or 'said of'] in rendering these technical Aristotelian phrases into Arabic.

47. Ibid., p. 11.

48. Ibid.

49. Ibid.

50. See my reference to the sentence, *dhālika 'l-muqbil huwa Zayd* (chapter 1, n. 7).

51. In the text: "Yudrak bi-'l-ḥiss," i.e., is comprehended by means of or, better, through sensation.

52. See also **Mūsīqā**, pp. 92 ff.

53. See Alfārābī's "Risālah fī-'l-ʿaql" in *Thamarah*, pp. 39–48. In this work Alfārābī refers to the first intelligibles as *maʿqūlāt bi-'l-fiʿl* [actual intelligibles], which he describes as forms [*ṣuwar*] detached from their matter [*mawād*]. He also describes the faculty of the mind that abstracts things from matter as the *actual intellect* [*al-ʿaql bi-'l-fiʿl*] and later in the same work (p. 45) he identifies it with the *acquired intellect* [*al-ʿaql al-mustafād*].

54. In **Ḥurūf** (p. 64, par. 6), Alfārābī says it is not clear whether there are first order concepts that are acquired through nonsensible things [*ḥāṣilah lā ʿan maḥsūsāt*]. His use of the term *mundhu awwal al-amr* in this context, however, is unclear. By it he could mean "at this stage of his theory" or "at the initial stages of man's development and encounter with objects," i.e., childhood.

55. In **Ḥurūf** (p. 63–64, par. 6) Alfārābī defines the Arabic term *maqūl* [lit. pronounced or said] as follows: "every utterance whether it signifies some thing or not." This definition is meant, I believe, to distinguish this term from the technical term *maqūlah*, which is the feminine form of the former term. The latter term is used as a technical term to mean "said of" or "predicated of" as well as "category."

56. The terms *first (second, . . .) order intelligible* or *first (second, . . .) order concept* are more appropriate than the exact translation "first (second, etc.) intelligible" when referring to these items as a group.

57. In **Thamarah**, p. 44.

58. Alfārābī puts it in a negative way that is very difficult to translate.

59. And to some extent also in "**Risālah fī 'l-ʿaql**."

60. These terms (*first [second, . . .] order intelligibles*) have traditionally been translated as "first (second, . . .) intentions" and Avicenna, rather than Alfārābī, is often credited as their originator. Kwame Gyekye is right in stating that "there is much in Alfārābī's writings, both of philosophy and terminology, to justify the view of his having anticipated Avicenna." Gyekye analyzed the source of this confusion rather well, despite the handicap of then-unavailable evidence from **Ḥurūf**, which was published shortly after Gyekye published his paper. Kwame Gyekye, "The Terms 'Prima Intentio' and 'Secunda Intentio' in Arabic Logic," *Speculum*, vol. 46, no. 1 (1971), p. 37.

61. We have explained the terms *first order intelligibles, second order intelligibles, . . .* , but have not yet spoken of "first order *terms*" (or utterances), "second order *terms, . . .* These roughly correspond on the language level with "first order intelligibles," "second order intelligibles," . . . , on the thought level. This correspondence will be discussed in more depth below.

62. My example.

63. A. I. Sabra, "Avicenna on the Subject Matter of Logic," *The Journal of Philosophy*, vol. 77 (1980), p. 756.

64. This is precisely what the expression *sharḥ al-ʾism* [exposition of the name] really means, as explained in chapter 1.

65. See chapter 1 of this study.

66. The meaning of the *wa* here is "or" rather than "and."

67. See Zimmermann's remarks (op. cit., p. xxxi, n. 2), concerning a possible relationship of Alfārābī's *mithāl awwal* to the "prototypon" of Dionysius Thrax.

68. The manuscript basis of the current edition of **Ḥurūf** is certainly a major problem in this regard.

69. Which in Arabic would be something like the term Alfārābī uses in this paragraph of **Ḥurūf**: *taqaddum fī-ʾl-ʿaql* [logical priority].

70. Prior, that is, to the utterances that signify first order concepts. We will refer to such utterances as first order utterances.

71. This is my interpretation of the phrase *aḥrā an takūn maḥsūsah* on line 15, which literally means "more appropriate to [be related] to sensible things."

72. The term *ʿalā ḥiyālih* appears also in the previous paragraph (par. 24) in a similar context.

73. I am indebted to Professor Wolfhart Heinrichs of Harvard University for this observation.

74. This claim can be contradicted by an argument of the following sort: There are certain verbs, such as *niʿma* [to be good], *biʾsa* [to be bad], *ʿasā* [may be], *ḥabbadhā* [it would be nice . . .], none of which has a verbal noun from which it is derived. This is indeed one of the arguments used by the Kūfian School of grammar in support of its position that the *maṣdar* [verbal noun] is derived from the verb (cf. Abū ʾl-Barakāt Ibn al-Anbārī, *Kitāb al-inṣāf fī masāʾil al-khilāf bayna ʾl-naḥawiyyīn al-baṣriyyīn wa-ʾl-kūfiyyīn* [Cairo: Maṭbaʿt al-saʿādah, 1961] vol. 1: 236). Alfārābī and the grammarians of the Baṣrian school can perhaps reply that these are not verbs in the strict sense of the term, since they do not express the action of an agent upon some thing, rather they all express certain attitudes or wishes of the speaker.

75. Thus al-Zajjāj, in defending the Baṣrian School in relation to the question of whether the verb is derived from the *maṣdar* or vice versa, states that if the verbs were the source, then every *maṣdar* should have a verb from which it is derived. But terms like *slavery* [*ʿubūdiyyah*] and *manhood* [*rujūliyyah*] are *maṣādir* and yet they are not derived from any verb. Al-Zajjāj concludes his arguments by stating: "It is evident that the *maṣādir* are the source [of the verbs]. In certain cases, a verb is derived [*ukhidha*] and in other cases no verb may be derived." (As reported by his student al-Zajjājī in *Īḍāḥ*, pp. 58–9.) In **Ḥurūf** (p. 77, par. 32), Alfārābī refers to this dispute, typically, without mentioning the names of the parties to which he is referring. A detailed description of the arguments of each of these schools regarding this question may be found in Ibn al-Anbārī, op. cit., vol. 1, pp. 235–245.

76. Perhaps a reference to the Kūfian Grammarians, who considered the participle form to be a *fiʿl dāʾim*, as we noted earlier in this chapter. It is also possible that this is a reference to and a criticism of Aristotle, who in *De Interpretatione* 16ª13 gave 'white' as an example of a verb.

77. Alfārābī's favorite expression in this regard is *yanṭawī fīh mawḍūʿah bi-ʾl-quwwah*, i.e., its subject is included implicitly or potentially in the term that signifies it.

78. "Primary substance" is a translation of the technical term *mushār ilayh lā fī mawḍūᶜ* which should be understood as an "individual material object" [i.e., a "this"] that is not 'in' a subject. But this is what we call (following Aristotle's *Categories*) a "primary substance."

79. Literally the term *aktharuhā* [mostly] modifies the term *mithāl awwal*, but then we will fall into the trap of implying that since they are *mithāl awwal*, therefore they are nondeclinable, an implication we have shown to be wrong in Alfārābī's system.

80. I.e., species and genera. See chapter 1 of this work.

81. Zimmermann's translation.

82. Similarly, the argument continues, with other forms such as the *mafʿūl* (i.e., passive participle) which may have the meaning of *fāʿil* (i.e., active participle). An example of this is *ʿalīm*, which literally means "capable of knowing" but actually is used to mean "he who actually knows"[*ʿālim*].

83. This point is not explicit in Alfārābī's writings. The closest Alfārābī comes to explaining himself is what he says in **Ḥurūf** (p. 79, par. 34). The point is explained, however, in several passages in Avicenna's writings. See for example: a) Ibn Sīnā, *Al-shifāʾ, al-manṭiq: 1. al-madkhal*, p. 150; b) Ibn Sīnā, *Manṭiq al-mashriqiyyīn* [*The logic of the Orientals*] (Cairo: Al-maktabah al-salafiyyah, 1910) p. 15.

84. Compare this with the grammarians' analysis of this issue, as summarized by W. Wright, op. cit., vol. 1, pp. 131–133.

85. Another significant topic is that of "predication," various aspects of which have been dealt with throughout this work (see particularly chapter 3 and chapter 5). To accord this topic the indepth treatment it deserves would require a book-length discussion beyond the scope of the present work.

86. W. Wright, op. cit., vol. 1, p. 165.

87. Ibid., p. 149.

88. Massignon and Kraus, "La formation des noms abstraits en arabe" in *Review d'Etudes Islamique*, 1934, p. 507 ff. Quoted in Soheil M. Afnan, *Philosophical Terminology in Arabic and Persian* (Leiden: E. J. Brill, 1964), p. 32.

89. Afnan, ibid.

90. It is surprising that all along Averroes talks about *huwiyyah* and *mawjūd* as synonymous. In fact *huwiyyah* parallels *wujud* both being abstract nouns or infinitives. The term *huwa* parallels *mawjūd* as we have seen earlier in this work. Alfārābī is more accurate than Averroes on this issue.

Conclusion

Logic has two sides—one mathematical, the other linguistic. The former is concerned with the systematic treatment of the logical truth of propositions and the relations that hold between them. This aspect of logic is governed by universal rules and principles. It is a formal system of purely mathematical interest that can be transposed easily from one natural language to another.

Logic in its broadest sense, however, cannot be separated from the language in which it is expressed. Language is the expression of mental entities (intelligibles, propositions, statements) that reflect the world, and as such it is not only the tool but also the subject matter of logic.

The debates that took place in the Arab world during the ninth and tenth centuries concerning the relationship between logic and language correspond roughly to the dichotomy outlined above. These debates led to an acute polarization between the logicians and the grammarians of that period.

The grammarians supported the view (expressed by Abū Saʿīd al-Sīrāfī in his debate with the logician Abū Bishr Mattā) that logic is derived from a particular natural language and that in fact there is no logic, except the logic of a given language. In modern linguistics, this view is referred to as *linguistic relativity,* or alternatively, as the "Sapir-Whorf hypothesis," since it is closely associated with contemporary linguists Benjamin Whorf and Edward Sapir.

Benjamin Lee Whorf (1897 – 1944), for example, believed that "a change in language can transform our appreciation of the Cosmos."[1] Language, according to him, influences the very way people perceive the world. In his words:

> We dissect nature along lines laid down by our native languages. The categories and types that we isolate from the world of phenomena we do not find there because they stare every observer in the face; on the contrary, the world is presented in a kaleidoscopic flux of impressions which has to be organized by our minds—and this means largely by the linguistic systems in our minds. We cut nature up, organize it into concepts, and ascribe significances as we do, largely because we are parties to an agreement to organize it in this way—an agreement that holds through our speech community and is codified in the patterns of our language.[2]

This linguistic relativistic view, closely approximating that of the Arab grammarian al-Sīrāfī, amounts to a complete denial of the formal side of logic, something the Arab logicians defended as universal and valid for all nations, regardless of their natural language. The opposing view held by Alfārābī and his fellow logicians comes very close to the modern notion of *linguistic universals,* brought into current vogue by Noam Chomsky.[3] In an almost Kantian vein, for example, Alfārābī posits that all human beings have fixed categories of the mind which determine their perception of the world, regardless of the language they speak. It is on this basis that Alfārābī, as we have seen, argues for intertranslatability.

Alfārābī, though clearly siding more with the logicians than with the grammarians, nevertheless took pains to resolve rather than exacerbate the conflict. As we have seen throughout his logical writings, Alfārābī's conciliatory aim was to show not the *mutual exclusivity,* but rather the *mutual interdependence* of the formal (or mathematical) and the linguistic sides of logic. He thereby suggests that both the grammarians and the logicians are right in observing the particularity and the universality of logic respectively, but wrong in claiming that the two aspects of logic are mutually exclusive.

According to Alfārābī, the logical form, i.e., the mathematical side of logic—which, in the eyes of medieval Arab thinkers, was identical with Aristotelian logic—is a constant and never changes, whereas the *expressions* of the mathematical forms change from one natural language to another. The content or matter of which these forms are composed is the different natural languages and the respective grammars (or sets of rules) that govern them.

The main purpose of the present study has been to show that Alfārābī intended to explore the interplay between the two aspects of logic as manifested in the Arabic language, i.e., when logical forms are expressed in this language.

It is true that Alfārābī, like the other logicians of this period, holds that the grammatical rules of any particular language are subordinated to the universal rules of logic, yet he maintains that logicians must deal with language, for it is a vital part of the study of logic: "As to the subject matter of logic . . . , it is the intelligibles signified by expressions and the expressions that signify intelligibles." (**Iḥṣā**', 59) and in **ʿIbārah** (p. 24), Alfārābī says: "The logician considers thought as relating to both sides, namely, to the entities outside the soul and to speech. He also studies speech by itself, but always in terms of its relationship to thought."

It is also true that for Alfārābī any natural language is a conventional, rather than a natural, set of symbols that can be changed when it does not agree with the laws of logic, yet Alfārābī knows that thought (i.e., the logical structure) must be expressed by means of a particular language and the logician must thus be aware of the specific rules and characteristics of the language(s) in which he chooses to discuss logic. Logicians, he says (**Iḥṣā'**, 62), must learn from the grammarians the rules of their language.

Languages correspond to the intelligibles in a conventional way rather than in a natural way, just as the intelligibles correspond to the world, and because language is a means by which to know the logical structures and consequently to know the world, one must be familiar with its rules and mechanisms. According to Alfārābī no natural language in and of itself is essential for logicians, yet no logician can dispense with all language.[4]

Alfārābī's extensive writings on logic and his many remarks about the relationship between logic and grammar are meant to show relationships in particular terms, i.e., by showing how logical theories and laws can be expressed in a particular language, the Arabic language in this case, and how a given language (Arabic) has all the elements that enable it to correspond to logical structures.

In so doing, Alfārābī disassociates himself from both the grammarians and the logicians. Alfārābī disagrees with the logicians' position that logicians do not need the particular meanings of terms in order to conduct logical research, but he also disagrees with the grammarians, who deny the existence of intelligible meanings detached from a particular language.

Alfārābī's main theme in his logical writings is to defend the thesis that although meanings (i.e., the domain of logic) are superior to utterances and to the rules that govern utterances, logicians cannot and should not ignore the natural languages, nor can they do without them, as Mattā in his debate with Sīrāfī was understood to contend. This does not mean, however, that Alfārābī abandoned his fellow logicians in favor of the grammarians' position. In fact, Alfārābī indicates throughout his logical writings that he strongly adheres to the position that the formal and universal rules of logic are superior to the rules of any particular language, just as they are superior to any other discipline. This amounts to saying that *natural languages must be logical* in the sense that their rules must conform to and agree with the logical structures, which exist in the domain of thought.

Alfārābī's enterprise may be divided into two major phases: 1) analysis of the semantic function of individual terms of the Arabic language in logical contexts, and 2) analysis of the Arabic language itself, in order to show that it possesses all the elements with which to express logical structures.

Alfārābī employs two methods in order to clarify and emphasize the logical semantic function of individual terms. First he classifies all the particles in a new way, completely different from any previous classifications undertaken by the Arab grammarians (**Alfāẓ**, 44–56). This classification is apparently based on the logical semantic function, rather than on the grammatical function of the expressions involved.

Thus, for example, the second category of this classification includes (ibid., 44) the terms *all* [*kull*] and *some* [*baʿḍ*], both of which are usually considered as nouns by the Arab grammarians, and yet are classified by Alfārābī as particles (*wāṣilāt* [connectives]), probably because of their use as quantifiers in logical contexts. Similarly, with the term *laysa* [it is not the case that], which Alfārābī classifies as one of the particles, whereas the grammarians place it among the verbs.

In this significant passage of **Alfāẓ**, Alfārābī makes clear his awareness of the fact that the expression *laysa* is a "verb" for the grammarians. He tells us also that many of the terms that he classifies as particles are called either nouns or verbs by the grammarians, adding that his primary concern in this classification is to satisfy the needs of the science under consideration, namely logic (**Alfāẓ**, 46).

This is a general principle attended to by Alfārābī in his treatment of language, particularly when he deals with the semantic aspects of terms. Alfārābī is very clear about this point and makes no secret of it: "We should not be taken to task when we use many of the expressions that are well known to the multitude to signify meanings [*maʿānī*] different from those these expressions signify for the grammarians, for the scientists and [different] from the language used by the multitude" (**Alfāẓ**, 44).

The logical function(s) and meaning(s) of a term are Alfārābī's only measure and criterion in his classification of particles, in particular, and terms, in general. But the classification of particles and terms is only one way in which Alfārābī differs from the grammarians. A second and more significant way is in his actual use of these terms in his logical theories.

Chapters 1 through 5 of the current study illustrate Alfārābī's use of certain terms in logical and philosophical contexts, in order to extract and identify their logical meanings, not necessarily identical to the meanings with which the grammarians are concerned. The science of grammar, according to Alfārābī (**Alfāẓ**, 43: 5–7), "studies the kinds of utterances according to what they signify as commonly known among people. The grammarians, therefore, deal with the signification of these utterances as they are known to the multitude, rather than as they are known to the practitioners of scientific disciplines."

The meanings of the question particles *mā* [what], *ayy* [which], *kayfa* [how], *lima* [why], and others, as well as terms such as *māhiyyah* [essence], *jawhar* [essence], *dhāt* [essence], *ḥukm* [judgment], *qawl* [logos],[5] *nawᶜ* [species], *jins* [genus], *ḥadd* [definition], *rasm* [description], *qismah* [division], *tarkīb* [classification], and many more are defined within their logical contexts. The meanings of these terms, as extracted from these logical contexts, is considered by Alfārābī as an *extension* of the common language rather than as "building a language within a language." As Alfārābī puts it (**Alfāẓ**, 43: 1 ff.):

> We ought to know that the science of grammar comprises kinds of utterances among which are those that the common people use to mean one thing, while scientists use them to mean something else. [Furthermore,] sometimes the practitioner of one discipline uses it with another meaning. . . . We have no need for meanings other than those used by the practitioners of this discipline [i.e., logic].

Logic, therefore, is a language within a language only to the extent that the meanings of its terms are not the same as those known to the grammarians or to the practitioners of other disciplines. In fact, Alfārābī argues (**Ḥurūf**, 164, pars. 163–164) that philosophy (and therefore logic) employs terms only in their original significations, i.e., those significations for which these terms were originally coined, whereas other disciplines (such as rhetoric and poetics) use terms with significations they acquire by "metaphor" [*istiᶜārah*], "extension" [*ittisāᶜ*], "license" [*tasāmuḥ*], and "figuratively" [*majāz*]. Philosophers cannot therefore be accused of building a language within a language. If anything, Alfārābī seems to argue, the philosophical language is the most accurate, since it uses terms in their primary sense only and does not appeal to any of the above-mentioned methods for extending and expanding meanings, as do the other disciplines.

In the final chapter of this work, we present Alfārābī's analysis of language from a logical point of view. From this perspective, Alfārābī analyzes the structure of the Arabic sentence in order to show that the particular logic of the Arabic language (i.e., its grammar) conforms to the Aristotelian principles of logic, which the Arab logicians (including Alfārābī) have adopted as the universal principles of thought.

Whether the details of Alfārābī's analysis are correct or incorrect is virtually immaterial. What is significant is the attempt in and of itself, which indicates that Alfārābī strongly desired to reconcile the structure of the Arabic language with Greek logic.

Alfārābī successfully defends, for example, the idea that the Arabic sentence basically agrees with the schema *'S is P,'* even when the copula is not explicitly manifest (as is generally the case in Arabic). By demonstrating this, Alfārābī actually shows that the nonformal side of logic *must and innately does* conform to the formal rules of (Aristotelian) logic, which is in principle a predicative logic (i.e., a logic according to which every atomic sentence fits the above-mentioned schema). In other words, the particular *expressions* of logic in a given natural language must and will necessarily, according to Alfārābī, conform to the formal principles this logic embodies.

The process of trying to solve logical and philosophical problems by analyzing the language itself (an approach which has characterized British and American "ordinary language" philosophy) is described by a contemporary philosopher of language, John R. Searle, as *linguistic philosophy:* "Linguistic philosophy is the attempt to solve particular philosophical problems by attending to the ordinary use of particular words or other elements in a particular language."[6]

In his very attempt to analyze certain terms used in Arabic logical (and more generally, philosophical) language, Alfārābī does just that. By analyzing terms such as *mawjūd, huwiyyah* (both used as a copula in Arabic logical writings), abstract nouns and their place in logical inquiries, and the particles and their role in logic, as well as by reexamining central issues concerning the structure of the Arabic language (such as the verb system), Alfārābī not only introduces the field of linguistic philosophy in Arabic, but also becomes the most significant contributor to this field of study. Linguistic philosophy is the resolution that Alfārābī reached in his attempt to harmonize the Aristotelian logic he so greatly admired, with the Arabic language he mastered so well.

Alfārābī was a logician who dealt with language and grammar (semantics, syntax) from a logical point of view. Yet he can also be considered a consummate grammarian who was thoroughly skilled in the art of logic and tried to apply what he considered to be universal principles of logic to the rules of the Arabic language. His profound knowledge of both disciplines and the task he undertook to harmonize them make him unique in the history of Arabic logic.

Notes to Conclusion

1. Benjamin Lee Whorf, *Language, Thought and Reality: Selected Writings*, ed. J. B. Caroll (Cambridge: MIT Press, 1976), p. vii.

2. Ibid., p. 213.

3. Cf. Joseph H. Greenberg, ed., *Universals of Human Language*, vol. 1 (Stanford, CA: Stanford University Press, 1978), pp. 228–229.

4. Avicenna, for his part, reaches the conclusion that all natural languages may be dispensed with (*Al-shifā᾿, al-manṭiq, 1: al-madkhal*, 22).

5. Like the Greek *logos*, the Arabic term *qawl* has several meanings and applications, as we have seen in chapter 2, section 1 (p. 37).

6. Searle, op. cit., p. 4. " 'Linguistic philosophy' is not the same as 'philosophy of language,' which has a broader meaning since it transcends particular languages." Philosophy of language deals with topics, such as 'truth' and 'meaning,' that are not related to particular languages; philosophy of language "is concerned only incidentally with particular elements in a particular language," (ibid.) although, as Searle explains, paying strict attention to the facts of actual natural languages is unavoidable.

Appendix I

Primary Substance in Aristotle

In *The Categories* Aristotle asserts that the basic elements of being are the primary substances, which he identifies with the individual material objects. There is no systematic attempt in this early work to find out what counts as an individual material object. No definition is given for these terms (*primary substance* and *individual material object*), although Aristotle does give certain characterizations of them, two of which I have mentioned before: 1) they are capable of receiving contraries while remaining one and the same (*Categories* 4^a10–14) and 2) "they are neither in a subject nor said of a subject" (*Categories* 1^b3 and 2^a11). Elsewhere in this work (2^b37) he introduces another side of the primary substances: "Further, it is because the primary substances are subjects for everything else that they are called substances most strictly." I will refer to this third characterization of primary substances as the *predicability test* in accordance with the terminology of modern logic. The predicability test is based on and actually equivalent to Aristotle's basic doctrine that a primary substance is neither said of nor in a subject, which means that anything else is in it as a subject (this man is white) or said of it as a subject (this man is an animal). In both cases, then, the primary substance is a subject of which other things can be predicated.

In *Metaphysics Z and H*[1] the search for a definition of the primary substance becomes Aristotle's main theme:

> Indeed, the question that was asked long ago, is asked now, keeps on being asked and always baffles us—'What is being?'—is the question 'What is substance?' (*Metaphysics Z*, 1029^a23–24)

In these works the concept of *matter* is introduced and examined as a candidate for this title. Aristotle is forced to do so because his analysis has led him to the conclusion that

> the predicates other than substances are predicated of substances, while substance is predicated of matter. (*Metaphysics Z*, 1029^a23–24)

And if we apply, as Aristotle does, the predictability test stated above we might think that matter has a better claim to the title of primary substance than the individual material objects.

In the *Metaphysics* Aristotle does not challenge the validity of this criterion for substancehood; on the contrary, he continues to use it in testing new candidates for the title of *oūsiā*. His new candidate is now matter, which emerges (as we have seen above) as the ultimate subject of predication: everything else, including the substance, which so far has been his candidate, is predicated of it.

However, it turns out that the predictability test is not a sufficient criterion for Aristotle to select his candidates for the title of *oūsiā*. It is only a necessary condition. There are two more requirements: "separability" and "thisness." Matter, Aristotle says, can be neither:

> If we adopt this point of view, then, it follows that matter is substance. But this is impossible; for both 'separability' and 'thisness' are thought to belong chiefly to substance. (*Metaphysics Z*, 1029ª26–31)

In chapter 3 of *Metaphysics* Z Aristotle says that the combination of form and matter cannot be his primary substance. Nor could the universal be a primary substance because by its very nature, he says, it is what is common to more than one thing.[2] (*Metaphysics Z*, 1038ᵇ9–12)

Aristotle's final conclusion concerning the nature of primary substance is put forth in the 16th chapter of *Metaphysics* Z (1031ᵇ21 ff.), where he identifies substance with its essence:

> Each thing itself, then, and its essence, are one and the same in no merely accidental way, as is evident both from the preceding arguments and because to know each thing, at least, is just to know its essence, so that even by the exhibition of instances it becomes clear that both must be one.

This conclusion is one of the most influential themes in the history of Arabic philosophy and logic, as becomes clear when one realizes that the search for substance is replaced by the search for essence and that for Aristotle as well as for Alfārābī and other Arab philosophers, *to state the essence of a thing is to define it*.[3]

Yet in order to understand what "essence" [*māhiyyah*] is, we must turn to an investigation of the other side of the individual/universal dualism, namely the secondary substances and the nonsubstantial universals, or as they came to be known, the "accidental universals." For the answer to the question What is the essence of a thing? or *What is the definition of a thing?* lies in understanding the relationships between secondary substances and the primary substance, whereas the answer to the question How is a thing? (inquiring about the *description* of that thing) lies in understanding the relationship between individuals and the nonsubstantial universals that are said of them.

Notes to Appendix I

1. All quotations from these two works will be from: Aristotle, *The Basic Works of Aristotle,* ed. Richard McKeon (New York: Random House, 1941).

2. Nor can the platonic solution to the Heraclitian challenge (namely the *forms* that are timeless and unchangeable) satisfy Aristotle's concept of substance. In fact, the platonic concept was totally rejected by Aristotle (see for example his *Metaphysics M,* Chapter 9, 1086^{b}30 ff.).

3. *Topics* I (5) 101^{b}37: "A *definition* is a phrase indicating the essence of something."

Appendix II

Avicenna (Ibn Sīnā) on the Concept of 'essential' [*dhātī*]

In his **Madkhal** (30 ff.) Avicenna distinguishes between an expression that signifies the essence of a thing and the parts of that expression which he calls "essential expressions" [*lafẓ dhātī*] which do not signify the entire essence but only parts of it. Just like Alfārābī, Avicenna says that the *dhāt* (i.e. the *māhiyyah*) comes about through certain composition of those essential parts (they both use the Arabic term *iltiʾām*).[1]

Avicenna asserts that the essential parts of the *dhāt* are *ontologically prior* [*mutaqaddima fī al-wujūd*] to the *dhāt* itself. He calls each of these parts *dhātī* ["the essential of," or simply "the essential"]. Avicenna then addresses the question whether the term *dhātī* also applies to the whole expression that signifies the *māhiyyah* or only to its parts.

The term *dhātī*, Avicenna explains, is bound grammatically to be a *dhāt* for something else, or in his words:

> *Dhātī* is an expression[2] the meaning of which stands in a certain relation to the *dhāt* of the thing, but the meaning of the *dhāt* of a thing is not relative to itself, rather it is relative to a thing which is not itself. Therefore, it is properly assumed that the expression *dhātī* is more appropriately applied[3] to the notions that constitute the essence, and that the expression which signifies the essence is not a *dhātī*. 'Man' is not essential [*dhātī*] for man, rather 'animal' and 'rational' [each of them separately] is essential for 'man.' (**Madkhal**, 31).

The rules of the (Arabic) language, Avicenna concludes, imply, therefore, that the expression *dhātī* should be confined only to the parts of the *māhiyyah*. Yet logicians have agreed among themselves to attribute to it a different meaning. For them the criterion for a universal 'x' to be essential for 'y' is the following: if 'x' is assumed [*tuwuhhimat*, literally "imagined"] to be nonexistent, then 'y' should be nonexistent, too. If the negation [*rafʿ*] of 'x,' in other words, leads by necessity to the negation of 'y,' then 'x' is essential for 'y's' existence.[4] 'X' can be either the true essence of 'Y,' or one of the components of this essence. In this sense, logicians term the *māhiyyah* and not only its components as *dhātī*, Avicenna says.

This criterion introduces a method to distinguish between the different kinds of predicates; essential predicates (genus, species, differentia), accidental predicates (both separable and inseparable), and property. The first two of these are obvious and need no elaboration.

Avicenna explains that, in the case of properties (which he calls in this passage *aʿrāḍ bi-ʾl-ṭabʿ*, i.e. accidents by nature), it might appear that the negation of a property negates the thing of which it is a property (just as in the case of an essential predicate). But this is not true, the argument continues, for what happens in this case is the following: since properties are *implied* by the things to which they belong (and not the other way around), the negation of the former can only be an *indicator* (not a cause) that the latter has been negated and that no longer exists. 'Laughter,' for example, is implied by the existence of 'man,' but when 'laughter' is negated (i.e., imagined as not existing) that indicates that "man" (the cause of laughter) has ceased to exist. (We have to remember, however, Avicenna would argue, that the relationships are conceptual and that therefore there is no temporal priority of 'man' to 'laughter' or vice versa.)

This of course differs substantially from the relationships that exist between essential predicates and their objects. In the latter case the negation of the essential predicate is negated when its essential predicate "animal" is negated, but not vice versa (a similar argument can be introduced concerning the other essential predicates; differential and that which represents the essence, i.e., the *hadd*, but we need not elaborate further at this point).

Notes to Appendix II

1. Which literally means: fitness, or the right combination. See Alfārābī's (**Ḥurūf**, 100, 195) and Ibn Sīnā (**Madkhal**, 30).

2. Literally he says: 'signifies an utterance.'

3. 'Yashtamilu,' which literally means 'includes,' or contains, but neither of these conveys the meaning meant by the Arabic term.

4. Compare this with Fārābī's **Burhān** (p. 39). There Alfārābī discusses the ontological priority of something over something else using the same criterion of negation [*rafʿ*].

Bibliography

Alfārābī's Works Used in this Study

Alfārābī, Abū Naṣr. **Iḥṣā' al-'ulūm**. Edited by 'Uthmān Amīn. Cairo: Maktabat al-anglo al-miṣriyyah, 1968(3). [= **Iḥṣā'**]

———. **Arā' ahl al-madīnah al-fāḍilah**. Edited by Albert Naṣr Nādir. Beirūt: Al-maṭba'ah al-kāthūlīkiyyah, 1959.

———. **Kitāb al-alfāẓ al-musta'malah fī 'l-manṭiq** [Book of Utterances Employed in Logic]. Edited by Muḥsin Mahdī. Beirūt: Dār al-mashriq, 1968. [= **Alfāẓ**]

———. "**Kitāb īsāghūjī ay al-madkhal**" [Al-Fārābī's Eisagoge]. Edited and translated by D. M. Dunlop. *The Islamic Quarterly* 3 (1956 – 57): 117 – 38. [= **Madkhal**]

———. "**Kitāb bārī armīniyās ay al-'ibārah**" [Short Treatise on Aristotle's De Interpretatione]. Ed. M. Kuyel [Turker]. *Arastirma* 4 (1966) 1 – 85. Ankara: 1968. [= **Bārī armīniyās**]

———. "**Kitāb al-burhān**" [Posterior Analytics]. In *Al-manṭiq 'inda Alfārābī* [Alfārābī's Logic]. Edited by Mājid Fakhrī. Beirūt: Dār al-mashriq, 1986. [= **Burhān**]

———. **Al-thamarah al-marḍiyyah** [Philosophical Papers]. Edited by Friedrich Dieterici. Leiden: E. J. Brill, 1890. The book is also known as: *Al-Fārābī's philosophische Abhandlungen*. [= **Thamarah**]

———. **Kitāb al-ḥurūf** [Book of Letters]. Edited by Muḥsin Mahdī. Beirūt: Dār-al-mashriq, 1970. [= **Ḥurūf**]

———. **Kitāb fī 'l-manṭiq: al-khiṭābah** [Book of Rhetorics]. Edited by M. S. Sālim. Cairo: Al-hay'ah al-miṣriyyah al-'āmmah li-l-kitāb, 1976.

———. "**Risālah ṣudira bihā 'l-kitāb**" ["Al-Fārābī's Introductory Risālah on Logic"]. Edited and translated by D. M. Dunlop. *The Islamic Quarterly* 3 (1956 – 57): 224 – 235. [= **Risālah**]

———. **Al-siyāsah al-madaniyyah** [The Political Regime]. Edited by Fawzi Najjār. Beirūt: Al-maṭba'ah al-kāthūlīkiyyah, 1964.

———. **Sharḥ Alfārābī li-kitāb Arisṭūṭālīs fī 'l-'ibārah**. Edited by W. Kutsch and S. Marrow. Beirūt: Al-maṭba'ah al-kāthūlīkiyyah, 1960.

———. "**Fuṣūl tashtamil ʿalā jamīʿ mā yuḍṭarr ilā maʿrifatih man arād al-shurūʿ fī ṣināʿat al-manṭiq**" [Al-Fārābī's introductory sections on logic]. Edited and translated by D. M. Dunlop. *The Islamic Quarterly* 2(1955): 264–282. [= **Fuṣūl**]

———. "**Kitāb qāṭāghūriyās ay al-maqūlāt** [Al-Fārābī's paraphrase of the *Categories* of Aristotle]." Edited and translated by D. M. Dunlop. *The Islamic Quarterly* 4(1957–58): 168–97; 5(1959): 21–54. [= **Maqūlāt**]

———. "**Kitāb al-qiyās** [Commentary on Aristotle's *Prior Analytics*]." In *Al-manṭiq ʿind Alfārābī* [Alfārābī's Logic]. Edited by Rafīq al-ʿAjam. Beirūt: Dār al-mashriq, 1986. [= **Qiyās**]

———. "**Kitāb al-qiyās al-ṣaghīr**" [Alfārābī's short commentary on Aristotle's *Prior Analytics*]. Edited by Mubahat Turker. *Ankara Universitesi: Dil ve Tarih-Cografya Fakültesi Dergisi* 16 (1958): 244–86. [= **Qiyās ṣaghīr**].

———. **Kitāb al-mūsīqā ʾl-kabīr** [The comprehensive book of music]. Edited by Ghaṭṭās Khashabah. Cairo: Dār al-kātib al-ʿarabī, 1967: 83–105. [= **Mūsīqā**]

———. **Mabādiʾ al-falsafah al-qadīmah** [The principles of ancient philosophy]. Cairo: 1910.

Works by Other Authors

Afnān, Soheil M. *Philosophical Terminology in Arabic and Persian*. Leiden: E. J. Brill, 1964.

Anscomb, G. E. M., and P. T. Geach. *Three Philosophers: Aristotle, Aquinas, Frege*. Ithaca, NY: Cornell University Press, 1961.

Aristotle. *Categories and De Interpretatione*. Translated with commentary by J. L. Ackrill. Oxford: Oxford University Press, 1963.

———. "Metaphysics" and "Topics." *The Basic Works of Aristotle*. Edited with an Introduction by Richard McKeon. New York: Random House, 1941.

———. *Aristotle's Posterior Analytics*. Translated by Jonathan Barnes. Oxford: Clarendon Press, 1975.

Averroes, See Ibn Rushd

Avicenna, See Ibn Sīnā

Badawī ʿA. R., ed. *Manṭiq Aristū* [Aristotle's Logic]. 3 vols. Cairo: Maṭbaʿat dār al-Kutub al-miṣriyyah 1948–52.

———., ed. *Arisṭūṭālīs, al-ṭabīʿah* [Aristotle's *Physics*] 2 vols. Translated by Isḥāq b. Hunayn. Cairo: Al-dār al-qawmiyyah li-l-ṭibāʿah wa-ʾl-nashr, 1964.

Bar Yoseph, ed. *Igrot ha-rambam* [Maimonides: Letters and Biography]. Tel Aviv: Mordechay Institute for Publishing Judaica, 1970.

Barnes, J.; M. Schofield; and R. Sorabji, eds. *Articles on Aristotle.* Vols. 1 & 3. London: Duckworth, 1975–1979.

Bielawski, Jozef. "Deux periodes dans la formation de la terminologie scientifique arabe." *Rocznik Orientalistyczny* (R.O.) 20(1956): 263–320.

Dancy, Russell. "On Some of Aristotle's First Thoughts About Substances." *Philosophical Review* (1975): 338–373.

De Boer, T. J. *History of Philosophy in Islam.* New York: Dover Publications, 1967.

Dieterici, F., ed. *Al-Fārābī's philosophische Abhandlungen.* Leiden: E. J. Brill, 1890. (See Alfārābī: *Al-thamarah al-marḍiyyah.*)

El Amrani-Jamal, A. *Logique Aristotélicienne et grammaire arabe: Etude et documents.* Paris: Librairie Philosophique Y. Vrin, 1983.

Edwards, Paul, ed. *Encyclopedia of Philosophy.* New York: Macmillan, 1967.

Encyclopedia of Islam. Leiden and Leipzig: Brill, 1913–38.

Encyclopedia of Islam, new edition. Leiden & London: Brill, 1960 ff.

Endress, Gerhard. "The Debate Between Arabic Grammar and Greek Logic." *Journal for the History of Arab Science* 1 (no. 2), November, 1977.

Frank, Richard M. "The origin of the Arabic philosophical term *aniyyah.*" *Cahiers de Byrsa* 6 (1956): 181–201.

Gätje, Helmut. "Die Gliederung der sprachlichen Zeichen nach al-Fārābī." *Der Islam* 47(1971): 1–24.

Georr, Khalil. *Les Categories d'Aristote dans leurs versions syro-arabes.* Beirūt: 1948.

Goichan, A. M. *Lexique de la langue philosophique d'ibn Sina.* Paris: 1938.

Greenberg, Joseph H., ed. *Universals of Human Language.* Vol. 1. Stanford, CA: Stanford University Press, 1978.

Gyekye, Kwame. "The Terms 'Prima Intentio' and 'Secunda Intentio' in Arabic Logic." *Speculum* 46(1971): 32–38.

Haddad, Fuad. "Al-Fārābī's Views on Logic and its Relation to Grammar." *Islamic Quarterly* 13(1969): 192–207.

———. "Al-Fārābī's Theory of Language." *American University of Beirūt Festival Book (Festschrift).* Edited by Fuad Sarraf and Suha Tamin. Beirūt, (1967).

———. *Alfārābī's Theory of Communication.* Beirūt: American University of Beirūt, 1989.

Hartman, Edwin. *Substance, Body, and Soul.* Princeton: Princeton University Press, 1977.

Hitti, Philip K. *History of the Arabs.* London: Macmillan & Co. Ltd., 1960.

Ibn ʿAdī, Yaḥyā. "On the Difference Between Philosophical Logic and Arabic Grammar." Edited by Gerhart Endress. *Journal for the History of Arabic Science* 2 (1978).

Ibn al-Anbārī, Abū ʾl-Barakāt. *Kitāb al-inṣāf fī masāʾil al-khilāf bayna ʾl-naḥawiyyīn al-baṣriyyīn wa-ʾl-kūfiyyīn.* 2 vols. Cairo: Maṭbaʿat al-saʿādah, 1961.

Ibn Fāris, Aḥmad. *Al-ṣaḥībī fī fiqh al-luqhah.* Edited by Muṣṭafā al-Shuwaymī. Beirūt: Muʾassasat Badrān, 1964.

Ibn al-Qifṭī, Abu al-Hasan ʿAli. *Taʾrīkh al-ḥukamāʾ*. Edited by J. Lippert. Leipzig: Dieterichsche Verlagsbuchhandlung, 1903.

Ibn Rushd. *Tafsīr mā baʿd al-ṭabīʿah.* [Averroes' commentary on Aristotle's *Metaphysics*] ed. Maurice Bouyges. 3 vol. Beirūt: Dār al-mashriq, 1938–48, esp. vol. 2, 1942.

Ibn al-Sarrāj, Abū Bakr Muḥammad. *Al-mujaz fī ʾl-naḥw.* Edited by M. al-Shuwaymī and B. Salīm Damirjī. Beirūt: Muʾassasat Badrān, 1965.

Ibn Sīnā. *Al-shifāʾ, al-manṭiq, 1: al-madkhal.* Edited by M. al-Khodeirī; F. al-Ahwānī; and G. Anawātī. Cairo: Al-Maṭbaʿah al-amīriyyah, 1952.]

———. *Al-shifāʾ, al-manṭiq, 3: al-ʿibārah.* Edited by M. al-Khodeirī. Cairo: Dār al-kātib al-ʿarabī li-l-ṭibāʿah wa-ʾl-nashr, 1970.

———. *Al-najāt.* Edited by al-Kurdī. Cairo: Maṭbaʿat al-Saʿādah, 1938.

Ibn Taymiyyah. *Kitāb al-radd ʿalā ʾl-manṭiqiyyīn.* Edited by al-Kutubī. Bombay: Qayyimah Press, 1949.

Kahn, Charles H. "On the Theory of the Verb 'To Be,' " in Milton K. Munitz, ed. *Logic and Ontology.* New York: New York University Press, 1973.

Al-Kindī. *Rasāʾil al-Kindī al-falsafiyyah.* Edited by Muhammad ʿAbd al-Hādī Abū Rīdah. Cairo: Dar al-Fikr al-ʿarabī, 1950.

Kneale, William and Martha. *The Development of Logic.* Oxford: Oxford University Press, 1962.

Kraemer, Joel L. *Philosophy in the Renaissance of Islam.* Leiden: E. J. Brill, 1986.

Lane, E. W. *Arabic-English Lexicon.* 8 vols. New York: Frederick Ungar Publishing Co., 1956.

Madkour, Ibrahīm. *L'Organon d'Aristote dans le monde arabe.* Paris: 1969(2). (= *Etudes Musulmanes*, x).

Mahdī, Muḥsin, tr. *Al-Fārābī's Philosophy of Plato and Aristotle*. Ithaca: Cornell University Press, 1969.

———. "Language and Logic in Classical Islam." In G. E. von Grunebaum, *Logic in Classical Islamic Culture*. Wiesbaden: Harrassowitz, 1970, pp. 51–83.

———. "Science, Philosophy and Religion in Alfarabi's Enumeration of the Sciences." In J. E. Murdoch and E. D. Sylla, eds. *The Cultural Context of Medieval Learning*, Boston Studies in the Philosophy of Science, vol. 26. Holland: D. Reidel, 1975, pp. 113–147.

———. "Islamic Philosophy: The Eastern and Western Schools." *Islam: The Perenniality of Values*. A special issue of *Cultures* 4, no. 1 (1977).

Makhzūmī, Madhī. *Madrasat al-kūfah wa-manhajuhā fī dirāsat al-lughah wa-ʾl-naḥw.* Baghdād: Maṭbaʿat dār al-maʿrifah, 1955.

Moody, E. A. *The Logic of William of Ockham*. New York: Russell and Russell, 1935. Reprint edition, 1965.

Patzig, Guenther. *Aristotle's Theory of The Syllogism*. Translated from the German by Jonathan Barnes. Dordrecht-Holland: Reidel Pub. Co., 1968.

Peters, F. E. *Aristotle and the Arabs: The Aristotelian Tradition in Islam*. New York: New York University Press, 1968.

Porphyry. *Isagoge*. English translation by Edward W. Warren, Toronto: The Pontifical Institute of Medieval Studies, 1975.

Quine, W. V. *From a Logical Point of View.* New York: Harper & Row, 1961.

Al-Rāzī, Abū Bakr. *Rasāʾil falsafiyyah*. Beirūt: Dār al-afāq al-jadīdah, 1975.

Al-Rāzī, Fakhr al-Dīn. *Mafātīḥ al-ghayb*. 8 vols. Cairo: Boulāq, 1872.

Ross, David. *Aristotle*. London: Methuen, 1949(5).

Al-Rummānī, Abū al-Ḥasan Ibn ʿĪsa. *Kitāb maʿānī ʾl-ḥurūf*. Edited by ʿA. F. I. Shalabī. Cairo: Dār nahḍat miṣr li-l-ṭabʿ wa-ʾl-nashr, 1973.

Russell, Bertrand. *Our Knowledge of the External World*. London: George Allen & Unwin, 1972.

Sabra, A. I. "Avicenna on the Subject Matter of Logic." *Journal of Philosophy* 77 (1980): 746–764.

Searle, John R. *Speech Act: An Essay in the Philosophy of Language*. England: Cambridge University Press, 1969.

Sībaweih, ʿAmr Ībn ʿUthmān. *Al-kitāb*. 5 vols. Edited by ʿA. S. M. Hārūn. Cairo: Dār al-qalam, al-hayʾah al-miṣriyyah al-ʿāmmah li-l-kitāb, 1966–1977.

Sommers, Fred. *The Logic of Natural Language*. Oxford: Clarendon Press, 1982.

Stebbing, L. S., *A Modern Introduction to Logic*. New York: Humanities Press, 1933.

Steinschneider, Moritz. *Al-Fārābī, des arabischen Philosophen: Leben und Schriften mit besonderer Ruecksicht auf die Geschichte der griechischen Wissenschaft unter den Arabern*. Amsterdam: Philo Press, 1966.

Al-Tawḥīdī, Abū Ḥayyān. *Al-imtāʿ wa-ʾl-muʾānasah*. 2 vols. Edited by A. Amīn and A. al-Zayn. Beirūt: n.d. (vol. 1, p. 104–129.)

———. *Al-muqābasāt*. Edited by M. T. Husein. Baghdād: Maṭbaʿat al-irshād, 1970.

Taylor, A. E. *Aristotle*. New York: Dover Publications Inc., 1955.

Throupeau, Gerard. *Lexique-index du kitab de Sibawayhi*. Paris: Klinck Sieck, 1976.

Versteegh, C. H. M. *Greek Elements in Arabic Linguistic Thinking*. Leiden: E. J. Brill, 1977.

Von Grunebaum, G. E., ed. *Logic in Classical Islamic Culture*. Wiesbaden: 1970.

Walzer, Richard. *Greek Into Arabic: Essays on Islamic Philosophy*. Oxford: Oxford University Press, 1963.

Whorf, Benjamin Lee. *Language, Thought and Reality: Selected Writings*. Edited by J. B. Caroll. Cambridge: MIT Press, 1976.

Wright, W. *A Grammar of the Arabic Language*. 2 vols. Cambridge, England: Cambridge University Press, 1975.

Al-Zajjājī, Abū ʾl-Qāsim. *Al-īḍāḥ fī ʿilal al-naḥw*. Edited by Māzin Mubārak. Cairo: Maktabat dār al-ʿurūbah, 1959.

Zimmermann, F. W. *Al-Fārābī's Commentary and Short Treatise on Aristotle's De Interpretatione*. Oxford: Oxford University Press, 1981.

Index

L

N